D. H. LAWRENCE: THE EARLY FICTION

D. H. LAWRENCE: THE EARLY FICTION

A Commentary

Michael Black

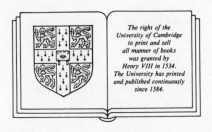

The right of the
University of Cambridge
to print and sell
all manner of books
was granted by
Henry VIII in 1534.
The University has printed
and published continuously
since 1584.

CAMBRIDGE UNIVERSITY PRESS

Cambridge

London   New York   New Rochelle

Melbourne   Sydney

Published in North America by the Press Syndicate of the
University of Cambridge
The Pitt Building, Trumpington Street, Cambridge
CB2 1RP, England
32 East 57th Street, New York, New York 10022
296 Beaconsfield Parade, Middle Park, Melbourne 3206,
Australia

Library of Congress Cataloging-in-Publication Data
Black, Michael H.
D. H. Lawrence, the early fiction.
Includes bibliographical references and index.
1. Lawrence, D. H. (David Herbert), 1885–1930—
Criticism and interpretation. I. Title.
PR6023.A93Z568 1986   823′.912   85–18968
ISBN 0–521–32293–6

Contents

Preface   vii

Cue-Titles   viii

1 The Criticism of Lawrence   1

2 Method   18

3 *The White Peacock*   41

4 *The Trespasser*   78

5 Short Stories I   111
    'A Modern Lover', 'The Shades of Spring', 'The Witch
    à la Mode', 'Love Among the Haystacks', 'Second Best'

6 *Sons and Lovers*   150

7 Short Stories II   188
    'Daughters of the Vicar', 'Odour of Chrysanthemums'

8 Short Stories III   211
    'The Prussian Officer', 'The Thorn in the Flesh'

9 Short Stories IV   233
    'The White Stocking', 'New Eve and Old Adam'

Notes   257
Index   272

For
Peter Burbidge
1919–85

Preface

I have not often referred to them explicitly, but I am very conscious of my debt to earlier writers on Lawrence. Indeed, I see myself as writing in a tradition which now goes back some seventy years.

Of the friends who have read early drafts I must mention Ronald Gray, who made helpful comments and gave encouragement, Julia Steward, Sam Goldberg and Jane Adamson. My debt to the scholarship and critical perception of John Worthen is very great indeed. He has corrected a number of errors and misstatements, and most generously made available to me some of the findings which readers will see in their fullest form in the volumes of the Cambridge Lawrence which he is editing.

To my friends and colleagues in that great enterprise I am also indebted. I have quoted the Cambridge texts which are so far available, with the kind permission of the Cambridge University Press and the Estate of Frieda Lawrence Ravagli represented by the Literary Executor Laurence Pollinger Ltd.

Cambridge   M.B.

Cue-Titles

All substantial quotations are followed by a reference to the source. Where it is available, the Cambridge edition is quoted. The following cue-titles are used:

Letters I   *The Letters of D. H. Lawrence, Volume I*, September 1901–May 1913, edited by James T. Boulton (Cambridge, 1979).

Letters II   *The Letters of D. H. Lawrence, Volume II*, June 1913–October 1916, edited by George J. Zytaruk and James T. Boulton (Cambridge, 1981).

WP(C)   *The White Peacock*, edited by Andrew Robertson (Cambridge, 1983).

T(C)   *The Trespasser*, edited by Elizabeth Mansfield (Cambridge, 1981).

PO(C)   *The Prussian Officer and Other Stories*, edited by John Worthen (Cambridge, 1983).

S & L(P)   *Sons and Lovers*, edited by Keith Sagar, Penguin English Library (Harmondsworth, 1981).

PI   *Phoenix: The Posthumous Papers of D. H. Lawrence*, edited and with an introduction by Edward D. McDonald (London, 1936).

PII   *Phoenix II, Collected, Unpublished and Other Prose works by D. H. Lawrence*, Collected and edited with an Introduction and notes by Warren Roberts and Harry T. Moore (London, 1968).

*P/H SS*I   (Phoenix-Heron Short Stories I) D. H. Lawrence: *Complete Short Stories Volume I* (London: Heinemann, 1955; and Heron Books).*

*P/H SN*I   (Phoenix-Heron Short Novels I) D. H. Lawrence: *Short Novels Volume I.* (London: Heinemann, 1956, and Heron Books).*

All elisions (. . .) are editorial

* Texts cited under these two cue-titles have been checked against the forthcoming Cambridge text (*Love Among the Haystacks and Other Stories*, edited by John Worthen) and its readings adopted.

1 The Criticism of Lawrence

Like all writers, Lawrence has been differently read at different times. While he was still writing, the books were received one by one, each adding to the public sense of what he was about. Each was new, and in some ways hard to grasp. Once he was dead, the public had to decide, with Lawrence as with other writers, what the whole work meant and whether it mattered. By now people were looking back over a number of years, and must have noticed that the first books already seemed different – because the others had been read since, and because they, his first readers, were older and the world had changed.

We now see that Lawrence is one of the writers who have helped the world to change – though not as much and not in the ways he wanted. That is to say, his readers have, from very early on, thought 'This man wants to change my way of seeing the world, and my life.' After an initial welcome, he was received with shock and opposition in his lifetime, and suffered for it. Since the world has changed, he does not now cause so much shock, but readers still feel his design on them, and many react in anger. It is one kind of tribute, to one of the few great writers with power to detain us at a deep level of personal involvement.

This was not yet clear in 1911, when *The White Peacock* was published. But Jessie Chambers (the original of Emily in *The White Peacock* and of Miriam in *Sons and Lovers*) had spent years growing up beside Lawrence, and loved him. When she sent some of his poems to the editor of 'The English Review' in 1909, it was out of the conviction that she was helping to establish a genius. When Catherine Carswell as reviewer came upon the first novels, she too perceived that this was no run-of-the-mill writer. Frieda Weekley, meeting one of her husband's pupils, and falling in love with him, knew that she was eloping to share the life of a genius. Aldous Huxley became a loyal friend, and to win the convinced and

1

lasting loyalty of that sceptical intelligence was to survive a real test. John Middleton Murry was a friend, of a sort, and convinced in his own way that Lawrence was a great man.

I have named the people who wrote the first substantial printed commentaries and memoirs. The stream of ephemeral and often unintelligent reviews which had greeted each of Lawrence's works was joined by a stream of books about him: so that his work was now being seen as a completed whole, by an author becoming a classic. His death in 1930 released this stream. The important first books are Murry's *Son of Woman*, 1931; Catherine Carswell's *Savage Pilgrimage* of 1932, which was partly a retort; Murry's *Reminiscences of D. H. Lawrence*, 1933, which was partly a riposte to Catherine Carswell, and Jessie Chambers's *D. H. Lawrence: A Personal Record* which was published under the pseudonym 'E.T.' in 1935, and was in places a reply to Murry's by now well-known diagnosis. Huxley's contribution was the important and admiring Introduction to the substantial volume of Lawrence's *Letters*, which he collected and edited in 1932. So, quickly after Lawrence's death there grew up a tradition of discussion about him: or rather, a controversy. This fierce argument to-and-fro was started by people who had known Lawrence as man, friend, and potential leader. It was conducted against the general background of slowly forming public opinion about Lawrence's nature as a writer, and helped to shape it.

His first novel and the first stories were well-received. There were people generously willing to recognise a new talent. Some thought, on the basis of the early stories and *Sons and Lovers*, that he was going to be the great working-class writer that the newly enfranchised and literate industrial population ought to produce. That hope soon faded. *Sons and Lovers*, reduced to a classic exposition of the so-called Oedipus Complex, offered others the hope that Lawrence would be the novelist of the newly discovered science of the mind. But Lawrence knew that his insights were deeper and broader than Freud's. Novels cannot be reductive in the way that theory must be. Another significance was that from the beginning there was great frankness in Lawrence's treatment of sexuality; the relations between men and women were his central concern,[1] and there was no way of avoiding the treatment of sexuality. He was bound to react against and suffer from the late-Victorian prudishness which insisted that sex was not a topic for open discussion. It is hard for anyone not born in that era or brought up by parents born in it even to conceive how many things might not then be said. One early reader of *Sons and Lovers* thought it was the dirtiest book he had read; yet he was a publisher, and might have been expected to be sophisticated. So, from the first, with *The White Peacock*, Lawrence had censorship trouble: the tale of Annable and his Lady Chrystabel was too rawly told for publishers anxious about the circulating library sale.

Unconventional or thoughtful people would thus see Lawrence as the standard-bearer of a necessary frankness. This seemed to link him with a progressiveness which he actually despised, and it was a shock to many to discover that Lawrence, who *ought* to be progressive, wasn't. The confusion lasted until after the legal case which made it possible for ordinary people to read the unbowdlerised original version of *Lady Chatterley's Lover*. That book, along with Joyce's *Ulysses*, was for years a rallying-point for people who were against censorship; and because of its nature Lawrence seemed the apostle, even the martyr, of a general liberalism (later called permissiveness) which he was against.

But Lawrence was the man who made it possible for others after him to describe sexual acts using the vernacular words. It has to be accepted as a liberation, of an equivocal kind. In the 1930s F. R. Leavis, writing his first brief study of Lawrence, was convinced that *Lady Chatterley's Lover* was the greatest of the works: partly because he applauded the 'hygienic' effect of using ordinary language to describe sexuality, partly because in that book Leavis could identify the linked themes of the industrial wasteland we live in and the personal lives thwarted by that blight. Yet Leavis lived to deplore the lawsuit against Penguin Books, since he could neither wish the prosecution to succeed nor support the terms in which the book was defended.

Since that case, sexual explicitness in fiction, sanctioned by Lawrence's example, has become a routine exercise, a cliché, or the exploitation of a lingering wish to be titillated. But Lawrence also begins to seem different again. Since it is now realised that he is not progressive, it has been a shock to some who wanted him as an ally to find how anti-progressive he is. He is not liked by feminists either, for good reasons. Those who admire him as the greatest English novelist of the century now see the sexual theme as only an aspect – though a central one – of something wider: a concept of personal development or fulfilment. That too is become an enlightened orthodoxy: part of the transvaluation of values or the rethinking of morality started by Nietzsche. In this area the central discussion of Lawrence as thinker or moralist must now be conducted, though it begs the question of the relationship between his thought and his art.

This evolution of the world's view of Lawrence – the history of his reception in its broadest terms – has been conditioned by the sharp debate about Lawrence's value and status mentioned above. Murry's *Son of Woman* was the book which dictated the original terms of this discussion. This is partly because Murry was endorsed by T. S. Eliot, who without having read much of Lawrence knew that he was against him, and welcomed Murry as having virtually disposed of him. Since Eliot was the most influential critic in England in the 1930s and 1940s, this position-taking, in *After Strange Gods* (1934) and elsewhere, was important, and meant that much discussion of Lawrence became apologetic or over-defensive. It was not until Lawrence was defended by Leavis, who took Eliot's place as the most influential critical voice in England in the 1950s and 1960s, that a convinced case *for* Lawrence was elaborated; and Leavis arguing against Eliot was arguing through him against Murry. But over the years he also changed the ground of his own championship of Lawrence.

Murry's case is not easy to summarise, because in places he is taking up his own stance against Lawrence as rival prophet, and the terms of his prophecy are as personal as any that he found in Lawrence. But briefly, he thought that Lawrence was born to be a religious leader, so that it does not matter that his writings are not 'art'. 'Art', we guess, has to do with the perfection of a form from which the artist has evacuated himself, leaving an exquisite and carefully-crafted structure which may be contemplated from an exclusively aesthetic point of view. Certainly Lawrence is not like that: his writings are always about life, and Lawrence himself is often present, sometimes obtrusively. Murry concedes the lack of art with such speed because he is interested in what he wanted to find instead: the scriptural writings left by the prophet of a new and personal religion. He thought that Lawrence was born to lead, though he led nowhere; he was born to love, though his love was tragically deflected; he was born to suffer, and so can by a rapid and frequent process of Murry's thought be seen as a Christ-figure. He was crucified on the cross formed by the intersection of his mission as Murry saw it, which was to love all mankind, and his own understanding of that mission, which was to introduce a new understanding of the sexual relationship – that is, to love women. But this was a doomed enterprise, since Lawrence was a 'case'. His self-revelation, in *Sons and Lovers* and elsewhere, is of a man whose mothering had made him fatally unable to love any woman sexually. This deflected him into the search for a virility which he could find only in a succession of fictional male alter egos with whom he could imagine a quasi-homosexual relationship; and the progression of the case led him into horrible imaginings in which the virile male brothers become adepts of human sacrifice and the loved women are required to be so abjectly submissive that they finally abjure their own sexuality.

Murry's case is in many respects very shrewd, and never less than plausible. It was based on personal knowledge of Lawrence, and what was for its time a wide and deep knowledge of the writings. It is full of acute insights into the books which even Lawrence's admirers must accept. If Lawrence was cast as a demonic Christ, who had to be forgiven because he knew not what he did, it was clear to others (including Lawrence) what part Murry played: he was Judas, who betrayed with a kiss. Catherine Carswell's *Savage Pilgrimage* was an immediate attempt at a counter-statement. It had some sting in it, and Murry had the first edition suppressed, and responded with his own further *Reminiscences*. *Savage Pilgrimage* was a straightforward brief biography animated by the desire to present Lawrence as normal – perhaps 'representative' is the better word; as a sympathetic human being; as an artist. These things are done mostly by implication. A sense of Lawrence's charm and greatness emerges, and a sense of his importance, but there is no sustained attempt to suggest the ways in which Lawrence was a great writer: there could not be at this stage. People felt, or had an inkling of, what they could not yet get into words.

But Murry could only be answered adequately by someone who would support the claim that Lawrence was a great literary artist. The assertion was finally made by F. R. Leavis, and widely accepted as true, though it was not demonstrated in convincing detail, in his first full-length book on Lawrence, *D. H. Lawrence: Novelist*.[2] The title asserts that Lawrence is important not as prophet, but as a writer of major works of fiction.

Leavis also claimed that Lawrence is the modern continuator of the 'Great Tradition' of the English novel – a claim which was hard in 1955 to understand. The difficulty can be explained in this way. Leavis's Great Tradition originally consisted of Jane Austen, George Eliot, Henry James, Joseph Conrad, and nobody else. These novelists were preeminent because they were centrally concerned with the moral difficulties of socially engaged individual consciences. Their characters are people trying to find their way and to make their choices in a life which continually faces them with problems of conduct, and where one of the main problems is how to judge the character and conduct of others. It is a tradition of strenuous moral discrimination by persons who are confirming their own nature in the struggle.

The fundamental reason why in 1955 it was hard to relate Lawrence to this tradition is that Lawrence quickly seems to thoughtful readers to have dropped the old moral tradition overboard: indeed to be against it. Jane Austen, for instance, whom he once called a 'narrow-gutted spinster', dramatises a social and moral world in which Lawrence's own ethos is at best 'sensibility', and at worst evil conduct. The contrast can be seen encapsulated in a single sentence in a letter from Lawrence to Louie Burrows of 12 April 1911: 'I say, only that is wicked which is a violation of one's feeling and instinct' – one's own feeling and instinct, not that of others. Jane Austen's characters act from principles which they receive from moral authority, though it is true that she shows, in Emma Woodhouse, that unless you learn for yourself the need for these things and their truth they are a dead letter, and that learning may mean growing, and that is painful. This is going on in an active verbalising component of the self which seems to live well above the midriff – indeed, up in the head. If in the end Mr Darcy proves to be a truly lovable person, then it becomes a pleasant duty to love Mr Darcy. Whether he is a sexual being as well as an estimable person is not to be dealt with in the pages of a book. Dickens drew nearer to these matters, but was not at first in the Great Tradition either. George Eliot and James indicated that sexuality was a moral vortex; but they remained at the outer ripples; and by and large their place in the tradition too has to do with conscious ethical strenuousness in the mature social being, where change is a matter of being convinced of the need to change, as a moral imperative.

Leavis had therefore either to accept the hiatus between Lawrence and these others, or to bridge it. Discovering the bridge was an important part of his endeavour, producing a coherence in his account of the English novel. But it took him many years.

He was born in 1895, only ten years after Lawrence, and was of an age to read Lawrence's works as they were published. He came on the first poems and stories in the 'English Review' before the 1914–18 war, and was reminded of them after it, when, shocked and intellectually dislocated like most of the survivors, he set about rebuilding an intellectual life in the 1920s. For him Lawrence became one of the clues in that chaos: T. S. Eliot was the other. Leavis wrote about these two as the most important writers in English of their age, which is still our age. His first writing about Lawrence appeared in 1930, but while it asserted Lawrence's importance, it did not assert Leavis's own understanding. It was nearly twenty years before he thought he was beginning to understand Lawrence: the important essays began to appear in *Scrutiny* in 1949, and were collected in the first book in 1955.

Leavis's indirect retort to Murry, and his explicit rebuke to Eliot, who had too readily accepted Murry's account as serving his own purpose, was to the effect that Lawrence *was* a great artist. But it was an equivocal reply. Leavis produced from the whole range of Lawrence's work a small canon of works of major art: specifically *The Rainbow, Women in Love*, 'St Mawr', and a few others among the longer tales such as 'Daughters of the Vicar' and 'The Captain's Doll'. Other books were commended in passing; but implicitly *Sons and Lovers* was ignored as good but not needing to have anything said about it. Leavis is very dogmatic in this book; he insists that Lawrence is great, and that he is an artist, and the reader gathers that he is so largely because he was deeply involved in, and tragically aware of, the state of modern industrial and urban civilisation.

This was Leavis's own concern. He was anti-Marxist, but had a radical hatred of the dehumanising aspects of modern life: it was as if he was against the means of production, whoever owned them. He felt that an important writer was not alive to his time if he ignored this dehumanisation; it was plain to him that in *The Rainbow* and *Women in Love* Lawrence gave a panoramic survey of English society which was a diagnosis of disease; and so he was predisposed to find these books great. But they are said to be great mostly by asserting that they are about modern society – which is not the same as showing that they have finely performed their function as novels, and may in any case be a distortion of emphasis. Leavis's preoccupations tended to make him slight the other novels; he felt he could admit, without paying it much attention, that a great deal of Lawrence's writing is flawed. He did explicitly criticise *The Plumed Serpent* at length, because Lawrence once said that he thought it the best thing he had done.

There is more than an underthought about Lawrence in the Leavises' book about Dickens, with its closely similar title, *Dickens the Novelist* (1970). For one thing, it seems that Leavis was aware of the need to explain the fundamental difference, or establish a fundamental link, between the writers of his Great Tradition and Lawrence. For Lawrence had a totally different view of the nature and growth of the individual human consciousness, the living being which is making its way in the world; he also had a challengingly different moral outlook; at this very fundamental level his art begins, and that is why it comes out perplexingly different. This was another reason why people brought up in the old tradition couldn't see him as an artist. In *Dickens the Novelist* Leavis bridged the gap by proposing a complementary moral and artistic tradition which runs from Blake through Dickens to Lawrence, and which is a valuable corrective to the Great Tradition of puritan moralism. The essential affinity between these three writers, far removed in time and not obviously linked, is a concept of the self not as a finished thing in a shell of selfhood, but as a growing identity which has to fulfil its own nature or be essentially frustrated. That is, the whole person has its needs; and these must be fulfilled, or development is thwarted.

This casts a retrospective light on the novelists of Leavis's Great Tradition. It was the tradition of the fine individual consciousness, a descendant of the old puritan conscience, the central Protestant thread in the Anglo-Saxon moral inheritance. Conscience is an active controlling force, typically thought of as in the soul or in the head, and linked to consciousness itself. It requires self-knowledge, and it insists on self-control or, if possible, self-transcendence. It tends heroically to say 'no, I must not', and to say it to the impulses which might claim to be needs. It tends to split the person into two parts: one is a conscience, a mind, and it controls the urges of the other – whether it is called the heart, the flesh, the body, or the instinctive impulses of the self. Naturally that includes the sexual impulses, automatically labelled 'lower' than the spiritual ones. Characteristically, the growth of conscience means learning to say 'no' to the mere self. Or, to put it more positively, moral identities are created and confirmed which have the strength to say that necessary no, in tribute to something which transcends the self, and is a social ideal recreated as a personal moral ideal.

The limitation in this tradition, the inherent potential morbidity, is seen in Henry James, where the beauty of saying no to oneself sometimes seems to be indulged at the expense of better things than those that are affirmed; and where the heroes and heroines are always making spiritual widows and widowers of themselves, and retreating into a safe sanctified niche with a satisfied conscience. The notion of the fineness of consciousness becomes so rarefied that the multiplying moral issues can, to a robust moral sense, begin to seem trivial, in the way, and often an excuse for doing nothing with a good grace. Contrad in his *Victory* gives warning of something similar: the central figure Axel Heyst, a fine conscience arrested in self-scrutiny, has become morally paralysed, and is scarcely able, for lack of the necessary coarseness and self-assertiveness, either to assent to simple love or to resist the crudest evil.

Blake proposed as a vital principle the spontaneity which can say yes to the life that Heyst learnt too late to say yes to. Sexuality is a main constituent of that life. Leavis saw Dickens – or one aspect of Dickens – as link between Blake and Lawrence. He suggested that Dickens's language is not just exuberance, but a constant tribute to its own origin: Dickens's sense of life, itself creative and creatively perceived, and strongly set towards the positives that Blake and Lawrence celebrated, and against the personal and social blights they both hated. Class-pride and money-pride are the most obvious, as barriers to open dealing with other whole personalities; but Dickens also showed with great depth of understanding and subtlety how these social attitudes are linked to corruptions of puritan strengths. The ego which congratulates itself on being part of a social elect, and reprobates those who are outside that group, is not just displaying a tribalism disguised as righteousness; within the tribe it will exert a dominating will on younger or weaker members, to form them as members of the elect. The asceticism will bear heavily on sexual self-expression. At the deepest level one is in contact with an exertion of the will, of conscious or unconscious grapplings, parasitism, underminings, dominance. The moral universe that

Dickens displays would be terrifying to the point of suicide if it were not also eruptively animated by counterforces which stand for life: a word which has born a heavy load in the discussion of Lawrence.

Reading Lawrence taught Leavis to go back and revalue Dickens. In the process, Blake's terms 'selfhood' and 'identity' were adopted, appropriated and given an extended programmatic sense. The self represses, but the identity responds to the 'creative flow from below'. The concept became important for Leavis, and is borrowed from Lawrence: it comes from 'Love was once a little boy':

> The individual is like a deep pool, or tarn, in the mountains, fed from beneath by unseen springs, and having no obvious inlet or outlet. The springs which feed the individual at the depths are sources of power, power from the unknown.[3]

The identity which is fed in that way feels responsibility to something other than itself. This is also derived from Lawrence, and the chief locus is the moment in *The Rainbow* when Tom Brangwen is alone outdoors at night in lambing-time and looks up at the sky and knows 'he did not belong to himself'.

'. . . Love was once a little boy' only became available in England when Secker reprinted *Reflections on the Death of a Porcupine* in 1934 in the New Adelphi library. Perhaps Leavis read it then. But the book soon went out of print, and it was not until 1968 that Warren Roberts and Harry T. Moore brought out *Phoenix II*, in which the piece was for the first time made widely and permanently available. It is important now to remember that some of Lawrence's more important 'doctrinal' writings appeared in ephemeral publications and were unnoticed at the time; and some remained uncollected or hard to find until the late 1960s, so they were not in any real sense available until then. When they were, they helped – as they helped Leavis – to get the discussion of Lawrence away from the terms proposed by Murry.

We can see this process continued in Leavis's second book about Lawrence, *Thought, Words and Creativity*, published in 1976, Leavis's 81st year. The same basic critical judgements are proposed, so that Leavis's canon of the 'great' Lawrence is unchanged. But the grounds of the argument are different: or rather they have now been stated because the work on Dickens had made them clear. Leavis's last two books have to be seen as a pair: *The Living Principle* is about Eliot, and *Thought, Words and Creativity* about Lawrence; and Leavis is saying that the two greatest writers in English of their generation both started from a similar point: the contemplation of a sick civilisation which threatens the health, indeed the moral life, of those born into it. As great writers, Eliot and Lawrence had to seek for something which they could offer to their readers as a countervailing good, and in this they were – in Murry's terms – the prophets called for by the times. Yet it could not have been done by mere prophetic assertion: it had to be done through art. To simplify: the alternatives were to revitalise Christianity, or to find some alternative. Eliot did the first thing, and the trajectory from *The Waste Land* to *Four Quartets* can be read as a single artistic testament, in which the search was at heart linguistic. The old Christian language and its images would not do; a new intuition had to be apprehended, and to apprehend it was to create the terms in which it could be expressed as art. The same thing was true of Lawrence: he had to find his own language, for the things he had to say were not at first known – not even to him. To discover what he was trying to say meant finding the way in which it could be said.

This must be true of all great artists. What they are for us is unique – like a voice, a face. It is indistinguishable from their message – what they say is also how they say it. This has been a cardinal aesthetic doctrine ever since the late nineteenth century: indeed it is a commonplace, but it is not common to find criticism which shows the identity. The critic wanting to be faithful to the work would in his own way have to replicate the artist's search, which is not the same as announcing the result by proposing a paraphrase or 'interpretation'. So, in retrospect, to say that Lawrence's critics have all been attempting to learn his language, and to follow the pathways he traced in his own mind, is the best way of characterising both their success and their failure. It is why honest readers have often said 'I don't know what Lawrence is trying to do here'. In honesty they have also said things like 'I find these repetitions boring and obsessive, and I think they indicate a failure'. From very early on they said 'Lawrence cannot create characters', or, more subtly, 'The principle on which Lawrence bases his apprehension of personality is obscure or unstable'. These are non-communications or non-understandings which start with the words, which are not understood.

Conversely, readers familiar with Lawrence begin to build up the sense of a personal language. It starts at the level of pet words like 'winsome', and moves on to something more like a set of technical terms: one begins to watch for words like 'lapse', 'immune', 'uncreated', 'fused', 'realised'. These are metaphorical; they have an active place in a personal system which we also learn, and which uses polarities such as ruddy and blanched, golden and white, with the suggestion that colour is also temperature, which either fosters or represses life. At a further point one realises that these things are emblematic of the largest polarities of all: sun, moon, light, dark. The reader finds that in this world people have some of the properties of flowers, and flowers of people. Other strange things lodge in the memory: if hands, the extremities of the body, are seen as like the tendrils of a plant, they also convey a kind of electricity, so that touch is a communication beyond speech. You become aware that though Lawrence's people speak to each other a lot, and dispute opinions with each other, the most important communication between them is not linguistic in the sense that it is a matter of logical propositions conveyed in neutral words.

After a further time, one realises that this must be so. Lawrence is committed by his genius to proceeding in this way. His medium, as language, must be figures of speech or forms of symbolism; for only in them can he escape the limited scope of the logical intellect, which he conceives as a living death. He has to offer a system of correspondences which constantly drop below ground or move into an upper air, to avoid the (so to speak) telegraph-wire of a thin linear communication of socially agreed meanings, taken in at the eye and ear and understood in the head. He is aiming at the rest of the body which a human being also is.

It is here that we leave the ground of argument staked out by Murry, and enter the one indicated by Leavis – and indeed by Lawrence. Whether Lawrence as a person was a 'case' remains a relevant issue. It is forced upon us by his presence in all his books, so that one often has to ask whether some urgent personal pressure in him forces him to put his thumb in the scale-pan. But the best way of arguing will be by detailed attention to the language or the structure. These are the places where the flaws will appear.

There is the problem also that Lawrence was an opinionated writer who wanted his readers to think, so that large tracts of his books are in the form of extended argument, and in novels like *Women in Love* the characters are locked in endless debate, bitter or leisurely, and the author also addresses us directly. The paradox is that this writer also felt that the great disease of the age is that we are all far too conscious, yet he had no way of conveying this except through our consciousness. He quickly came to believe that the 'blood' (whatever that means) is wiser than the intellect: but in what sense do we read with the 'blood'? Well, perhaps we do, in some way; but he would have to show this, and the first step would be a definition of the 'blood'.

In the fiction we have therefore a complex situation. The author as argumentative person addresses the reader directly; and his characters also argue with each other on intellectual matters. Here they can only use the language of argument. But this vein of debate runs through a living tissue of motifs and metaphors which give a continuous set of hints and directives about mysterious other goings-on, instinctive, non-verbal, which matter more than the surface argument. By these means Lawrence, like any poet, exploits the metaphorical properties of his writer's language which make it unlike the formal language of logicians and which cause the thread of discourse to branch into other than logical paths. This was more essential to his whole undertaking than it might be for other writers, for his developed sense of the individual human being was of a living creature that was always unfolding from some nucleus that was certainly not up in head, with the mediating mind: it was in unmediated contact with the world from other centres of the body. It may have been a tactical error that at one stage Lawrence named these centres (the solar plexus, the lumbar ganglion and so on) and formalised his imagined psycho-physiology. The general principle is still serious, original and important. Lawrence's individuals are not classical selves, moral entities whose principle of coherence is the reflective memory, a process in the head which tells the person remembering that he is the same person that he was in the past, and all the experience he can remember is *his* experience. That is a process in which the consciousness is retentive of the past, and holds on to it as the assurance of continuity of being. For that reason the philosophers' self has a vested interest in remaining as he remembers himself, for fear of not knowing who he is. For

Lawrence that consciousness is suspect *because* it is conservative, and wants to hold people stable. He is aware of a different centre of being where what one does is not so much to think thoughts as to receive immediate senses of the world, or urgent messages from deep in the psyche, which come as impulses or images. This image-making capacity is the condition of an ever-new experience, the unfolding as of a plant which evolves its whole sequence of structures from the original seed, and where the growing-point can be successively shoot, stem, leaf, flower, seedpod. In human life, ever-new experience produces successive selves which are sloughed off at crucial times of life, and new selves are born in a process which is conceptualised as an analogy with perpetual resurrection. In this way we are like trees, or the perennial plants. At important moments we 'lapse out' as seed or nut again, passing through the air to lodge and germinate in the death that is necessary to rebirth.

Here I am anticipating later commentary and argument; but it is useful to say so much by way of introduction. It takes me back to Leavis, the critic who has taken us farther with Lawrence than anyone yet. There were two central perceptions in his second book on Lawrence. The first was his formulation of something like the point I have just made: but characteristic in that Leavis did not use Lawrence's plant analogy; he used instead Blake's notion of the identity as a growing thing which escapes the self-defensive ploys of the ego which only wants to be its safe old self, and to make demands on others and the world. The identity is a braver dynamic being, in process, which has the courage to believe that realising one's needs is not just an egoistic demand. This is an extremely difficult ethical point, a crux; indeed the place where you either follow Lawrence as disciple or criticise him as adversary.

Leavis's other central perception was that all his life Lawrence was seeking for the thing he wanted to say. He was trying to intuit profound apprehensions about the nature of consciousness in the living being, part of a living universe which had to be recovered from the dead abstractions of nineteenth-century rationalism or twentieth-century positivism. These things would finally come to him as the way of expressing them. For part of the time, therefore, he was bound to be failing to say it. The failures were many, and necessary.

Leavis   expresses   this   struggle   as   'the   whole   intuited

apprehension striving to find itself, to discover what it is in words';
or as 'the emergence . . . of original thought out of the ungrasped
apprehended – the intuitively, the vaguely but insistently
apprehended: first the stir of apprehension, and then the
prolonged repetitious wrestle to persuade it into words'.[4] When
the thought had been expressed as art, it could also be seen as
what we should now call a system, where the whole both supports
and demands each part.

This system has as its centre or starting-point the individual
centre of life, the person growing and changing in time. This
monad, as the philosophers might call it, or this soul, as Christians
would call it, lives in a universe of which it is part. It is not a pure
mind puzzled by its separateness from a physical universe which it
merely perceives: nor is it split between an intelligence and a body
which somehow provides lodging for this spiritual entity. The
world is not just seen with the eyes, it actually begins at the middle
of the body and at the fingertips. Hence part of the significance of
the strange phrase which Leavis recovers from *The Plumed Serpent*
as a key to the system: 'It comes from – from the middle – from the
God.'[5]

What goes on in us is not exclusively the accepted process of
thought or reflection up in the top storey, though that does go on;
the more important process is like tides which ebb and flow,
perhaps in the blood. Since we are of the world we are in, we are no
more merely economic and industrial beings than we are merely
intellectual beings. Leavis's sympathy for Lawrence sprang from
his own recoil from a society that reduces our transactions with
the world to economic, political, and at best intellectual
relationships: these proceed by their own logic to identifiable,
quantifiable, manipulable relationships. Acting on political
simplifications, managing the economy, finding technological
solutions, seeking by analysis to find the greatest good of the
greatest number of social beings: all this led to the technologico-
Benthamism that Leavis hated.

And certainly Lawrence hated it too. He was a radical critic of
what Eliot called the Waste Land; in his very first novel we find
him looking for answers to the question that gives no peace: What
for? Leavis was right to bracket Eliot and Lawrence as the most
ambitious and searching writers in English since the first World
War. We have ultimately to ask, both of Eliot and Lawrence, is
their 'answer' coherent, and do we accept it? I put the word in

quotation marks to indicate its provisionality or unsatisfactori-
ness. To face the problems of the twentieth century is banal
because it is inevitable. We all face them, since we are living now,
and the notion of coming up with solutions is absurd. The
problems of any period are its ineradicable difficulties. But a great
writer may make us see them and think about them, and his way of
looking at them will open a mental space around them. Does
Lawrence do that? We read him in order to find out.

There is a paradox in saying that he has a system. Everything
said above was meant to break down the idea that what Lawrence
'meant' was instantly stated, or could ever be instantly grasped –
at a glance – either by himself or by anyone else. Fifty years after
his death we have still not collected or published everything that
he wrote. Any reader needs years in order to take him in, even
using the short-cuts published as criticism. Nonetheless Lawrence
will soon be all there as a writer, available to us; and we do have
some seventy years of writing about him. He is taking shape, and
the shape is surprisingly consonant with the idea of system.

Two other recent critics have developed this idea of his
coherence. J. C. F. Littlewood put it too neatly: 'Lawrence's
development reveals this principle of continuity at work
everywhere, as if all that he had to say was from the beginning
waiting to get itself said.'[6] Carl Baron says something similar:

> The works by Lawrence most widely read are his four
> outstanding novels, *Sons and Lovers*, *The Rainbow*, *Women in Love*,
> and *Lady Chatterley's Lover*. I suggest that it has become a critical
> challenge worth taking up, to understand whether and in what
> ways these very different novels are exploring the same
> fundamental material as *The White Peacock*.[7]

In some respects the position is counter-intuitive. The young
Lawrence who wrote the first draft of *The White Peacock* had not in
1906 left Eastwood, had not before 1912 left England; had not met
his wife; had not suffered the near-madness of the period 1914–18;
had not read the books he later read, or met the later friends and
enemies; had not seen Italy, Australia, New Mexico – and so on.
How could these things not have affected him profoundly? More
simply: he had not had all his 'thoughts', to use that word, and
had not engaged in the profound struggle with them that Leavis
intuited. Yet the paradox is familiar, and personal to us all: it is

one person to whom all this happens, and at the end the person who dies is either the completion or the wreck of the person who was born. It is then, if you are a genius, that the system is complete, and can be contemplated.

Lawrence himself had, very early, been struck by the apparent paradox, and had his own answer. Writing to Helen Corke, who had accused him of inconsistency or fickleness, he replied:

> Why should things that were real to me become false? I don't understand you perfectly. Surely it has always been one of my tenets, that a truth, or a vital experience, is eternal, in so far as it is incorporated into one's being; and so is oneself. How am I one thing today, and another tomorrow? It is an absurdity. Yet you urge it against me very often: it is almost my chief characteristic, in your eyes. You never believe that I have any real unity of character.
>
> An illness changes me a good deal – like winter on the face of the earth: but that does not mean that I am shook about like a kaleidoscope. It would be to deny identity. One may seem very different from one's past, but one is nevertheless the new child of one's yesterdays. (1 February 1912, in *Letters I*, 359–60)

2 Method

In the chapters which follow, my intention is, through the analysis of the early fictions, to establish and develop the general critical position stated by Leavis, and hinted at by Littlewood and Baron. I aim to show the extent to which Lawrence's writing discovers a personal universe which can finally be seen as a system – but also the extent to which the discovery was a life-long search which the reader cannot expect to receive instantaneously. The coherence no more bursts immediately upon us than it did upon him.

From the theoretical point of view, one interest of what follows is that I use the classic 'close reading' techniques of the so-called New Criticism, with an important qualification. I do not take the single work as a closed-off entity to be explicated, relating each part internally to all the others in a closed system whose relations with the world and indeed with the author cannot properly be discussed. My commentary cannot take the works as autonomous, since I am committed to exploring the stages of Lawrence's search: his attempts to realise at various times the things he was always trying to grasp.

Lawrence was also a peculiarly open or instinctive writer, who wanted his intellectual processes to interfere as little as possible with what, deep within him, was trying to come out. This introduces an important psychological dimension. I note below associations much deeper and more extended than the analyst can usually liberate, and we are dealing with psychic products much more dense and elaborate than dreams and fantasies. I have no psychoanalytical scheme of my own which I wish to illustrate by the interpretation of Lawrence. I am simply trying to construct his internal universe by way of his language.

My special interest is in figures of speech – what is often called 'imagery'. This is a convenient term with a very general application, and should be taken to mean not only classical rhetorical forms (simile, metaphor, and larger structures such as symbol and allegory) but anything which presents itself instinctively to the writer as a way of representing which is not literal description, reportage or logical analysis. It can include elements of visualisation such as choice of posture or the imagined features of a character, or imagined or recreated scene. I am not interested in these as attempts to provide descriptions of the outside world. They are often that, but even so the figures which press themselves on a writer come from within, and they strike the reader as original because of this. We can all find the apt cliché, but the poet makes available a direct transcript of his immediate experience, by which he enlarges ours. In these uses of language we feel, as we do in the great soliloquies of Shakespeare's or Racine's dramatic characters, in direct contact with the workings of another mind in a way that ordinary social language does not convey.

In principle I ought to take the writings one by one in chronological order, submit my mind to them as tabula rasa, and report the gradual building-up of the system. In practice this is not possible. The chronological relationship between the works is much more complicated than the sequence of publication dates suggests. To insist on the method would have involved dealing with all the drafts of all the works, for only in that way can strict chronological order be preserved. That is impractical. To act as tabula rasa is also impossible now, and it is sensible to accept that one has some knowledge: helpful also to the reader, since strict insistence on the method would make it improper to point out a significance until a class of phenomena had established itself by repetition and one was then entitled to go back to the first instance and say 'now we understand why he introduced this feature'. This is what I have done in my own reading, but I must spare the reader some tedium.

Looking for signs of a 'system' I start from the position of one who has read the whole work, and a good deal of previous commentary. There is a danger therefore of seeing early things as merely prefiguring later ones – as unsuccessful shots at later successes, or crude statements of later refinements. This is sometimes true, but I try to avoid saying it too often, and the obviousness and boringness of saying it makes it fairly easy to avoid. Each work has to be treated as interesting and complete in itself, and seriously offered.

The system shows itself in parallels, continuities and developments, and so in noticing in one fiction things which bear a relationship to another. Merely noticing parallels can also be mechanical; on the other hand it is rarely a mere parallel that is in question: more often a significant development.

The recurrences which one notes as another example of something met before, and beginning to constitute a class, often seem like trivialities or oddities. I note what look like personal obsessions: certain words are repeatedly used, producing a certain range of association; gestures are repeatedly made, properties (in the stage sense) repeatedly introduced. I record these in all seriousness, for reasons which are worth stating.

In the first place, nothing of this kind is merely odd. Perhaps nothing of a personal kind is: the things about our friends which strike us as odd are what make them them, like their features, their voices and their fingerprints. Since it is one of Lawrence's beliefs that a living being should always be seeking to be more and more itself – unique, for all that it belongs to a species – one must pay due heed. ('Every human sameness is different' as Leavis put it).

Moreover, Lawrence was committed, as a matter of conscious belief, to writing in a particular way. The 'art speech' which was for him, as he said, the 'only speech' could not be a matter of a logical procession of propositions, culminating in considered generalisations or laws of behaviour or morality valid for the sociologically, legally or administratively defined citizen. He was not aiming at the social intelligence. His writing came from, and was aimed at, that point in the middle of a whole person which he called 'the breast', even though he had to use words, taken in at the eye. He was not, as a matter of principle, your ordinary thinker, cogitating a philosophy which could be stated as maxims: though he did this too, quite freely, on the way. He was committed to using words differently, so that they came from deeper in him and strike deeper in us.

For this reason his language needs to be learnt, and one has to look without preconceptions for its key terms. In a letter to Gordon Campbell of 20 December 1914, Lawrence quotes this text from Job:

Who is he that hideth counsel without knowledge? therefore have I uttered that I understood not: things too wonderful for me, which I knew not. (*Letters II*, 246. Cf Job xiii, 3)

The man who as a matter of conviction made himself available as a channel for words to pass through would thus find himself watching his fictions spring 'unbidden from his pen'. Reading after him, we have to be careful not to make premature judgements to the effect that something is merely idiosyncratic. I have, in what follows, taken the line that anything which seems personal or strange should be held in the mind as authentic, and a potential source of power. Such things are mere obsessions if they are only repeated (and there are some); but repetition can manipulate the object until it finally makes the sense which was once merely intuited.

The place from where these things come is, Wordsworth said, the hiding-place of the writer's power. This is so especially with writers like Lawrence who are in their ordinary moments perfectly capable of intelligent discourse about matters of opinion – or also the matters on which they write prophetically or poetically. If you simply summarise his opinions, that is what they are, and he is an opinionated person like you and me, but more intelligent and more articulate. The relationship between these opinions and his gift is what is in question. You don't in the first place *go* to the works for opinions – or if you do, you are treating them wrongly. The novels and stories are more like visions than essays or newspaper articles; and in them you meet a linguistic gift so organised and so available that it transforms the language it uses, and through it the universe of sensation. It is like being given a different way of feeling the world, through that transformed language. The thoughts that we derive ultimately from Lawrence should seem more like the fruits of that world, its feel or its weather – not like official reports from it.

Leavis managed to convince the reader that Lawrence is 'about' certain important topics while never demonstrating in detail how the major fictions convey this. Leavis proceeds by a mixture of hints, rather insistent assertions, apt quotation and a binding element of conclusion, but the reader never finally sees how these conclusions emerge from the data, while agreeing perhaps that they do.

There is no deception here: Leavis himself pointed out that the mature Lawrence does not lend himself to systematic serial commentary. If you were to try to notate all the effects and unpack all the implications, the commentary would be much longer than the original, and very tedious. The commentator is forced back to some such method as Leavis used, or he finds himself doing what other critics have had to do for lack of space – which is to offer a summary paraphrase or a network of key quotations rapidly connected by elliptical comment.

I am attempting to demonstrate what these others seem to me not quite to have managed to demonstrate. I face the same difficulties, and hope that the scale on which I have chosen to work gives me a better chance of success. This volume considers the early works only, and so can give reasonable (I will not say adequate) space to each. I give extended attention to fictions dismissed as apprentice works. Certainly these are not mature or developed specimens of Lawrence's art: but if you believe that from the beginning he was enormously talented and going in the right direction, and was always conscious that there was something he wanted to realise in his work, then it becomes specially interesting to reconsider these first attempts, because there is much in them which was more overt than the later works, and much which later he took for granted. The later books are by the writer who had already said these things.

But we should read them not as early expressions of ideas which later he expresses better. It seems dubious to me that important writers deal in ideas – though a reader may precipitate out an idea-like formulation. What the poet produces is collocations of words, figures of speech. Valéry called these the echoes in an internal cistern, dark reverberations which have shaped themselves as rhythms or phrases. For a novelist they come out both as imagery and as repeated gestures by his characters, repeated poses, groupings; a certain favoured scenery; related predicaments. I do see the early Lawrence repeatedly butting up against insoluble personal problems in his characters which were related to his own; and that is not surprising. But I also see him as bringing out of his memory-well characteristic crystallisations which are hard to place, but which it would be wrong to dismiss as odd or obsessive. It is as if they had to go back into the well, to get more and more accreted crystals; brought out again and turned around in the light, they finally flashed more and more facets of significance. Having recorded these oddities in the commentary on the individual works, I try to show how some of these things acquired their place in this mental world, and how, used and reused, they acquire a weight of significance as members of a family, or the features of a single face.

This book follows Lawrence's writing up to the point when it is generally agreed that his maturity begins. These are unfamiliar works for most readers, and there is good hope that because of this I can realise my intention of making Lawrence strange again. To generalise before the commentary seems premature and prejudicial: on the other hand I should offer some guiding principles before plunging the reader into a dense thicket of detail.

I comment as one who has seen a point in the text before me because I am also familiar with texts I comment on later. The reader may be attending to the text for the first time, and may therefore find the point being made too ponderous for the immediate context. Consider 'A Prelude', Lawrence's very first publication: the little story – hardly more than a sketch – which was one of the entries for the Christmas competition which the *Nottinghamshire Guardian* ran in 1907. Lawrence won the prize for the best Christmas story, and it was printed in the paper. At the simplest level of attention, the reader of 1907 could pass over it with a shrug, perhaps saying 'Nice, but sentimental. A local author. Some local colour.' After the publication of *The White Peacock*, still more of *Sons and Lovers*, alert readers would have recognised the locale and some of the characters as familiar. Almost any reader of Lawrence today can see that Lawrence is here making his first use of the Haggs Farm and the Chambers family: that he was therefore in this very first publication declaring his tendency to create from his own experience. The father and mother of the story are prototypes of the Saxtons in *The White Peacock* and the Leiverses in *Sons and Lovers*. Readers sensitive to smaller recurrences will see Lawrence recording for the first time young miners coming home in their pit dirt, and remarking the strange redness of the lips, and the whiteness of teeth and eyes in the black faces. He found a poignant significance, later, in this strangeness, and readers of 'Daughters of the Vicar' will recognise an attempt to grasp it. So much is relatively easy. But the story itself has a deep point, and it is only after reading the later fictions that the reader is likely to see it.

The eldest son, Fred, works on the land, and is the first sketch of George Saxton in *The White Peacock*. He is in love with Nellie, who lives some distance away, a superior girl, prototype of Lettie Beardsall. He decides to court her, by going to her house as a 'guyser' or mummer in the old play of St George. (Had Lawrence been reading *The Return of the Native?*) His visit makes an

impression on Nellie, who realises that she wants him, despite the
social distance between them. Fred, though, thinks his initiative
has failed, and returns home, cast down. But Nellie then goes to *his*
house, and sings carols outside, as a way of indicating her feelings.
In this way they find each other by managing to make the right
gesture and to interpret the gesture of the other across the social
barrier and the handicap of verbal inarticulacy or
incomprehension. That last sentence comes to me as
interpretation of the point because I have read 'Love Among the
Haystacks', 'Daughters of the Vicar' and other stories. Together
these stories reveal one of Lawrence's preoccupations: with
reaching across, making contact. That impulse itself leads to a
minor theme, a preoccupation with gestures of the hands.

At a certain point in one's reading one can go yet further. When
Fred dresses up in his guyser's costume, there is a perceptible
glamour about him. We notice that he rolls his sleeves up to the
shoulder, and holds his sword in 'one naked muscular arm'. He
'looks at himself with approval' as Lawrence's male heroes in
expansive moods are apt to do.

> "Oh, that is grand," exclaimed his mother, as he entered the
> kitchen. His dark eyes glowed with pleasure to hear her say it.
> He seemed somewhat excited, this bucolic young man. His
> tanned skin shone rich and warm under the white cloth. . . . His
> eyes glittered like a true Arab's, and it was to be noticed that the
> muscles of his sun-browned arm were tense with the grip of the
> broad hand. (*PII* 7)

To dwell too much on that now would be premature, and to
seem to over-interpret. But the reader who comes back to this
passage after reading the other early fictions will recognise the
first use of observations or motifs or images which are the
immediate or sensual substance of Lawrence's writing, and are
the fine structure which ultimately shapes itself into themes or
subjects.

Thanks to the work of the scholars who are establishing his texts,
it is clear that the notion of Lawrence as an impulsive or artless –
even a careless – writer must be abandoned. Few writers worked
harder. Most people know that there are three drafts of *Lady
Chatterley's Lover*, for all three have been published. Few people

realise that *Women in Love* went through at least seven drafts. The early works considered in this volume show Lawrence embarking on his career in the way that he meant to carry on. *The White Peacock* was laboriously rewritten more than once: *The Trespasser* was drastically revised; the important early stories also evolved slowly, sometimes over several years, from early drafts or early published versions, and the final version is often radically different from the first.

Yet Lawrence was reacting against a too conscious art. He said explicitly that it would bore him to 'plot out' a novel in the manner of Henry James. For him there was no question of using a notebook in order to work out in substantial detail a plot, and a cast of characters, or settling down to elaborate notes for a worked-out structure, calculated to fulfil that plan. Still less did he want to illustrate a preconceived theme which had come to him as a product of thought.

He said that the fictions came 'unbidden' from the pen. Writing, he watched them arrive, and welcomed them as interesting but hitherto unknown kinsfolk. This was not inconsistent with art, since if they didn't feel right he had to sit down and write them out again and again, until they *did* feel right. Since he lived by selling his work, he could be persuaded of the need to tinker and patch small details to satisfy commercial requirements, but he was often unwilling to do it himself and turned aside, resigned, while Garnett 'barbered' *Sons and Lovers*. He never let that degree of revision by another hand happen again. All the evidence shows that his own method was successive complete redrafting. For a man who died young, produced in a relatively short writing-career an impressive number of works, yet also had some long barren or fallow patches, he therefore worked with daemonic energy. It was the daemon that he counted on, and wanted to liberate; the redrafting process was an enabling device, which could release the required spontaneity in combination with a reconsidering process which would produce the eventual form. This was not planned so much as finally recognised.

It follows that the formal devices such as we can identify in the early fictions had to be as simple and unconstricting as they are. The basic elements of *The White Peacock* are two contrasted young couples and, in Parts I and II, the procession of the seasons. George Saxton and Lettie Beardsall, Emily Saxton and Cyril Beardsall are introduced to us in summer, and begin to work out their lives as the cosmic time-scheme unfolds through autumn, winter, spring, summer again, and so on. The attention given to skies and trees and flowers means that the human protagonists are naturalised as part of the scene, blooming and withering like the plants, and trapped and frustrated like wild animals caught in snares, or domestic animals manipulated by invisible stockmen. The interplay between sentient beings and the setting in which they are no longer fully at home gives the first novel, for all its failure and excesses, an extraordinary breadth of implication, and an ambition which only a great writer would propose to himself.

The Trespasser, like many of the short stories, is based on a very simple temporal device: introduction or prelude in the present; flashback to the recent past which has produced the present; climax; postlude back in the present. It is a scheme which could become mechanical, but it is simple enough to be unobtrusive, to permit the daemon to work, and to survive redrafting.

Sons and Lovers shows Lawrence settling down to his mature form: the well-paced sequential narrative in very substantial chapters each made up of scenes or incidents simply juxtaposed. *The White Peacock* showed the first attempt to write in such chapters. It is remarkable how many components each may have, and how un-banal their choice and juxtaposition can be. The effect is to make the chapter a strikingly original movement (to borrow the musical term).

The staple medium throughout is Lawrence's prose: that of a poet whose prose was always better poetry than his poetry. At the outset, in *The White Peacock*, it is often intrusively 'poetic'; but the real objection is not that it *is* so, but that it often verges on bad poetry, when Lawrence is borrowing, unassimilated, the pose, manner and idiom of poetic prose-writers and poetasters of the 1890s. It can be bad in *The Trespasser* when it is too consciously or intensively developing the thematic web which forms the fine structure of that novel. Here again *The White Peacock* was preparatory; its network of references to plant- and animal-life turns the simple temporal sequence of the seasons into a more elaborate symbolic scheme, assimilating the human characters more closely to the other forms of life around them. In *The Trespasser* the image-web or symbolic structure is denser, more worked out, and felt more intensely, if not more truly or deeply. It also differs importantly in that the network in *The White Peacock* is largely homogeneous: consisting of references to plant and animal life in a simple analogical scheme. In *The Trespasser* the elements are more multifarious, and the metaphoric life of the prose is such that the elements metamorphose more freely into each other, so that the effect of those passages is not 'descriptive' but an organic life like the verse medium in English renaissance drama, but more heavy-laden, more conscious and more cloying.

The writer – even the genius – who stands aside to let the deep hidden thing come out is making genuine originality possible;[1] but he may produce automatic writing, trivia, or, as I suggested above, unassimilable oddities. It is here that the willingness to rewrite becomes important: the product can go back into the well. Here also the idea of an unfolding oeuvre becomes important. The individual works have two signifiances: one in their own right, and one as part of the total unfolding which can only be received from the whole shelf-full of books: the works of D. H. Lawrence.

From this point of view, all the works become interesting again, and there opens up the possibility of an appeal against Leavis's drastic reduction of the oeuvre to a few works which are great because 'achieved', and the rest which are not. The approach I have adopted does give a reason for reassessing neglected works, and it can award them a special status as stages (if only as false steps) in a sequence. But it does not rule out one critical approach so much as to suggest another: it could supply one criterion for a revaluation.

I do not take the simple view that each individual work is like a single sentence; and the whole work a paragraph (a 'structure') in which the last words of the last book reach a premeditated full stop, and a single large clear message is at last revealed. It is true that the whole life's work, being the product of one mind, has the unity of a mind. But that includes the mind's growth and decay, its profusion and miscellaneousness, changes of mind, and a certain amount that turns out to have a momentary life which is not sustained.

This can produce both continuities and discontinuities. The continuities cross the boundaries of the single works, and one can watch them with interest and profit. But they can also just stop; drop out of sight; Lawrence has worked out the vein and finished with them, or else he has taken them into his bloodstream, and something else is now his concern. I can give a relatively trivial example of this, and a more serious one, a lasting and deep preoccupation.

The first is one of the themes or motives identified in the commentary and it concerns flowers or berries in a woman's hair. Some actual experiences of Lawrence's which gave him the idea are recorded in *Sons and Lovers* – providing an example of how early events in the biographical record are given a written form which is relatively late. I cite two instances in the chapter on *Sons and Lovers* below: the first is the occasion when Paul Morel threads daisies in the hair of Lily Western and says she looks like 'a young witch-woman'; the second is when he scatters cowslips over Clara Dawes' hair, saying 'Ashes to ashes, and dust to dust, / If the Lord won't have you the devil must.' If the devil must, perhaps it is because she is a witch (or so we learn to think, by picking up Lawrence's own associations). I might have quoted also the later occasion on which Paul picks cherries, high up in the tree and pelts Miriam Leivers with them. 'She ran for shelter, picking up some cherries. Two fine pairs she hung over her ears; then she looked up again.' (*S & L*(P) 34). Within a page of this incident Paul takes her 'in among the trees' where 'it was very dark among the firs', and she gives herself to him in sacrifice. The collocation of incidents is not accidental, and reflected forward over it are the implications of these earlier remarks:

> There were some crimson berries among the leaves in the bowl. He reached over and pulled out a bunch.
> 'If you put red berries in your hair,' he said, 'why would you look like some witch or priestess, and never like a reveller?'
> She laughed with a naked, painful sound.
> 'I don't know,' she said.
> His vigorous warm hands were playing excitedly with the berries.
> 'Why can't you laugh?' he said. 'You never laugh laughter.'
> (*S & L*(P) 240)

Witch, priestess and reveller are here associated in a ternary opposition. Miriam as priestess is unhappily presiding over the sacrifice of herself: so we learn from the story.

Jessie Chambers with cherries in her ears was an actual memory; there is a poem about it in a letter to Blanche Jennings in January 1909.[2] There is also a literary reminiscence which Lawrence may have had at the back of his mind while writing the novel. In a letter written in February of the same year to Louie

Burrows on her twenty-first birthday, he sent her a volume of Ibsen, containing *Hedda Gabler*. It is a strange, wild letter, rejoicing in Louie as an Atalanta, healthy and strong, an Amazon, a Bacchante, in her 'comparative jolly savagery of leopard-skins and ox-hide buskins'. She can 'tell Ibsen's people they are fools.' The letter ends 'Be jolly – be a woman.'[3]

Hedda Gabler, we remember, longed for a mate who would come home to her from some Bacchanal with vine-leaves in his hair, flushed and fearless, a free man. Lawrence's mind has moved from the gift, to a contrast between Hedda's wish and Louie's actuality. He imagines her as a Bacchante, an Atalanta, because that is what Jessie Chambers (Miriam) was *not* like.

Lawrence was revising *The White Peacock* at this time, and the incident with Jessie found its way into the book. Cyril puts berries in Emily's hair:

> I plucked a few bunches of guelder-rose fruits, transparent, ruby berries. She stroked them softly against her lips and cheek, caressing them. Then she murmured to herself
> "I have always wanted to put red berries in my hair." . . .
> She thrust the stalks of the berries under her combs. Her hair was not heavy or long enough to have held them. Then, with the ruby bunches glowing through the black mist of curls, she looked up at me, brightly, with wide eyes. I looked at her, and felt the smile winning into her eyes. Then I turned and dragged a trail of golden-leaved convolvulus from the hedge, and I twisted it into a coronet for her.
> "There!" said I, "You're crowned." . . .
> "Not Chloë, not Bacchante. You have always got your soul in your eyes, such an earnest troublesome soul."
> The laughter faded at once, and her great seriousness looked out again at me, pleading.
> "You are like Burne-Jones' damsels. Troublesome shadows are always crowding across your eyes, and you cherish them. You think the flesh of the apple is nothing, nothing. You only care for the eternal pips. Why don't you snatch your apple and eat it, and throw the core away."
> She looked at me sadly, not understanding, but believing that I in my wisdom spoke truth, as she always believed when I lost her in a maze of words. She stooped down, and the chaplet fell from her hair, and only one bunch of berries remained. (*WP*(C) 68–9)

This is long and heavy, and done too much through Cyril's sermonising, as Lawrence soon realised (compare the rapidity of the notation in the *Sons and Lovers* variant). But it has its own force, and even more as the first of a number of motivic recurrences. Emily's serious effort to be a reveller, his wish to crown her, are against the grain of her nature. The Burne-Jones damsel will recur in 'The Witch à la Mode' and elsewhere as Tennyson's Lady of Shalott. The apparently wild remarks about 'the flesh of the apple' move from one theme to another more important one: Emily is an old, not a new Eve. The new Eve has primroses, not berries, in her hair in the story of that name, so is associated with spring, not autumn.

The note is repeated in *The White Peacock* in the chapter called, appropriately, 'The Forbidden Apple'. It is the one in which Lettie is tempted by George, but can overcome the temptation because it is not strong enough. Here it is Lettie who makes the gesture. She has said 'Shall we go into the wood for a few moments?', and they turn aside.

> "If there were fauns and hamadryads!" she said softly, turning to him to soothe his misery. She took his cap from his head, ruffled his hair, saying:
> "If you were a faun, I would put guelder roses round your hair, and make you look Bacchanalian." (*WP*(C) 214)

But she insists that they are not free: indeed, contemplating the possibility of freedom, she is frightened of it: 'If we were free on the winds! But I'm glad we're not.'

Evidently this was a notion that Lawrence was much taken with, as the recurrence in *Sons and Lovers* shows. But the later recurrence in 'New Eve and old Adam' shows the motive dropping into its place, seeming there to be merely a strange little detail, unexplained and unrelated to other elements of the local imagery. It is something which is not carried forward when Lawrence moves out of the world of Jessie, Louie and Helen Corke. Or rather, the incidental touch – berries/flowers in the hair – first associated with Jessie and Louie as failed or successful revellers has now become assimilated into the larger and more important motive, which does recur in later works, of the Dionysian, the Bacchanalian, or Pan himself; or else it is diverted another way – towards the Biblical reference, to Eve. Through her it is linked to the truly vital theme: is the woman, as Adam's rib, 'flesh of his flesh'? So what seemed at first no more than an oddity has a small but organic place in a long process of not exactly thought, but a mutation of images which carry a preoccupation, a tension.

My second example is fundamental to Lawrence's internal personal life because it touches on his deep sense of his own viability as an identity sometimes threatened with chaos and slipping towards death. I analyse below the passage at the end of *Sons and Lovers* where the notion of his alter ego Paul Morel as 'a tiny upright speck of flesh' mutates kaleidoscopically: the speck becomes an ear of wheat in a huge field; and by a natural verbal association becomes a 'grain', like the 'little stars' and the sun. They make the scale immense, and himself even smaller; but like him, they are threatened by the vastness of the immense night of space. This is because his mother is dead. She has taken with her into the void his sense of a comfort behind him; and by a personal association of his own, this comfort was seen as a light. The association came from his childhood fears and dreads, where that light was once identified with a particular remembered lamppost which stood upright, as he now stands upright, and which cast around it a circle of safe illumination. Beyond that illumination lay – still lies – the realm of dread, and this can at times suggest predatory animals prowling round. By a natural inversion, very confident barbarians can be imagined bursting out of a circle of darkness into the light of a new world.

This strange phantasmagoria in *Sons and Lovers* is related to the experience of Paul Morel, and it expands kaleidoscopically all over his mental sky at the moment of crisis which Lawrence is willing into a victory at the end of *Sons and Lovers*. It does, to me, seem willed there rather than a natural flow of spontaneous association. There is something over-grandiose about it which is like similarly Hardyesque moments in his other early fictions. Making your characters fit the scale of the whole universe need not necessarily imply humility, but titanism; or it can become a stock mechanism. But there are other uses of the scheme which are less willed towards a conclusion, more spontaneous.

You can find elements of this same image-syndrome persisting throughout Lawrence's mature writing. It can also be found as a common-sensical self-diagnosis, to the effect that he needed a woman 'at his back' if he was to do anything effectual. While true, this is banal, and no more than other people can manage to say for themselves. What is interesting about Lawrence is that he can show the kind and depth of the original internal currents which may also come out later as a piece of banal social wisdom. He can go back and catch the pressure of actual experience which judgement summarises and may defuse. For instance, the notion of a circle of light which may be crossed can by one of Lawrence's surprising associations transform itself into the notion of the bodily envelope, the 'sheathing', which may leak, or which may be pervious. The reader who is attuned to these circuits, if I can use the phrase, learns to be affected by subliminal or potential unfoldings when certain words set them working. For instance, in 'The Witch à la Mode' the Lawrence-figure-hero says: 'I've got such a skinful of heavy visions, they come sweating through my dreams.' That makes him the kin of Siegmund McNair in *The Trespasser*, as well as of Paul Morel, and also of George Saxton in *The White Peacock*, some of whose words acquire a different force when the reader comes back to them after reading *Sons and Lovers*. In this early writing, Lawrence had not yet got deeply enough into what he is trying to say: partly because his mother had not yet died, and so he had not felt, or not felt fully, a horror which was to seize him when he felt that with her his own light was gone. But George Saxton is as if prophetically attuned to this state. In his last appeal to Lettie he says:

> "I was only a warmth to you . . . so you could do without me. But you were like the light to me, and otherwise it was dark and aimless." (*WP*(C) 302–3)

George finds related and more urgent words when he defines his metaphysical dread to Cyril:

> "I am like this sometimes, when there's nothing I want to do, and nowhere I want to go, and nobody I want to be near. Then you feel so rottenly lonely, Cyril. You feel awful, like a vacuum, with a pressure on you, a sort of pressure of darkness, and you yourself – just nothing, a vacuum – that's what it's like – a little vacuum that's not dark, all loose in the middle of a space of darkness, that's pressing on you." (*WP*(C) 287–8)

The distance between what is hesitantly grasped at here and the orchestral statement which concludes *Sons and Lovers* is a measure of Lawrence's development between the two books. What links the two passages is a direct intuition of Lawrence's, which starts from his personal experience, is made more anguished by his bereavement, which is equally personal, but is always striving towards the status of valid statement about the relationship between the single focus of life and the universe it inhabits. The reader who rejects it as over-intense and grandiose still remains directly in touch with the movements of this other mind – Lawrence's – through having been dominated by his associative procedures. In this way one is swayed by something not normally recognised as persuasion or even thought.

These thematic chains are the naked or unmanipulated internal experience which is the substance of a large part of the life of the mind. This is continuous, so that most of the time we do not think discrete thoughts; what is going on in the active consciousness, either before thought or underlying it, is this procession or stream, intermittently verbal, and very much like a kaleidoscopic metamorphosis. The thoughts we verbalise have become social because they have to be put into a shared language. The original process is personal: it is only Lawrence for whom that lonely lamp-post, radiating a semi-circle of light before it, becomes a central meeting point of his associations. The taxonomist–collector of such phenomena will recognise in the 'single upright at the centre of a circular plane' an archetype or universal; but such universals have already become concepts, with a merely notional importance. The particular lamp-post in Eastwood becomes a direct contact with Lawrence's own mental world. As figure of speech, it is part of his language-system, which is a personal metaphor-system.

For instance, the single light radiating its beams around it has natural associative links with his other central metaphor, which issues from his sense of opposed possibilities: the individual life as baffled smoky burning, as banked-up fire, or as clear flame, as candle-flame. We can see the metaphors issuing in doctrine in the very important letter to Ernest Collings, written a few weeks after he had sent *Sons and Lovers* off to Garnett. It contains a simple statement of his self-knowledge: 'It is hopeless for me to try to do anything without I have a woman at the back of me.' Almost at once that is turned into the remembered sensation of physical dread: 'I daren't sit in the world without a woman behind me. And you give me that feeling a bit: as if you were uneasy of what is behind you.' Then there is the statement of his present position, now that his lack or weakness is supported by Frieda: 'But a woman I love sort of keeps me in direct communication with the unknown, in which otherwise I am a bit lost.' Maintaining this orientation towards 'the unknown' despite the dread of doing so is essential to his art, in which 'the unknown' is being invited into the circle of light; and that is the purpose of his method of writing.

The letter goes on to make his routine disclaimer: 'Don't ever mind what I say. I am a great bosher, and full of fancies that interest me.' We learn how to treat that: he must be talking in complete earnest. A paragraph later comes the classic utterance which every reader remembers and quotes:

> My great religion is a belief in the blood, the flesh, as being wiser than the intellect. We can go wrong in our minds. But what our blood feels and believes and says, is always true. The intellect is only a bit and a bridle. What do I care about knowledge. All I want is to answer to my blood, direct, without fribbling intervention of mind, or moral, or what not.

This is a letter, we remember; written swiftly as an expression of the moment's mood, and not on oath. So it is free and emphatic and without afterthought. We, reading now, may have our own afterthoughts before we start taking this as a rule of life. For the moment however, it is worth saying that direct access to the association process, and the fictions in their larger aspect, give us a sense of what is meant by the 'blood'. We can read 'The Prussian Officer' and see what happens; or 'New Eve and Old Adam', where the Lawrence-figure Peter Moest is a conscious sufferer who attends to the tides contending in his 'blood' and is in danger of being pulled apart by them. Just 'answering to my blood, direct' seems to have tragic consequences in one story, and to be importantly qualified as a possibility in the other; we reflect that the artist speaks in the letter, and has told us not to trust him, but to 'trust the tale'. The artist, however, continues in his vein of central utterance, and veers into one of his great metaphors:

> I conceive a man's body as a kind of flame, like a candle flame forever upright and yet flowing: and the intellect is just the light that is shed onto the things around. And I am not so much

concerned with the things around; – which is really mind: – but with the mystery of the flame forever flowing, coming God knows how from out of practically nowhere, and being *itself*, whatever there is around it, that it lights up. We have got so ridiculously mindful, that we never know that we ourselves are anything – we think there are only the objects we shine upon. And there the poor flame goes burning ignored, to produce this light. And instead of chasing the mystery in the fugitive, half lighted things outside us, we ought to look at ourselves, and say 'My God, I am myself!'

I shall show that the candle-flame, golden and warm, associated with the sweetness of honey and the warmth of the sun, is a cardinal point to which Lawrence's compass naturally sets. It is opposed in Lawrence's associative world to the fierce white light of the pressure lamp, to the coldness of moonlight, and the corrosive power of salt glittering in that light like the pillar which once was Lot's wife. The cold white light is identified with mind, the warm gold one with being. He goes on:

That is why I like to live in Italy. The people are so unconscious. They only feel and want: they don't know. We know too much. No, we only *think* we know such a lot. A flame isn't a flame because it lights up two, or twenty objects on a table. It's a flame because it is itself. And we have forgotten ourselves. We are Hamlet without the Prince of Denmark. We cannot *be*. 'To be or not to be' – it is the question with us now, by Jove. And nearly every Englishman says 'Not to be'. So he goes in for Humanitarianism and such like forms of not-being. The real way of living is to answer to one's wants. Not 'I want to light up with my intelligence as many things as possible' – but 'For the living of my full flame – I want that liberty, I want that woman, I want that pound of peaches, I want to go to sleep, I want to go to the pub and have a good time, I want to look a beastly swell today, I want to kiss that girl, I want to insult that man' – Instead of that, all these wants, which are there whether-or-not, are utterly ignored, and we talk about some sort of ideas. (17 January 1913, in *Letters I* 502–4)

Lawrence liked Collings, who he never met, but who was a sympathetic distant correspondent, to whom he could overflow.

He has here had an inspired spillage, a moment of seeing everything clearly and getting it on paper in an easy run of words. The letter sums up as conscious doctrine a lot that he had worked at in the early fictions: the flame metaphor, the candle-light, come from all three first novels. But it is also a forward-looking set of remarks, even if the generalisation about the Italians may have had its origin in a visit to the Italian opera in Croydon at the end of March 1911, and his intuition then that Italians 'run all on impulse, and don't care about their immortal souls, and don't worry about the ultimate', and the thought that he himself was 'just as emotional and impulsive as they' (*Letters I* 247). Idle then, as later, to say 'do you mean some Italians or all Italians?' and idle for actual Italians to say that they care very much about their immortal souls. He carried that doctrine with him to Italy and found it confirmed: in 1913 he was engaged in the metaphysics of *Twilight in Italy* where this notion of unconsciousness is crucial, and it was to be the underlying datum of the first part of *The Rainbow*, where the first Brangwens are given that kind of unconsciousness.

The image of the candle-flame, flowing off the upright body of the candle as a natural process is an apt figure for a happy luminous being, untormented by self-consciousness, and an apt way of symbolising one of Lawrence's talents, which is to come at what people are, as distinct from what they think and say, or what they drive themselves to be, think and say. The associations of honey and sunlight are with pleasure, happiness and natural flowering and fruiting. Natural happy being, as distinct from thinking, is (to enter into Lawrence's central paradox) what one ought to think about preserving against thought. It is a shrewd, conscious and pertinaciously pursued perception – dramatised in *Women in Love* – that the intellectual or social goals people set themselves may be a compensation for the lack of such being, or even a self-thwarting. It is bound up with Lawrence's rejection of self-sacrifice in *Sons and Lovers*. If you were to add to his catalogue in his letter the things that he wanted himself: 'I want that other man's wife, and I want her to forget her children' it is not a merely *ad hominem* argument. If you were to add: 'I want to murder that Prussian Officer', or 'I want to rape and murder this ten-year-old girl' you face a difficulty in his position which he is not at this moment concerned with.

There is however a basic consistency in Lawrence's position.

The willingness to let the writing come directly in metaphor, and gradually to shape itself in fictions through successive phases of rewriting, is his willingness to become himself as a writer, and to discover what that might mean through the writing. It implies openness and courage. As a subsequent stage, he can announce to Collings in his letter what this is beginning to mean, and to express this as something like ordinary opinion, maxim or generalisation. It is still an image-generated form of discourse. Challenged on the morality of his utterance, he would accept that his wants had taken him where he was and given him the troubles that he had, and he was not disowning them. As for other people's extreme wants, or what might be the issue of a 'blood' which had been thwarted or tainted or corrupted – that might be the subject of later fiction. Meanwhile, it seems to me that he wants the exclamation 'My God, I am myself!' to be said in wonder and admiration, and that presupposes a self one can identify oneself with. Other people can, or should, say it in an entirely different tone of voice, or might not be able to face saying it at all.

Lawrence, contemplating himself, could discover genius, and I think most of his readers will agree (perhaps after thought) that he was a good man.[4] The doctrine of spontaneity and self-fulfilment meant that in standing aside to let the writing come, or to let the daemon speak, or to let that which was perfectly himself take place within him, what spoke, what took place, was Lawrence himself.

This seems obvious; but there is a potential equivocation in the doctrine of spontaneity. The tarn in the hills, which Leavis thought of approvingly as a type of valuable spontaneity, is fed from below by unseen springs. The water comes in from some physical source with which the tarn is in direct though hidden touch because it is there, situated in the rock. The figure won't really do for people, who walk about, and are not literally pervious to anything. When Lawrence stood aside to let his writing take place, it was a valuable discipline for him, and it justified the very acute piece of criticism which Frieda wrote to Garnett (one of the best pieces of Lawrence-criticism):

I also feel as if I ought to say something about L's formlessness. I don't think he has 'no form'; I used to. . . . I think the honesty, the vividness of a book suffers if you subject to it 'form'. I have heard so much about 'form' with Ernst, why are you English so keen on it, their own form wants smashing in almost any direction, but they can't come out of their snail-house. I know it is so much safer. That's what I love Lawrence for, that he is so plucky and honest in his work, he dares to come out in the open, and plants his stuff down bald and naked, really he is the only revolutionary worthy of the name, that I know, any new thing must find a new shape, then afterwards one can call it 'art'. I hate art, it seems like grammar, wants to make a language all grammar, language was first and then they abstracted a grammar; I quite firmly believe that L is quite great in spite of his 'gaps'. Look at the vividness of his stuff, it knocks you down I think. It is perhaps too 'intimate' comes too close, but I believe that is youth and he has not done, not by long chalks! . . . I am sure he is a real artist, the way things pour out of him, *he* seems only the pen . . . (19 November 1912, *Letters I* 479)

But he is not only the pen, but the person holding it, and what it writes comes from him. It comes from further back than with a smaller writer, and it is, as Frieda says, vivid and new in consequence, but it is not from anyone or anything beyond him.

This is a matter on which Lawrence could equivocate. In a letter to Helen Corke written in his days as a teacher he wrote:

> I was thinking today: how can I blame the boys for breaches of discipline. Yet I must not only blame, I must punish. Once I said to myself: 'How can I blame – why be angry?' Then there came a hideous state of affairs. Now I say: 'When anger comes with bright eyes, he may do his will. In me, he will hardly shake off the hand of God. He is one of the archangels with a fiery sword: God sent him – it is beyond my knowing'. (21 June 1910, *Letters I* 164)

A metaphor has all its implications, and to argue that way can be dangerous. Lawrence knew that his anger was there, and if it was provoked, it must come out. So much we all learn; it is useful for children to learn that the teacher in front of them may change from Blake's horse of instruction into his tiger of wrath. Most of us do well to fear our anger and to try to hold it back. To say that it is sent by God is not something the recipients of the punishment will accept as anything but our self-justification. They will say that responsibility is not so easily displaced.

Meanwhile it is possible to look at the early fictions as a group of writings given shape and consistency not only by their relationship to Lawrence's life, but by their own progression. It is dangerous to take the programmatic utterances thrown out in the letters as if they were sober formulations having the same status as the fictions. There is a relationship: but the letters are the product of a single spontaneity, while the works are more meditated, and more complex in consequence.

The young Lawrence could say to Blanche Jennings in a letter in 1908: 'Real independence and self-responsibility are terrifying to the majority; to *all* girls, I think' (*Letters I* 62). Another writer might have proposed it as a theme, but the long working-out of *The White Peacock* gives a depth even beyond the comment of the author contemplating Lettie's marriage-choice and its effects. And George Saxton's very convincing decline and collapse in that novel is a prophetic comment on the assumption that any person can say 'My God, I am myself!' with true self-knowledge or self-approval, or have the energy and the gift to take a self blown off-course and steer it back to harbour. Similarly it was not enough for George to know that he 'wanted that girl', Lettie. He would have had to be somebody different to get her; and getting her would only have been a different disaster.

The total and tragic frustration of Siegmund Macnair in *The Trespasser* is like an admonition from the real world to the Lawrence who in March 1911 wrote to Helen Corke, who lived with the consequences of stepping 'out of the common pale':

> But entre nous, and entre nous alone – we can make our own laws. Step out of the common pale, and the old laws drop obsolete – you know that – and new laws suddenly reign. (*Letters I* 240)

Lawrence, about to start on the revision of *Paul Morel* which was to turn it into *Sons and Lovers*, wrote in a letter to Edward Garnett of 22 July 1912:

> I *don't* want to go back to town and civilisation. I want to rough it and scramble through, free, free. I don't want to be tied down. . . . I'm only coming out wholesome and myself. (*Letters I* 427)

Paul Morel looks, at the end of *Sons and Lovers*, as if he *is* going back to town and civilisation, to take some part in the enterprise of being socially human. The novel ends there, but in the light of all that has happened in its course we wonder what he might make of that enterprise. It is possible that he has come out 'wholesome and himself', and it is certainly Lawrence's intention that he should now be in some sense free. He will not accept the obligation, the servitude, of paying back those who have sacrificed themselves to him, and he will not sacrifice himself to them; yet with his history behind him a *need* for freedom is one thing, but achieved freedom is another: he seems damaged for life. That was Murry's conclusion about his creator, who went through that experience himself. What Lawrence's genius has shown is a triumph of consciousness, which seems the best recourse in the circumstances. In the letter to Collings Lawrence seemed to be repudiating consciousness ('we know too much. No, we only *think* we know such a lot'). But the effect of his extraordinary labour to create spontaneously was to bring things out into the light; and what is that but a form of consciousness? And what are the fictions but an address to 'town and civilisation'?

But Lawrence must be given the last word. It was both his intellectual conviction and his habit of life that one must always be ready to move into another phase. A crystallised consciousness of something lived through must always become something one collects in the mind like a set of dead facts. He touches on this in the story 'A Modern Lover': '. . . thought – that's not life. . . . We've got to begin again . . .'. The same perception gives force to the sentence in a letter to Helen Corke which I quoted above: Lawrence always expected to be, at every next phase, 'the new child of his yesterdays'. So Paul Morel is not the psychoanalyst's patient who after a long stasis has by analysis struggled back to discover, recognise, and if possible exorcise the infantile trauma which arrested his growth and removed his freedom. He is a being in process who has by an internal personal evolution decisively cast his early life behind him and entered the next stage of his life. This is evidently a kind of faith. Like all faith it runs the risk of being an illusion, but is the foundation of Lawrence's ethic.

3   The White Peacock

'In the first place it is a novel of sentiment – may the devil fly away with it – what the critics would call, I believe, an 'erotic novel' – the devil damn the whole race black –, all about love – and rhapsodies on spring scattered here and there – heroines galore – no plot – nine-tenths adjectives – every colour in the spectrum descanted upon – a poem or two – scraps of Latin and French – altogether a sloppy, spicy mess.' Lawrence was the first to deprecate his first book in April 1908 in this letter to Blanche Jennings (*Letters I* 43–4).

But we learn to see behind Lawrence's self-deprecation. What he wrote mattered to him greatly, but he was uncannily able to anticipate criticism by stating it himself as a concessive move. In later letters to her he went on retreating into her presence with his draft of *The White Peacock*, at that time called *Laetitia*, and in between the self-dispraise reminding her that 'In Laetitia there is, I would declare it in the teeth of all the jabbering critics in the world, some beautiful writing – there are some exquisite passages, such as I shall not write again' (13 May 1908, *Letters I* 53).

In 1908 and 1909, during the later stages of the writing, one difficulty that faced him was that, in his first year of teaching, his daily work was an exhausting demand on him, and he could only write at intervals. The book was not naturally falling into the sort of spontaneous unity he wanted but did not yet know how to achieve. He had to accept this: 'I'm afraid it will be a mosaic. My time's so broken up. . . . It will have to be . . . a mosaic of words' (Chambers: *Personal Record*, 104).

The 'mosaic effect' in *White Peacock* is certainly damaging. The reader finds that there is an impressive overall pattern, but within it some pieces contribute little. So for instance one gets quickly tired of young Alice Gall, a portrait of the real-life Alice Hall,[1] put in as a 'character-piece'. Her would-be sprightly chatter is boring and intrusive. The whole story of Cyril Beardsall's suddenly rediscovered father, who enters only to die, should have relevance as illustrating alienation from the family and drunken failure, but is separable from the overall structure and weakly handled. More important, the story of Annable the gamekeeper also fits uneasily. It mattered to Lawrence: there is something working below the surface here, so that the account is highly charged and disturbing, and Annable has an important role as substitute-father for Cyril, an analogue of George Saxton, and in wider terms a representative of thwarted male life, a baffled Pan. But he too suddenly looms up, tells his story, dies, and disappears in little more than a chapter; another separable element. The attempt to give his 'note' a continuing reverberation leads to a further separate piece – the story of his wife and family after his death, and especially the story of little Sam, his son, a Dickensian set-piece of comedy and pathos, also un-integrated. There is another tiny set-piece, entirely gratuitous, about the spinster Miss Sleighter (and I suppose few readers even remember who she is or where she comes).

There are also, as Lawrence said, too many lengthy conversations. That is a good fault, in a writer who wants to show things working themselves out and not just to assert that they happened; but a conversation can be pointed and economical and many in *The White Peacock* are rambling or pointless. There are other superfluous characters who appear and disappear, having done nothing but be characteristic. And there are too many set-piece descriptions which draw attention to themselves as writing-for-effect, and are sometimes weakly literary. Finally, pedants will point out that Cyril, the narrator, is impossibly omniscient. By the end of the first chapter he is telling us things that he cannot have witnessed or have had recounted to him.

One can say all that, and it is a serious adverse case. And yet: *The White Peacock* was written by Lawrence; it was his first book; and the first book by a genius is not likely to be trivial. There is much in it which has the imprint of that genius. Sometimes one has to think to see the point, and it is often with hindsight that one attaches significance, but most readers come to this book with some knowledge of the later writings. If one concedes and has done with the criticisms, one can attend to what is good.

At the elementary level of the plot, taken as a whole and allowed to have its natural human force, the novel is not only ambitious, it starts the reader off on some of Lawrence's life-long preoccupations, though it does not yet give his mature view of them. It deals with a patterned group of young people entering adult life, leaving the sheltering environment which has made their childhood on the whole secure and happy. They find they have to make fundamental choices, including what to *be*, and who to link with that process of self-development – who to choose sexually, as mate for life.

George and Emily Saxton at Strelley Mill Farm are based on Lawrence's childhood friends, Alan[2] and Jessie Chambers at the Haggs Farm near Eastwood. For both of them he felt a deep love. Cyril and Lettice Beardsall, also brother and sister, are more complicated: more imaginary and less solidly based. Cyril is the first Lawrence-figure in the fictions,[3] though not very substantial as a person. We gather that his emotional life is blocked, that this has to do with a past conflict between his separated parents, and that he cannot manage to love Emily; but he says little about this and seems mainly there in order to tell the story. Since the central figure of the story and the most deeply imagined character is George, that is partly why Cyril's momentary recovery and final loss of his despised father seem only a side-show. Conversely, Cyril's relationship with Annable acquires more force because it affords a parable-commentary on the attraction Lettie has for George, and Annable's decline is prophetic of George's. But Cyril is more than a mouthpiece, because he *feels* the story as well as telling it: as narrator he supplies that steady stream of poetic observation and moral comment which is the binding element in the whole structure and an ambitious attempt to set the human passions in a universal frame. Lettie might possibly be based on Lettice Ada, Lawrence's sister, but not very substantially. She might be, as Jessie Chambers very shrewdly pointed out, an aspect of Lawrence himself. She is mainly a creature of the imagination; but she has some life and complexity and her evolution, her life-course, has a convincing power and pathos. She is the first fatal woman in Lawrence's fiction.

The novel has three Parts. The first two contain the earliest and the weakest writing, and are set in the country round Eastwood: not the grimy mining-town itself, but the pleasant woods and hills a few miles out: the 'country of my heart' as Lawrence called it. The opening scene is set at Strelley Mill Farm (the Haggs) and the choice is important. From the beginning the Farm is more actual than the idealized cottage in which the Beardsalls live with a softened, more genteel version of Lawrence's mother. The Farm is real; but the cottage is an out-of-focus calendar picture, as if Lawrence's family had suddenly become E. M. Forster's – hence better off and more cultivated – but in the transformation had ceased to be physically or socially real (one reason for having the father out of the way is that Arthur John Lawrence could not be accommodated in this idyll).

The main formal or structural element of the book is Lawrence's very accurate and loving accounts of the procession of the seasons, noted precisely in terms of what blooms when. This moves from one summer through autumn and winter to the following spring, and on through a second year. This scheme with its ambitious implications has to be loosened if not entirely abandoned when the time-scale is expanded in Part III. This traces the later life of George and Lettie in their marriages, through a further fifteen years or so. There are inconsistencies here, if one thinks about them: Parts I and II seem set in a very recent past, so is Part III in the future, or is one suddenly to imagine the first Parts set back in the 1890s? But there are motor-cars. And if Lettie and George have in the end been married for so long, how are their children still so young?

But this too is pedantic. One need only say that when he came to *The Rainbow* Lawrence took more care with that sort of plotting; meanwhile it makes no difference to the essential truth of his story. And Part III, which was much less of a reworking of earlier material is, despite this awkward fit, a powerful element of the book; more mature and strong. The first Parts attract attention because of the reader's interest in Lawrence's youth, and because of the vein of sometimes over-lush poetry supplied by the pageant of the seasons. Part III is more freely projected, imagining what might happen to the persons concerned: it is a tragic prediction told with disheartening power. It rings very true, and it is more maturely Lawrentian than Parts I and II – even if it dislocates the original pattern. Among other things it includes an evocation of the wider world – especially the London that Lawrence went to work in in 1908. He knew that his characters, left in the idyll of the Mill, the lake at Nethermere and the woods and hills, would not have properly set out, would not be in the world. Marriage is essentially linked with being launched into that world, where people have to join society at the same time as they discover how to live together. The launch is long delayed in Parts I and II in a series of hesitations, untaken opportunities, doubts, and challenges to make up one's mind. In Part III the decisions are taken, and fifteen years of disastrous consequences rapidly unfold as a kind of nemesis.

So the lives of all four young people are decided (even Cyril's empty life is a kind of decision) and mostly for ill; this is a story of mismatch, personal defeat, bafflement and even disintegration, especially in the main characters George and Lettie. They find that their marriages are in related ways failures. It is repeatedly shown that they might have married each other. It would have been across a class-barrier, since Lettie is refined – over-refined – and George is presented as the opposite: a countryman, almost a yokel. But he is not stupid, indeed he has a keen sensitivity. Until the end of the book, he is not at ease in elegant drawing-rooms, and never occupied with the interests – music, literature and so on – treated there as subjects of conversation, though in the fields he listens willingly to Cyril talking about Schopenhauer and William James; and when Cyril shows him some Beardsley drawings he is responsive to the point of inflammation, and instantly wants to approach Lettie. As he says at one moment to Cyril: 'You and Lettie have made me conscious,' and that is a word that indicates a lot for Lawrence, mostly damaging. The essential point about George is that at the beginning of the book he is living naturally, happily and freely in the healthy body which he is glad to *be*, and which he is pround of. But he is latent: he has not begun to live, therefore to change. At the end of the book this body is corrupted as a tree is corrupted by fungus, and the change, though horrifying, is natural. The cause is the fall into consciousness precipitated by friendship with Cyril and love for Lettie. As living body, George is contrasted with Cyril, who is delicate, inhibited, and 'mental'; and with Lettie, who is as beautiful and healthy, but is also overbred; inhibited by being a lady at a time when that might mean denying one's sexuality, and rejecting the physicality, the sexuality, of a husband who was valued for his mind, or for his social self only. There are also moments when one suspects that Lettie's trouble is simply that she is a woman. That is one implication of the violent cynicism that Annable introduces into the story, the mild bafflement of Cyril, and the disaster which overtakes George.

Lettie is what the French call an *allumeuse* and the British a coarser name. She knows she has power over men, and uses it for sheer pleasure. She ensnares both George and Leslie Tempest, an overbred young man (so contrasted with George) whose wealth comes from the family firm, and who is the first of Lawrence's managers, officers, and gentlemen (Anton Skrebensky in *The Rainbow*, Gerald Crich in *Women in Love*, Rico Carrington in 'St Mawr' and Clifford Chatterley are of the same species). But Lettie is not just a tease, because she is not entirely in control. She feels a deep pull towards George, which George is frightened to respond to, even when she gives the plainest hints. She represents for George a doubly fatal challenge: fatal either to accept or to avoid. Losing her leads to his decline; but we cannot believe that winning her would establish him in life. As it is, the consciousness which she initiates in him sets off a process of growth which is malignant or corrupting; and this unavoidable tragedy gives the book an undertone of sheer horror. She for her part becomes fatally enmeshed with Leslie, half-knowing that he cannot in human or sexual terms satisfy her. Leslie is at first catastrophically dependent on her, and in a very convincing scene[4] uses emotional blackmail to secure her. So there comes a moment when only a decisive gesture by George can pull her away from Leslie. This is the dramatic focus of Part II. George twice nearly makes the gesture, but fails to be commanding enough. It is clear to the reader that Lettie half-wants George to master her, to command her, to make her submit, as to a fate. He is too gentle, or too passive, or too muddled, or too appalled at the momentousness of it all, but manages to make a declaration, which she welcomes but is able to reject. So Lettie marries Leslie. He becomes an industrialist and MP; she becomes a society hostess and mother, living in a 'white' marriage which Leslie accepts. They have separate rooms, Cyril notices; if they have children it is because Lettie needs them to give her a role in life. George falls back on a second best: on Meg, the girl at the Ram Inn who loves him in an uncomplicated way, but whom he cheats by not giving her the best part of himself. This marriage too is a failure, for reasons to do with Meg's demands on him and his refusal to meet them. The failure is complementary to Lettie's; as a result the woman negates the man as man; uses him as instrumental to her own motherhood; takes consolation in the children and even uses them against him. He feels both used and refused. Leslie is content to be MP, industrialist and face at the head of the family table. George has no ground of his own to stand on; he makes some money horse-trading; he inspects politics and sees through the vocal progressivism that is the opposite of Leslie's complacent conservatism. He begins to drink.

There is a crucial last encounter. He visits Lettie at her London home, and once more, and more powerfully, makes the demand on her which he had tried to make fifteen years before. He now needs her desperately as the only light in his darkness; they cannot only be friends, it is love or nothing. She puts him off in a last frivolity: she will not really hear what he is saying, or respond to the depth of his need. In a curious symbolic gesture, she combs his hair into another style (as if to say 'Let me turn you into an acceptable social hanger-on')[5] and finally points to the children and the way of the world as being insuperable obstacles to an affair: she will not dare. He goes away and starts to drink himself to death.

At this level, of the plot and the extractable prose meaning – even the moral – the story is serious, imaginative and original. The literary ancestors might be George Eliot's pairs of young people in *Middlemarch*, or Tolstoy's pairs in *Anna Karenina*; or one might see George Saxton as a failed version of Hardy's Gabriel Oak in *Far from the Madding Crowd*. More strikingly, the strong rustic pair at the farm (George, Emily) set against an overbred pair from a cultivated drawing room (Lettie and Cyril) may remind the reader of *Wuthering Heights* – Lettie's wilfulness and charm and her disastrous choice are very like Catherine Earnshaw's. But from the beginning Lawrence is in his own world, and what he owes to his models is a minor matter compared with what he has to say on his own.

That leads us to what might be called Lawrence's beliefs or preoccupations; and these are what give us the overt moral content. When Lettie has become a wife and mother, she makes her own comment on her life, and Lawrence adds his. At a dinner where George is present she expresses the cynical and deadly world-weariness which Gudrun Brangwen will later express in *Women in Love*:

"Really!" Lettie was saying, "I don't see that one thing is worth doing any more than another. It's like dessert: you are equally indifferent whether you have grapes or pears or pineapple."

and then as a postscript, she says what Gerald Crich will say: 'The only thing worth doing is producing.' This is her answer to what Leavis called the torment of the eternal question 'what for?' – the peculiarly modern but unsatisfying answer. Lettie adds a mordant self-perception. She is talking to writers who agree that *their* work is 'a real source of satisfaction', and she has to agree:

> "... I am a failure there. Did you know I have a son, though? – a marvellous little fellow, is he not, Leslie? – he is my work. I am a wonderful mother, am I not, Leslie?"
>
> "Too devoted," he replied.
>
> "There!" she exclaimed in triumph. – "When I have to sign my name and occupation in a visitor's book, it will be '– Mother.' I hope my business will flourish," she concluded, smiling. There was a touch of ironical brutality in her now. She was, at the bottom, quite sincere. Having reached that point in a woman's career when most, perhaps all of the things in life seem worthless and insipid, she had determined to put up with it, to ignore her own self, to empty her own potentialities into the vessel of another or others, and to live her life at second hand. This peculiar abnegation of self is the resource of a woman for the escaping of the responsibilities of her own development. Like a nun, she puts over her living face a veil, as a sign that the woman no longer exists for herself: she is the servant of God, of some man, of her children, or may be, of some cause. As a servant, she is no longer responsible for her self, which would make her terrified and lonely. Service is light and easy. To be responsible for the good progress of one's life – is terrifying. It is the most insufferable form of loneliness, and the heaviest of responsibilities. (*WP*(C) 283–4)

'To be responsible for the good progress of one's life': it is a direct comment from Lawrence himself, and a weighty one. 'Service is light and easy' seems a paradox, but means that any duty imposed from outside only requires submission, in people all too inclined to submit. Later, the word 'sacrifice' will be substituted for 'service'.

This rather abstract moral gets amplified into a living theme in the rest of the novel. For women in particular, the idea of being servant to the children might seem to imply passivity; but in Meg certainly, and also in Emily, there is displayed a wholehearted eagerness to worship the tiny child which startles and shuts out the man. Cyril has just watched Meg and Emily bathing George's twins, and something emerges in Emily which has already emerged in Meg:

> Emily, delighted, began to undress the baby whose hair was like crocus petals. Her fingers trembled with pleasure as she loosed the little tapes. . . . A distinct, glowing atmosphere seemed suddenly to burst out around her and the child, leaving me outside. The moment before she had been very near to me, her eyes searching mine, her spirit clinging timidly about me. Now I was put away, quite alone, neglected, forgotten, outside the glow which surrounded the woman and the baby.
>
> "Ha! – Ha-a-a!" she said with a deep-throated vowel, as she put her face against the child's small breasts, so round, almost like a girl's, silken and warm and wonderful. She kissed him, and touched him, and hovered over him, drinking in his baby sweetnesses, the sweetness of the laughing little mouth's wide wet kisses, of the round, waving limbs, of the little shoulders so winsomely curving to the arms and the breasts, of the tiny soft neck hidden very warm beneath the chin, tasting deliciously with her lips and her cheeks all the exquisite softness, silkiness, warmth and tender life of the baby's body.
>
> A woman is so ready to disclaim the body of a man's love; she yields him her own soft beauty with so much gentle patience and regret; . . . shrinking from his passionate limbs and his body. It was with some perplexity, some anger and bitterness that I watched Emily moved almost to ecstasy by the baby's small, innocuous person.
>
> "Meg never found any pleasure in me as she does in the kids," said George bitterly, for himself. (*WP*(C) 277–8)

Lawrence is here giving to Emily his own experience of being delighted with the baby Hilda Mary Jones, in Croydon,[6] from whom he realised something essential about touch – a quintessential truth for him, and a theme in much that he wrote. But one is left wondering: is this just a common male jealousy, or has Lawrence laid his finger on something eternal and universal in women in relation to children, or something local and of his time in their relation to men? And finally, suppose Meg were to say 'But that *is* the good progress of my life. If you are jealous, too bad'?

For men, at any rate, the good progress of their life must involve
something else. When Lettie has announced the date of her
marriage to Leslie, George declares that he will marry Meg,
almost in revenge:

> "Well", said the father "I suppose we can't have everything
> we want – we generally have to put up with the next best thing –
> don't we Lettie?" – he laughed.
> Lettie flushed furiously.
> "I don't know", she said. "You can generally get what
> you want if you want it badly enough. Of course – if you *don't
> mind* – –." (*WP*(C) 188)

A few pages later, Cyril attacks George for not having insisted
at that moment, which offered a real chance that Lettie might
have been won back:

> "It's no good now," said I. "You should have insisted and
> made your own destiny."
> "Yes – perhaps so," he drawled, in his best reflective manner.
> "I would have had her – she'd have been glad if you'd done as
> you wanted with her. . . . You should have had the courage to
> risk yourself – you're always too careful of yourself and your
> own poor feelings – you never could brace yourself up to a
> shower-bath of contempt and hard usage, so you've saved your
> feelings and lost . . . (*WP*(C) 195)

So 'the good progress of one's life' requires 'the courage to risk
oneself', and that means that 'you can generally get what you
want if you want it badly enough', and 'she'd have been glad if
you'd done as you wanted with her'. It implies a morality of a
special kind: the reverse of 'service', which is what slaves are for,
and the reverse of 'sacrifice', which calls for victims. Or at any rate
the victim is going to be someone else.

And we here begin to touch on the network of meanings in the
book. These remarks link back with something George says quite
early on, in the chapter called 'The Scent of Blood' (part I,
chapter V). The title is indicative, for the main theme is killing – a
preoccupation throughout the first two Parts – and it is introduced
as a background note:

Lately, however, she [Lettie] had noticed again the cruel pitiful crying of a hedgehog caught in a gin, and she had noticed the traps for the fierce little murderers, traps walled in with a small fence of fir, and baited with the guts of a killed rabbit. (*WP*(C) 44)

During the chapter Lettie and Leslie watch, she with fascination and horror, he with condescension, as George, harvesting oats, kills the rabbits which come out of the dwindling cover provided by the crop. George is swift and vigorous enough to chase and catch them as they are headed off by the others standing around, Cyril included. Cyril is excited, but cannot bring himself to kill another creature. George can, with no hesitation, and incidentally breaks open a nest of mice, and kills the mother and her nine babies with no qualm, though a sort of fellow-feeling ('Poor brute', said George, looking at the mother, 'What a job she must have had rearing that lot!').

On the second page of the book, George had killed some bees in their nest out of mere curiosity; and within a few pages more had put an injured cat out of its misery by drowning it. The point is made, heavily enough: he is a farmer; some animals are vermin; some are stock; some are pets. He has power over all of them, of life and death. It is his job – perhaps a vocation – to deal out that life and death. It is also sport at times.

The developing thought about the good progress of one's life, and getting what you want if you want it badly enough shades into these other thoughts, which are also about the sort of person one is; where the capacity for acting decisively may turn into the capacity to take a life:

"I don't know", said Leslie. "When it comes to killing it goes against the stomach."

"If you can run," said George, "you should be able to run to death. When your blood's up, you don't hang half-way."

"I think a man is horrible," said Lettie, "who can tear the head off a little mite of a thing like a rabbit, after running it in torture over a field."

"When he is nothing but a barbarian to begin with – –," said Emily.

"If you began to run yourself – you'd be the same," said George
. . .
"Well," said George, "what's the good finicking! If you feel like doing a thing – you'd better do it."
"Unless you haven't courage," said Emily, bitingly. (*WP*(C) 52)

These ponderings, doubts and criticisms in Lawrence's first book can be seen as the prelude to a major strand in his whole work.

There are also three or four chapters where one can discern the beginnings of Lawrence's later gift of natural sequence within a large unit. One such is this chapter 'The Scent of Blood'. It opens with a reference back to 'the death of the man who was our father', which has produced a change in the family's life because it is felt as 'the unanswered crying of failure'. This metaphorical sound is at once metamorphosed into, or imagined as drowned for a moment by, natural peaceful sounds (water, leaves, wood-pigeons). But this is broken across by the 'cry of the hedgehog caught in a gin'. So the thematic prelude introduces thoughts of predation and death.

Lettie is then introduced visually, sitting by the window. It is a weaker passage, rather lush: 'The sun clung to her hair, and kissed her with passionate splashes of colour . . .'. 'The sun loved Lettice, and was loth to leave her,' Lawrence says, and it is a link with a number of references to the sun as ancestral favouring power. I suggest that this 'stands for' something male, mature and favourable; like a father-totem. Several things in *Sons and Lovers*, for instance, support this identification. But consider also this very direct and poignant remark of Cyril, which can be taken as Lawrence's own feeling, working in London:

It seemed almost as if, at home, I might lift my hand to the ceiling of the valley, and touch my own beloved sky, whose familiar clouds came again and again to visit me, whose stars were constant to me, born when I was born, *whose sun had been all my father to me*. But now the skies were strange over my head, and Orion walked past me unnoticing, he who night after night had stood over the woods to spend with me a wonderful hour.[7] (Italics added. *WP*(C) 260)

Leslie enters, and kisses Lettie as she sleeps. This too is a weak passage, though her offence at having been taken physically unawares is real. After a too-long and too-arch conversation they go out with Cyril and walk towards the Mill. They hear the sound of a scythe being whetted, and see George at work, scything oats. The tableau is powerfully symbolic:

> ... his black hair was moist and twisted into confused half-curls. Firmly planted, he swung with a beautiful rhythm from the waist . . . ; his shirt, faded almost white, was torn just above the belt, and showed the muscles of his back playing like lights upon the white sand of a brook. (*WP*(C) 47)

Leslie gives himself away by saying 'I should think mowing is a nice exercise', and trying to do it himself, though warned that he will sweat and make his hands sore. Lettie, uneasy and stirred, conceals her unease by asking 'How do you bind the corn?' As George shows her, 'Instead of attending, she looked at his hands, big, hard, inflamed by the snaith of the scythe'. Hands are a key-topic in Lawrence (some such phrase, however awkward, is needed); and that can be well illustrated by showing what happens next:

> "Do you know," she said suddenly, "Your arms tempt me to touch them. They are such a fine brown colour, and they look so hard."
> He held out one arm to her. She hesitated, then she swiftly put her finger-tips on the smooth brown muscle, and drew them along. Quickly she hid her hand in the folds of her skirt, blushing. He laughed a low, quiet laugh, at once pleasant and startling to hear. (*WP*(C) 48)

This can be linked with other places in other chapters. For instance, at the end of Annable's account, made to Cyril, of his passionate life with his Lady Chrystabel,

> He held out his arm to me, and bade me try his muscle. I was startled. The hard flesh almost filled his sleeve.
> "Ah," he continued "You don't know what it is to have the pride of a body like mine". (*WP*(C) 150)

Cyril's gesture is like Lettie's. In Annable's narrative the other
woman, Lady Chrystabel, is shown to have been first besotted and
then sated with his body. She had wanted to stare at it, to draw it,
to touch it, to possess it, but never (it seems) properly to love the
man it actually *was*. Chrystabel is a more fatal woman than Lettie;
but the book as a whole makes the reader think them sisters. So
Lettie in yet another part of the book reacts against her
undisclosed physical relationship with Leslie, and makes the
gesture she had made after touching George:

> "I don't see why – why it should make trouble between us,
> Lettie," he faltered. She made a swift gesture of repulsion,
> whereupon, catching sight of her hand, she hid it swiftly gainst
> her skirt again.
> "You make my hands – my very hands disclaim me," she
> struggled to say. (*WP*(C) 176)

There is a third tiny example of the same gesture, seeming
trivial, but deeply indicative. Lettie watches George leading the
bull-calf from the stall to the yard. He offers a finger, which the
calf 'with its shiny nose uplifted was mumbling in its sticky gums'
like a dummy, and so consenting to be led:

> Then he returned, rubbing his sticky finger dry against his
> breeches. He stood near to Lettie, and she felt rather than saw
> the extraordinary pale cleanness of the one finger among the
> others. She rubbed her finger against her dress in painful
> sympathy. (*WP*(C) 231)

At this point Lettie has behind her the traumatic experience,
presumably a sexual fiasco, which took place when Leslie had
stayed one night at her home. (Cyril for once does not know what
actually happened, though he can narrate the scene the morning
after in which Lettie says her 'very hands disclaim her'.) To
Leslie, with the knowledge of their failed night together, Lettie
makes an absolutely crucial statement:

> ". . . I want you to let me go; I don't want to ——"
> "To what?"
> "To get married at all – let me be, let me go."
> "What for?"
> "Oh – for my sake."
> "You mean you don't love me?"

"Love, – love, – I don't know anything about it. But I can't –
we can't be – don't you see – Oh, what do they say, – flesh of one
flesh."

"Why?" he whispered, like a child that is told some tale of
mystery. (*WP*(C) 196)

The charged phrase 'flesh of one flesh' becomes a theme in the
whole of Lawrence's early fiction, and the recurrences are
noticed in the chapters which follow. Here it is clear that Lettie
has a basic difficulty in acting as a sexual being at all; and it may
be this which led Jessie Chambers to say that there was something
of Lawrence in her. Her deepest needs and instinctive blocks are
his: also her conscious wish, her will, to be normally sexual.

To return to the moment at which she touches George's arm,
something is being not said, but conveyed in a more powerful way
about a mingled attraction and repulsion. Lettie who, at the
beginning of the chapter did not want to be kissed by Leslie, is now
magnetised by George as the Lady Chrystabel had been by
Annable; but the thrill of his animality is for her at first a mental
thrill. When it is communicated as a physical force, like
electricity, through the hand, the messenger of the body, it is then
repudiated: and not just once. This is a powerful set, of the whole
person. Such women are fatal to the men on whom they exercise
their power.

But Lettie is not only fatal: she is attractive, intelligent,
troubled by her own misgivings, and anxious to be whole. She
wants something, as all the young people do; and in this same
chapter, she expresses her wish for stability and integration into
the life she sees before her:

"I wish I could work here," she said, looking away at the
standing corn, and the dim blue woods. He followed her look,
and laughed quietly, with indulgent resignation.

"I do!" she said emphatically.

"You feel so fine," he said, pushing his hand through his
open shirt-front, and gently rubbing the muscles of his side.
"It's a pleasure to work or to stand still. It's a pleasure to
yourself – your own physique."

She looked at him, full at his physical beauty, as if he were
some great firm bud of life.

Leslie came up, wiping his brow.

"Jove," said he "I do perspire." (*WP*(C) 48)

So much for Leslie. But the sentences about the other two are full of implication and feeling: and especially his pleasure in his body.

The chapter goes on, through a succession of notations, mostly fairly deft, to reach the rabbit hunt, very vividly narrated, and culminating in this:

> George began to mow. As I walked round I caught sight of a rabbit skulking near the bottom corner of the patch. Its ears lay pressed against its back; I could see the palpitation of the heart under the brown fur, and I could see the shining dark eyes looking at me. I felt no pity for it, but still I could not actually hurt it. I beckoned to the father. He ran up, and aimed a blow with the rake. There was a sharp little cry which sent a hot pain through me as if I had been cut. But the rabbit ran out, and instantly I forgot the cry, and gave pursuit, fairly feeling my fingers stiffen to choke it. It was all lame. Leslie was upon it in a moment, and he almost pulled its head off in his excitement to kill it. (*WP*(C) 50)

The nest of mice is laid open and the occupants killed, after which the scything is finished ('together they soon laid the proud quivering heads low').

Evening falls; they all return to the farm, and there follows the discussion about killing, the girls being superior, mental, and hostile, the men complacent, since they have all, even Cyril, felt the urge in their fingers. Lettie is left looking 'very glum'. We infer that her genuine wish to be able to live like George, perhaps with him, in an idealised pastoral world of handsome brown country-folk making the graceful gestures of mowing has had a check. These people not only have bodies, about which her feelings are confused: they kill things, and even the harvest is a slaughter in which proud heads are laid low. If it is not murder, it is at least sacrifice.

The mood changes with the lighting, from the soft blue and gold of the September sun to a night scene which is more ambiguous and disturbing, since it mingles profusion with waste and corruption, so that one can hardly tell which is which. The familiar becomes strange, disturbing and emblematic, and is rendered in direct and powerful writing. Lawrence is already in possession of his power:

After a while we went out also, before the light faded altogether from the pond. Emily took us into the lower garden, to get some ripe plums. The old garden was very low. The soil was black. The cornbind and goosegrass were clutching at the ancient gooseberry bushes, which sprawled by the paths. The garden was not very productive, save of weeds, and perhaps, tremendous lank artichokes or swollen marrows. But at the bottom, where the end of the farmbuildings rose high and gray, there was a plum-tree which had been crucified to the wall, and which had broken away and leaned forward from bondage. Now under the boughs were hidden great mist-bloomed crimson treasures, splendid globes. I shook the old, ragged trunk, green, with even the fresh gum dulled over, and the treasures fell heavily, thudding down among the immense rhubarb leaves below. The girls laughed, and we divided the spoil, and turned back to the yard. We went down to the edge of the garden, which skirted the bottom pond, a pool chained in a heavy growth of weeds. It was moving with rats, the father had said. The rushes were thick below us; opposite, the great bank fronted us, with orchard trees climbing it like a hillside. The lower pond received the overflow from the upper by a tunnel from the deep black sluice. Two rats ran into the black culvert at our approach. We sat on some piled, mossy stones to watch. The rats came out again, ran a little way, stopped, ran again, listened, were reassured, and slid about freely, dragging their long naked tails. Soon six or seven grey beasts were playing round the mouth of the culvert in the gloom. They sat and wiped their sharp faces, stroking their whiskers. Then one would give a little rush and a little squirm of excitement, and would jump vertically into the air, alighting on four feet, running, sliding into the black shadow. One dropped with an ugly plop into the water, and swam towards us, the hoary imp, his sharp snout and his wicked little eyes moving at us. Lettie shuddered. I thew a stone into the dead pool, and frightened them all. But we had frightened ourselves more, so we hurried away, and stamped our feet in relief on the free pavement of the yard.[8] (*WP*(C) 52–3)

This note of lushness turning into waste and then decaying, to reveal an underside of verminous predation, rot and death, recurs more than once. It is surely very powerful. Lawrence senses a

natural force, the power of growth and life, that has an equal
capacity for corruption. The two things must go together: what
lives must die, or the world will be strangled with its waste
fertility; and what grows most rankly must corrupt as swiftly.
Predators have their place in the world: they keep the population
down and keep it lively; and scavengers keep the place clean. This
is a natural tragic principle: we need not look up from the earth to
find it. Any thing which is started into life, as George is, may by a
hairsbreadth be misdirected, and started into death.

The human herald of this theme is Annable, while he plays a
part in the story, but it surfaces again in the London scenes in Part
III. Indeed George succumbs to this force in the end: it gets him as
it got Annable. In this passage it is fully notated, but the focus of
attention quickly changes. Lettie, Leslie, Emily and Cyril sit in
the evening light, and George joins them, announcing that the
moon is going to rise. This is usually a crucial event in Lawrence,
though it is never easy to say what is involved – except that the
moon is a feminine influence, and often disruptive, as here:

> "Yes – I like to see it come over the wood. It lifts slowly up to
> stare at you. I always think it wants to know something, and I
> always think I have something to answer, only I don't know
> what it is," said Emily.
>
> Where the sky was pale in the east over the rim of wood came
> the forehead of the yellow moon. We stood and watched in
> silence. Then, as the great disc, nearly full, lifted and looked
> straight upon us, we were washed off our feet in a vague sea of
> moonlight. We stood with the light like water on our faces.
> Lettie was glad, a little bit exalted; Emily was passionately
> troubled; her lips were parted, almost beseeching; Leslie was
> frowning, oblivious, and George was thinking, and the terrible,
> immense moonbeams braided through his feeling. At length
> Leslie said softly, mistakenly:
>
> "Come along dear" – and he took her arm.
>
> She let him lead her along the bank of the pond, and across
> the plank over the sluice.
>
> "Do you know," she said, as we were carefully descending
> the steep bank of the orchard, "I feel as if I wanted to laugh, or
> dance. Something rather outrageous."
>
> "Surely not like that *now*," Leslie replied in a low voice,
> feeling really hurt. (*WP*(C) 54–5)

He has been solemnly wooing her, and wants a religious hush of
a self-satisfying sort in which he can propose, and be given a
maidenly 'yes'. But the moon has entered her blood, as it does
habitually in Lawrence's women, and made her wild and wilful.
She does dance, as a deliberate put-down for Leslie; and she
dances with George, 'tremendous, irresistible dancing', which
expresses the thing in both of them that is never going to have an
outlet except in this way. The scene is allowed to make its own
point, a vividly imagined quarter-hour which has a significance
which is coarsened if put into other words.

The chapter needs to be read as a rapidly moving whole. It has
weaknesses, archnesses and longueurs at the beginning; but it is
still a striking sequence of strongly imagined notations which
succeed each other with ease and naturalness and are always
deploying and relating the main thrusts of the whole book. This
is done without obvious allegorising, such that properties
remorselessly 'stand for' stateable meanings. I cannot say what
the swimming rat means, nor exactly what the sun and moon are
doing, or the act of dancing. They have their element of
gratuitousness and naturalness, and are part of the process of a
universe in which these young people are looking for meaning.
Emily puts it felicitously when she says of the moon that it wants
to know something, not to tell something, and that she has the
answer, if she only knew what it is. The answer would be the
meaning, but it would need words from the conscious self.

It is a chapter in which one feels that Lawrence is finding his
personal mode. The natural unit, for him, is the long chapter, a
seemingly natural sequence of events and effects. Within the
sequence there are descriptions, events, conversations, but this is
never a matter of realist scene-setting, merely veracious-seeming
action, the neutral record of action. It is a live universe that these
characters inhabit and question, and the sense they make of it is
never statable: for statements might be positivist or scientist or
utilitarian propositions. Such sense as the characters manage to
elicit is, from those points of view, primitive or supersititious. And
actually, they are more conscious of a lack or a question than of an
answer, as Emily's feeling about the moon suggests. They are
aware of needs or yearnings: the first stage of a religious belief.

These hesitant feelings are expressed by way of the network or
system of images and motifs, and it is time to attempt to sketch it.
To do so is destructive, since it breaks down Lawrence's own

sequence, as he moulded it into his succession of chapters. However, there are chapters in which these hints or intimations are dropped with greater profusion and coherence than elsewhere, and many of the examples I quote below come from Part II of the book; and especially Chapter I, 'Strange Blossoms, and Strange New Budding'; Chapter II, 'A Shadow in Spring', which deals with Annable; and Chapters VII and VIII which have parallel structures. In VII, 'The Fascination of the Forbidden Apple', George finally makes his effort to win Lettie away from Leslie, and fails. In VIII, 'A Poem of Friendship', a number of notations closely resemble those in VII, but here Cyril and George manage to express their David and Jonathan love, passing the love of women, and George is given a visionary significance.

The overall movement of Part II is from Spring to harvest-time – the second harvest season in the book, so that at the end of the Part George is again at work in the fields, with Cyril to help him in what turns out to be his last harvest at the Farm. Chapter I, 'Strange Blossoms . . .', presents the year's first flowers, and especially the snowdrops; and both Cyril and Emily are looking for their meaning.

> Below, in the first shadows, drooped hosts of little white flowers, so silent and sad; it seemed like a holy communion of pure wild things, numberless, frail, and folded meekly in the evening light. Other flower companies are glad; stately barbaric hordes of bluebells,[9] merry-headed cowslip groups, even light, tossing wood-anemones; but snowdrops are sad and mysterious. We have lost their meaning. They do not belong to us, who ravish them. The girls bent among them, touching them with their fingers, and symbolising the yearning which I felt. Folded in the twilight, these conquered flowerets are sad like forlorn little friends of dryads.
>
> "What do they mean, do you think?" said Lettie in a low voice, as her white fingers touched the flowers, and her black furs fell on them.
>
> "There are not so many this year," said Leslie.
>
> "They remind me of mistletoe, which is never ours, though we wear it," said Emily to me.
>
> "What do you think they say – what do they make you think, Cyril?" Lettie repeated.
>
> "I don't know. Emily says they belong to some old wild lost

religion – They were the symbol of tears, perhaps, to some strange hearted Druid folk before us"

"More than tears," said Lettie "more than tears, they are so still. Something out of an old religion, that we have lost. They make me feel afraid."

"What should you have to fear?" asked Leslie.

"If I knew I shouldn't fear," she answered "Look at all the snowdrops" – they hung in dim, strange flecks among the dusky leaves – "look at them – closed up, retreating powerless. They belong to some knowledge we have lost, that I have lost, and that I need. I feel afraid. They seem like something in fate. Do you think, Cyril, we can lose things from off the earth – like mastodons, and those old monstrosities – but things that matter – wisdom?"

"It is against my creed," said I.

"I believe I have lost something," said she.

"Come," said Leslie "don't trouble with fancies . . .". (*WP*(C) 129–30)

This is not just 'poetic': or if such remarks as 'forlorn little friends of dryads' are weakly so, the rest is serious. It turns the universal adolescent yearning from a commonplace into a serious questioning with more than a hint of the kind of answer needed. Leslie is deftly placed on the way; and a few minutes later is given a foretaste of the annihilation dealt out to Anton Skrebensky in the later book:

"Don't you care for me?" he asked softly.

"You?" – she sat up and looked at him, and laughed strangely. "You do not seem real to me," she replied, in a strange voice. (*WP*(C) 130)

Annable then makes his first real appearance as a force in this world. He is given some rather stagey and obvious remarks to make; but then all his words and actions are falsely theatrical and rather crude. The note he insistently strikes is that of animality, and here he refers to his brood of children as 'a lovely little litter', a 'pretty bag o' ferrets', 'natural as weasels', a 'bunch o' young foxes'. Lawrence is determined to pursue this note ('Be a good animal', and 'They can be like birds, or weasels, or vipers, or squirrels, so long as they ain't human rot'.) It is the word 'rot' that Annable is leading to, and it is here that his schematic figure becomes more interesting, for it is rot which he finally stands for, in his noisy way. 'I won his respect one afternoon when he found me trespassing in the woods because I was watching some maggots at work in a dead rabbit', Cyril says.

There follows the narrative of Annable's marriage with the fatal Lady Chrystabel. The prelude to that story is Cyril's exploration of the abandoned church, which is a place of horror, linked with the gamekeeper by its 'ragged confusion of feathers, and broken nests and remnants of dead birds.' This sounds again the note of another scene of rank desolation, a few pages after the strange horror of the pond with the rats. It had described how George and Cyril had one night walked to a deserted farm:

> We pushed open the gate, and as we walked down the path, weeds and dead plants brushed our ankles. We looked in at a window. The room was lighted also by a window from the other side, through which the moonlight streamed onto the flagged floor, dirty, littered with paper and wisps of straw. The hearth lay in the light, with all its distress of grey ashes, and piled cinders of burnt paper, and a child's headless doll, charred and pitiful. On the border-line of shadow lay a round, fur cap – a game-keeper's cap.

There is the link, too obviously established. In the outhouses

> . . . here and there we saw feathers, bits of animal wreckage, even the remnants of a cat. . . . As we entered the stable, there was an ugly noise and three great rats half rushed at us, and threatened us with their vicious teeth. I shuddered, and hurried back, stumbling over a bucket, rotten with rust and so filled with weeds that I thought it part of the jungle. There was a silence made horrible by the faint noises that rats, and flying bats give out. (*WP*(C) 60–1)

The theme of rank decay and vicious animal life in the moonlight links the three scenes, and is projected forward into Part III in ways which I touch on below. For the time being this tonality is expressly associated with Annable; and in the third such scene he tells Cyril his story. He makes the heavy link himself:

> ". . . Oh my God! – I'm like a good house built and finished and left to tumble down again with nobody to live in it." (*WP*(C) 149)

Annable's story is that of a man who offered his body to a
woman, who thought she wanted it, but not him in it. So she cast
him out, to use a Biblical phrase, and the goodly house went to rot.
Since he has an intense pride in his body, her rejection of it was a
rejection of him.

During the phase of her infatuation she made drawings of him:
expressing a mental infatuation that wants to know, and to
possess: it is a hubris. Having 'known', she passed on. Pressing
Cyril to feel the muscle of his arm, as Lettie had felt George's,
Annable is inviting or miming another hubris, the irresponsible
touch which is not a humble or reverent gesture.

> "Ah," he continued "You don't know what it is to have the
> pride of a body like mine. But she wouldn't have children – no,
> she wouldn't – said she daren't. That was the root of the
> difference at first. But she cooled down; and if you don't know
> the pride of my body, you'd never know my humiliation . . .
> "She began to get souly. A poet got hold of her, and she began
> to affect Burne-Jones – or Waterhouse – it was Waterhouse –
> she was a lot like one of his women – 'Lady of Shalott', I believe.
> At any rate, she got souly, and I was her animal – son animal –
> son boeuf". (WP(C) 150–1)

The reader remembers that Lettie has called George a fatted
calf, a stalled ox and a bull, and the parallel between the two
relationships becomes plain: the later tableau in which George
leads the bull-calf by offering it a finger to suck, and Lettie
observes with painful sympathy, is a complex analogue, with
striking sexual undertones. The parallel established by Annable is
fundamentally tragic; for its suggests that even if George had won
Lettie by managing to do what he 'felt like', and 'getting what he
wanted', he would have found that he was 'running to death' by
being the prey, not the hunter. Lettie is the kind of woman that the
Lady Chrystabel had been. And so, in the event, is the woman he
does marry, Meg: seeming natural, easy and physical, she turns
out to be a woman, and above all a mother. So Annable's violent
cynicism about women, 'all vanity and screech and defilement',
like the white peacock soiling the gravestones, seems dangerously
like an underlying moral of the whole book, not at all mitigated by
his concession 'I suppose . . . it wasn't all her fault.'

The animal-imagery which centres on Annable veers

constantly away from the bull, the vigorous male, and towards vermin. It seems extraordinary that a gamekeeper should think of his own children as vermin, but he does: they are not the stock he is paid to preserve, but the predators he is paid to destroy. And although he appears and disappears in little more than a single chapter, that note, of trapped vermin, links 'the unanswered crying of failure' associated with Cyril's defeated father, with the cries which come from the 'traps for the fierce little murderers.' It is strange, and perhaps not quite conscious or under control, but it comes wholeheartedly from Lawrence. And since he said, and it is commonly agreed, that he was 'unfair' to his own father, it is worth reflecting on the way that the absent father is here half-absolved and half-incriminated by the implications of the imagery. Was he vermin? But are vermin all bad? Is it their fault that they follow their nature and are trapped? In Annable's view, they are better than white peacocks.

One of the wordless feelings which George enjoys is wonder at being this particular body. We have a record of Lawrence's own wonder at the same experience. He worked in the fields haymaking in late July and early August 1908. In a letter to Blanche Jennings in which he asked at one point 'Have you anything to say on the Annable part? Is it really coarse?' he also wrote this:

> My hands are brown, hard, and coarse; my face is gradually tanning. Aren't you glad? I have really worked hard; I can pick alongside a big experienced man; indeed I am fairly strong; I am pretty well developed; I have done a good deal of dumb-bell practice. Indeed as I was rubbing myself down in the late twilight a few minutes ago, and as I passed my hands over my sides where the muscles lie suave and secret I did love myself. I am thin, but well skimmed over with muscle; my skin is white and unblemished; soft and dull with a fine pubescent bloom, not shiny like my friend's. I am very fond of myself. I like you because I can talk like this to you.
>
> You tell me I have no male friends. The man I have been working with in the hay is the original of my George – lacking, alas, the other's subtlety of sympathetic discrimination which lent him his nobility. (*Letters I* 65)

I don't know what Miss Jennings made of that: perhaps she blushed, perhaps she laughed; but surely she was surprised. She would not have known that she had received a central text; or that the thought of a naked man passing his hands over his own sides was an almost religious imagining for Lawrence.

In *The White Peacock* this type-scene is foreshadowed when George pushes his hand through his shirt and strokes himself as he rests from haymaking; it is turned into a sexual ploy when Annable tells how he stood drying himself on the river-bank where Lady Chrystabel could see him; it has its fullest expression in the scene where George and Cyril go swimming; Cyril is taken with the nobility of George's body, and George, like a father, holds Cyril to him and rubs him dry. Inevitably the thought has occurred – is that not latent homosexuality? But the idea is too simple: George looks like a god and acts like a father, and Cyril's attitude to him is reverence without overtones of simple desire.

The link which helps here was given in that first scene of mowing, where George had essentially been expressing his content, his naturalness, a self-satisfaction which could easily become stagnant. Lettie was the beholder and Lawrence gives her the perception that he is 'some great firm bud of life'. She herself makes an amplifying comment on this figure, and it may also have been this passage that Jessie Chambers was thinking of when she suggested that Lettie was an aspect of Lawrence. Certainly Lawrence himself could have said this:

". . . You never grow up, like bulbs which spend all summer getting fat and fleshy but never wakening the germ of a flower. As for me, the flower is born in me, but it wants bringing forth. Things don't flower if they are overfed. You have to suffer before you blossom in this life. When death is just touching a plant, it forces it into a passion of flowering. You wonder how I have touched death. You don't know. There's always a sense of death in this home. I believe my mother hated my father before I was born. That was death in her veins for me before I was born. It makes a difference – – " (*WP*(C) 28)

The figure links the twin-themes of animal life and plant life. George 'in the flesh' is a 'great firm bud'; but it is now suggested that this bud will never flower, and nor may Lettie's – she says so herself. What is wrong with him is a latency or dormancy which never finds its season. What is wrong with her is that something like a frost has nipped her in the bud. An implicit term here, an essential factor, is the sun; but it is only felt as an absence. For George has become a bulb, which has its life underground. The strange negativity of the whole complex is that flowering of a hectic kind is associated with death. If George is to blossom, he must suffer; and even if he does blossom it will be the prelude to death. Lettie for her part feels death in her veins from the start of life, because of the negation of the father (subliminally associated in the book with the sun). Implicit as a moral for action is the thought: seek out the sun which will not so much warm as burn you into blossoming; and accept the necessary sequel, death. It is better than stagnation, or rotting: which is the dominant note in the Annable story, and presented to Cyril as a parable of George's ultimate fate, though he cannot know this yet.

At the end of Annable's narration, Cyril moves away, disturbed, having no words for his complicated feelings, and resorting to an instinctive gesture:

> Over the hill, the big flushed face of the moon poised just above the tree-tops, very majestic, and far off – yet imminent. I turned with swift sudden friendliness to the net of elm-boughs spread over my head, dotted with soft clusters winsomely. I jumped up and pulled the cool soft tufts against my face for company, and as I passed, still I reached forward for the touch of this budded gentleness of the trees. The wood breathed fragrantly, with a subtle sympathy. The firs softened their touch to me, and the larches woke from the barren winter-sleep, and put out velvet fingers to caress me as I passed. Only the clean, bare branches of the ash stood emblem of the discipline of life.[10] (*WP*(C) 152)

The real trees, the real plants, are always there, and never distorted or thwarted by anything but natural external forces: unlike us, considered as plants. Cyril's gesture here is the hopeful assertion of a kinship. He wants to be like these trees, as he feels accepted by them. The trouble is that he is a particular kind of animal: a human being started into consciousness.

In the very emblematic chapter, laden with meaning, called 'The Fascination of the Forbidden Apple' (Part II, chapter VII), Lettie moves about, dealing out significances. She has to draw out of George the declaration of love that she wants. She also wants to be pressed to leave Leslie, breaking her engagement; but *does* she ultimately want to do that? The social self in her does not: it claims to be responsible, and is quick to point out that we 'have to consider things.' But the other part of her wants to be 'free' like the birds which have built their nests and laid their eggs in a hoofprint in the meadow, or in an old kettle, or in a tin. To be free like the birds would also be to blossom like the flowers which are doing that all round them. During the whole chapter she is dropping hints which George humbly picks up and follows, so that she is ensnaring him, and running a risk. Yet her hints or texts can also be tragic insults: for instance:

. . . In the hedge was an elm tree, with myriads of dark dots pointed against the bright sky, myriads of clusters of flaky green fruit.

"Look at that elm", she said, "you'd think it was in full leaf, wouldn't you? Do you know why it's so prolific? . . . It's casting its bread upon the winds – No, it is dying, so it puts out all its strength and loads its boughs with the last fruit. It'll be dead next year. If you're here then, come and see. Look at the ivy, the suave smooth ivy, with its fingers in the tree's throat! Trees know how to die, you see – we don't."

With her whimsical moods she tormented him. She was at bottom a seething confusion of emotion, and she wanted to make him likewise.

Having introduced the theme of death, she finds another text in the wayside pulpit that the countryside momentarily becomes: and Lawrence is able to switch from the 'plant' circuit to the 'animal' circuit:

. . . Lettie stooped over a wood-pigeon that lay on the ground on its breast, its wings half spread. She took it up – its eyes were bursten and bloody; she felt its breast, ruffling the dimming iris on its throat.

"It's been fighting", he said.

"What for – a mate?" she asked, looking at him.

"I don't know," he answered.

"Cold – he's quite cold, under the feathers! I think a wood-pigeon must enjoy being fought for – and being won;

especially if the right one won. It would be a fine pleasure, to see them fighting – don't you think?'' she said, torturing him. (*WP*(C) 209–10)

She gives the dead bird a little funeral ceremony. ' "There," she said . . . "he's done with. Come on." He followed her, speechless with his emotion.' She progresses to even plainer hints ('When I've had my way, I *do* want somebody to take it back from me'). The chapter moves to its poetic climax in a wood whose ridings are filled with flowers, which move Lettie as well as the narrator to a too-pretty descant on the beauty of it all which is also the pity of it all for Lettie and George. The problem here is that the 'poetry' will do very well for Lettie: its prettiness and whimsicality match her childlikeness and her manipulative fancy. But it is also too like one vein in Cyril's own narrative poetry, which can veer disconcertingly from this prettiness to the sombre and the startling notes he can introduce at Lawrence's most original and profound. The result is that the symbolic structure of the book is affected in places by being too lush or too decorative, or striving too obviously for a symbolic effect which becomes mere emblem or allegory – as with the convenient pigeon.

This chapter is what the experts on construction would call the *scène à faire*: it is the moment where Lettie has to come forward and *make* George declare himself, but has also to maintain a social commitment, her previous engagement, unless he can produce some prodigy of conviction and authority. And he can't; he requires her to go on directing him.

". . . could you get free?"
"Tell me what to do – yes, if you tell me."
"I can't tell you – so let me go."
"No Lettie," he pleaded, with terror and humility. "No Lettie, don't go. What should I do with my life! Nobody would love you like I do – and what should I do with my love for you? – hate it and fear it, because it's too much for me."
She turned and kissed him gratefully. He then took her in a long, passionate embrace, mouth to mouth. In the end it had so wearied her, that she could only wait in his arms till he was too tired to hold her. He was trembling already.
"Poor Meg!" she murmured to herself dully . . . (*WP*(C) 215)

That is well enough *stated*, but the earlier symbolic parts of the chapter don't have the strength which would make it the centre of the book which it needs to be. What is extraordinary, and what the experts on construction could not have postulated at all, is that the next chapter 'A Poem of Friendship', offers a formal parallel, in that Cyril and George enter the same magical territory, even see some of the same things; that their love for each other is at an unspoken level cemented where the love of Lettie and George had been frustrated; and at the end of the chapter George is apotheosised.

Just as the previous chapter had effectively begun with Lettie setting out for the Mill, so now, after a thematic prelude 'Such a morning, I went up to George, on the top fallow.' And just as Lettie and George had come upon nests filled with fledgelings, over-emblematic of life, so now Cyril comes upon a lark's nest, and the writing becomes intensely simple:

> . . . I became conscious of something near my feet, something little and dark, moving indefinitely. I had found again the larkie's nest. I perceived the yellow beaks, the bulging eyelids of two tiny larks, and the blue lines of their wing quills. The indefinite movement was the swift rise and fall of the brown fledged backs, over which waved long strands of fine down. The two little specks of birds lay side by side, beak to beak, their tiny bodies rising and falling in quick unison. I gently put down my fingers to touch them; they were warm; gratifying to find them warm, in the midst of so much cold and wet! I became curiously absorbed in them, as an eddy of wind stirred the strands of down. When one fledgeling moved uneasily, shifting his soft ball, I was quite excited; but he nestled down again, with his head close to his brother's. In my heart of hearts, I longed for someone to nestle against, somone who would come between me and the coldness and the wetness. I envied the two little miracles exposed to any tread, yet so serene. It seemed as if I were always wandering, looking for something which they had found even before the light broke into their shell. (*WP*(C) 220)

This is an introduction to the next section, which is the bathing-scene. Cyril's questions are like Emily's feeling about the moon, or Lettie's sense that the flowers have 'something' which she has lost. What they don't have is human consciousness, and especially the modern sense of unease at not quite belonging. They can just be, direct from the centre of life which they are. And the essential thing about the young George in the early part of the book is that, for all his wakening consciousness, he is for the most part content to be. His disaster is that he loses that content, even though Lettie could criticise it as his bulb-like latency, his stagnation.

The bodily contact which Cyril and George enjoy is not overheated or suggestive, even if it is a little arch. George mocks Cyril gently for being thin, and Cyril replies that his slenderness is 'more exquisite than his [George's] grossness':

> But I had to give in, and bow to him, and he took on an indulgent, gentle manner. I laughed and submitted. For he knew how I admired the noble, white fruitfulness of his form. As I watched him, he stood in white relief against the mass of green. He polished his arm, holding it out straight and solid; he rubbed his hair into curls, while I watched the deep muscles of his shoulders, and the bands stood out in his neck as he held it firm. I remembered the story of Annable.
>
> He saw I had forgotten to continue my rubbing, and laughing he took hold of me and began to rub me briskly, as if I were a child, or rather, a woman he loved and did not fear. I left myself quite limply in his hands, and, to get a better grip of me, he put his arm round me and pressed me against him, and the sweetness of the touch of our naked bodies one against the other was superb. It satisfied in some measure the vague, indecipherable yearning of my soul; and it was the same with him. When he had rubbed me all warm, he let me go, and we looked at each other with eyes of still laughter, and our love was perfect for a moment, more perfect than any love I have known since, either for man or woman. (WP(C) 222–3)

This seems exactly stated, so that the most apt comment is to make the parallel with the two fledgelings in the nest just before. The scene is succeeded by another in which they return to the fields where George's true role, and his place in life, are established. The momentary reference to Annable reminds us that George is linked by his physicality to the gamekeeper, who is a lord of life in the animal world. The strange tonality of the Annable motif, always in the minor, associates him not just with animal life, but with its inversion: verminous death and rotting corpses; and this is appropriate in that he has exiled himself as if he were vermin and the enemy of social order; and he is in any case defeated, thwarted and stagnating. George has it in common with Annable that he can deal out life and death to the animals which he guards as stock or hunts as vermin. But his role as farmer gives him also a positive role: he nurtures growth in the fields, and so a whole range of the network of images – those to do with plants and flowers – also naturally centres in him as human representative. This long passage immediately after the bathing scene, not lush and emphatic as many others are, has power and grace:

> The cool, moist fragrance of the morning, the intentional stillness of everything, of the tall bluish trees, of the wet, frank flowers, of the trustful moths folded and unfolded in the fallen swaths, was a perfect medium of sympathy. The horses moved with a still dignity, obeying his commands. When they were harnessed, and the machine oiled, still he was loth to shatter the perfect morning, but stood looking down the valley.
>
> "I shan't mow these fields any more," he said, and the fallen, silvered swaths flickered back his regret and the faint scent of the limes was wistful. So much of the field was cut, so much remained to cut; then it was ended. This year the elder flowers were wide-spread over the corner bushes, and the pink roses fluttered high above the hedge. There were the same flowers in the grass as we had known many years; – we should not know them any more.
>
> "But merely to have mown them is worth having lived for" he said, looking at me. (*WP*(C) 223)

He then makes a reference which parallels Lettie's remark in the previous chapter about the dying tree in its hectic luxuriance. She might have been referring to her own dangerous mood. Now George makes a prophecy of the same kind:

> "You see that sycamore," he said, "that bushy one beyond the big willow? I remember when father broke off the leading shoot because he wanted a fine straight stick. I can remember I felt sorry. It was running up so straight, with such a fine balance of leaves . . . it seemed a cruelty. When you are gone and we are left from here, I shall feel like that, as if my leading shoot were broken off. You see the tree is spoiled. Yet look how it went on growing. I believe I shall grow faster". (*WP*(C) 223)

George's conscious, almost solemn resumption of his task begins to look like a ritual. So it is, in a straightforward way: the task has to be skilfully done. But there is something deeper:

> The machine started. The bed of the knife fell, and the grass shivered and dropped over. I watched the heads of the daisies and the splendid lines of the cocksfoot grass quiver, shake against the crimson burnet, and drop over. The machine went singing down the field, leaving a track of smooth velvet green in the way of the swath-board. The flowers in the wall of uncut grass waited unmoved as the days wait for us. (*WP*(C) 223–4)

It was probably in Lawrence's mind that all flesh is grass, and man cometh forth like a flower and is cut down.[11] The mower has always been a powerful figure of speech, and here is one of its most poetic uses. It is given a further richness in this last paragraph:

> Later, when the morning was hot, and the honeysuckle had ceased to breathe, and all the other scents were moving in the air about us, when all the field was down, when I had seen the last trembling ecstasy of the harebells, trembling to fall; when the thick clump of purple vetch had sunk; when the green swaths were settling, and the silver swaths were glistening and glittering as the sun came along them, in the hot ripe morning we worked together turning the hay, tipping over the yesterday's swaths with our forks, and bringing yesterday's fresh, hidden flowers into the death of sunlight. (*WP*(C) 223–4)

It is a beautiful and subtle touch: 'into the death of sunlight' enacts the paradox of the farmer as lord of life. What he brings to fruition he also brings to its appointed death; the sun which ripens also withers, as it rots the overripe fruit or the animal carcass. The whole system coheres and it is natural; the Bible sees it as 'the spirit of the Lord' at work. Where man intervenes he either assists the natural course or momentarily impedes it to no purpose. But the farmer is committed to the seasons and processes of life; and if he is in harmony with what he does, he has what George briefly assumes, a priest-like or even god-like function as ally of the sun, or of the Lord (however He is understood). He presides at a sacrifice which lasts the year through.

Part II is coming to an end. The next chapter 'Pastorals and

Peonies' is very weak in comparison. It contains two notations which matter: the one about the bullcalf being led by George, and this:

> ... turning from the profferred cup he lay down flat, put his mouth to the water, and drank deeply. She stood and watched the motion of his drinking, and of his heavy breathing afterwards. He got up, wiping his mouth, not looking at her. Then he washed his hands in the water, and stirred up the mud. He put his hand to the bottom of the trough, bringing out a handful of soft silt, with the grey shrimps twisting in it. He flung the mud on the floor where the poor grey creatures writhed.
> "It wants cleaning out," he said.[12] (*WP*(C) 229)

That disturbing little scene finds its echo in Part III. The whole drive of this Part is towards collapse and decay: primarily in George, who retains the centrality he acquired in Part II, but in the other characters too. And the movement out into the larger world, of the metropolis, of modern living, of industry, of the modern state, is also a move into squalor and tragedy. Lawrence was excited by London: he was moved by the beauty of the evening lights softening the great city so that it became more like something he could love: the lights were like flowers, or like bees, and so by metaphor they put him in touch with the natural world again. He could also be stirred by its energy, ingenuity, human panache. But for the most part, he could not deceive himself: nearly all of it was ugly, harsh, trivial and cruel.

> At the Marble Arch Corner we listened to a little socialist who was flaring fiercely under a plane tree. The hot stream of his words flowed over the old wounds that the knowledge of the unending miseries of the poor had given me, and I winced. For him the world was all East-end, and all the East-end was as a pool from which the waters are drained off, leaving the water-things to wrestle in the wet mud under the sun, till the whole of the city seems a heaving, shuddering struggle of black-mudded objects deprived of the elements of life. I felt a great terror of the little man, lest he should make me see all mud, as I had seen before. (*WP*(C) 281–2)

The implications are grim. Life in the city breeds these creatures of the mud, which are a sheer superfluity from the farmer's or gamekeeper's point of view (it's life, but not useful life), and an entirely natural process from a larger point of view (if you have mud, you must have the creatures that the mud produces). The socialist exposes the picture; but he can do nothing fundamental about what is as much one of the processes of city life as of pond-life. A farmer can clear his pond out, and kill his rats, but what do you do with what Annable called 'human rot'?

Nor could Annable prevent himself becoming human rot; nor can George. At the end of the book his state is presented in the kinder alternative of the plant/tree part of the image-network, while Annable always belonged to the animal/vermin part. Yet the kindliness is minimal:

> Like a tree that is falling, going soft and pale and rotten, clammy with small fungi, he stood leaning against the gate, while the dim afternoon drifted with a sweet flow of thick sunshine past him, not touching him. (*WP*(C) 324)

The network which I have been pursuing in some of its ramifications provides a harmonisation which accompanies and deepens the succession of events which makes the plot, and those few crucial conversations which provide what I called the doctrines, the moral preoccupations. In fact, the harmony is not separable from the melody. It is not a frame or a cement for the separable pieces of the plot. It turns out to be the most important element in the structure, both because it is continuous, and because it is powerful and full of meaning. It is a curious circumstance that all these things are said by the ineffectual Cyril, whose own emotional problems never come into focus. But he is the narrative voice which is mediating the texture to us, and whether he is an 'I' or an unidentified authorial voice only matters at one or two places. (One of them is the important bathing-scene). In the end the reader accepts that there is a strong identity between the author and his mouthpiece, and it is inevitable that in an immature book they have the same weaknesses. Consequently, when the 'network' strikes us as lush, literary or mannered, it may be Cyril speaking, or it may be Lettie; and the weakness is not a dramatic irony; it is a momentary lapse by Lawrence.

The lapses are outweighed by the strengths, and the final impression of this book is of its excess of energy; it is *too* weighted, too charged with significance; it is extraordinarily ambitious. For a young man in his first book to try to take on the nature of the universe and the course of human life shows that whatever he is, he is no palterer. He moves straight into the league of those dramatists, poets and novelists who, as Virginia Woolf once put it, seem to be making the largest of all gestures, as if to say 'We, the human race . . .'.

From the beginning, Lawrence is reaching beyond the circumstances in which his characters are engaged. They are the individual and personal embodiment of something impersonal. The challenge of Emily Brontë, as of Hardy, was that they too involved the universe. Their characters can at moments be reduced to tiny figures in a large landscape, which can itself dwindle to a point on the globe, which is a speck in the universe. The human passions need not be diminished by this; they are the spiritual force of that universe, and assimilated to its natural forces.

Lawrence from the start shows his people as torn between a known impulse – to behave as social beings, by marrying suitable people and doing conventional things like running businesses and becoming an MP and being generally 'successful', as on the surface Leslie Tempest is – torn between that and something which is more powerful because more fundamental and natural, but which is not yet known, not realised. If it were realised it would come as words, and inevitably as the product of the consciousness; and that is likely to be a betrayal, for we are in the realm of the things we do because of what we are, not what we know.

But it is an implication of the book that even in 1910 his people have been born too late: they can't help being conscious, and must interrogate themselves and each other. Lawrence's young men and women hunt for this thing which they are half-aware of as a lost wisdom which the flowers have, or an old religion, or the question that the moon is asking. They resort inevitably to poetic speech; and Cyril's equivocal position, as person who sees and hears everything and then tells us, means that his voice and his language are not inappropriately spread over everyone else like a cloak. Since he is the unacknowledged poet of the group, we receive it all as his poetry, sometimes lush and sometimes faded and mannered, but quite often direct and startling. The medium therefore, is not 'character' or 'plot', but the web of reiterated and developing allusion, reminiscence and motif. The network is woven, link by link, into the sequence of brief passages, incidents, descriptions, conversations, which at their best cohere in the chapters, making them natural groupings.

The characters through this medium question the being of the life around them, in its fullest aspect: the life of plants and animals as well as humans. The flowers, trees, birds, vermin, farm animals offer in their natural being the possibility of some knowledge. These things are not 'ours': they are other, unknown, sundered from consciousness. Yet they are also living creatures, existing in a whole living universe, with a confident simplicity which humans envy. They are themselves from a pure impulse which runs direct in them, from a universal source to which they have access, and from which we are cut off by the fact of consciousness.

George and Annable are defeated human representatives. Annable has been broken before he appears; George is broken during the course of the book, which ends 'He sat apart and obscure among us, like a condemned man.' He had had, at the beginning, a security rooted in his physical self-satisfaction. He forms the link with the plants and animals; he is as near to being like them as it is now possible to be. What Lettie represents is a feminine principle attracted to George as 'good animal' because it lacks that deep unconscious self-adjustment. Lettie and Cyril bring George into the consciousness necessary to enter into modern active life and growth; it is part of that process that he suddenly utters phrases about it. Unsettled from his self-content (which was static, and could not itself lead into growth) he is unsettled from his natural role. As originally lodged in his world, George was a kind of priest of life. The words are heavy, but the scenes in which the meaning is given are accurate and beautiful. He is the natural mediator of germination, fruition and death to the plants and animals he tends. They are all one life, and he needs few words for it, since he knows what to do with them.

But he does not know what to do with Lettie. There is no woman in the book who answers to his need. It is implied that women generally, or the young women of the time, are so bred that, though excited, they are repelled by the man's body, as Lettie is. If they are like Meg they want of the man more than he is willing to give to such as them.[13]

Both Meg and Lettie move to being mothers, so shutting the man out except as begetter and provider. The condition of life in this world at this time is therefore tragic, because men and women cannot meet each other in a natural relationship which fulfils them and locks them into an equally natural outward life. Lawrence has gone straight to his central preoccupation: love and marriage; and he has stated a fundamental problem: in modern society marriage is thrown out of equilibrium, and most people cannot manage it right. Therefore they cannot manage the good progress of their life. It would be foolish to expect that in his first book he would get much beyond seizing the problem. To have done it so boldly was already a striking achievement.

4 *The Trespasser*

The Trespasser is the most ignored and slighted of Lawrence's novels, but is far more interesting than people admit. As with *The White Peacock*, Lawrence anticipated the criticism. Over-impressed by Hueffer's reaction, and feeling as usual self-protective and willing to say it first, he wrote to his publisher:

> You are going to tell me some nasty things about it. I guess I have told them, most of them, to myself – amid acute inner blushes. The book is execrable bad art: it has no idea of progressive action, but arranges gorgeous tableaux-vivants which have not any connection one with the other: it is 'chargé' as a Prince Rupert's drop (if you know that curiosity): its purple patches glisten sicklily: it is, finally, pornographic. (to Frederick Atkinson, 11 February 1911, in *Letters I* 229)

This was written of the first version. Lawrence revised the book substantially in 1912, encouraged by Edward Garnett, to whom he then wrote more judiciously:

> At the bottom of my heart I don't like the work, though I'm sure it has points and I don't think it retrograde from the *White Peacock*. It surprises me by its steady progressiveness – I hate it for its fluid, luscious quality. (19 January 1912, in *Letters I* 351)

Later in the same month he wrote this:

> It really isn't bad, is it – but too florid, too 'chargé'. But it can't be anything else – it is itself. I must let it stand. At any rate, not many folk could have done it, however they may find fault.[1] (29 January 1912 in *Letters I* 358)

Lawrence's earlier remarks, and Hueffer's ('a rotten work of genius') have stuck in people's minds. The book is written off as a mistaken direction, with no relevance to the main work.

78

I must not go too far the other way: this is not a representative work of Lawrence's, indeed it is like nothing else in the canon. It *is* still immature, though less diffuse and more controlled in its impact than *The White Peacock*. It is too much in one very intense tone, and it is dominated by its subject, in that Lawrence was working from the documented story[2] and the conversational reminiscences of Helen Corke, recovering from the trauma of her lover's suicide. This faithfulness to actual events seems at first to give the novel less breadth of implication than *The White Peacock*, where although Alan Chambers in some sense 'was' the original of George Saxton, George's story was Lawrence's imaginative extension of what might have happened to such a person, so that he could invent a whole chain of events, leading to a collapse; and could involve a larger cast of characters.

The Trespasser, also a young man's book, is as morose in its outcome. The bafflement and disaster in which *The Trespasser* ends is like that of *The White Peacock* in that a man has been destroyed by the failure of his love for a woman; and this seems fated, since the woman is shown to be unable to meet his need. Again, this need is sexual. But expanding the over-simplification involved in using the word 'sexual' gives us one deeper meaning of the book. As in *The White Peacock*, the wider implications are provided by the whole texture of the writing, and not just by the thoughts and conversations of the characters or direct address by the author. When Lawrence said that the book was too 'chargé', he was pointing to its power as well as its relentless burden of intensity and its ultimate anguish. When he talked of its 'steady progressiveness' he was pointing to its strength, and his method; its 'fluid luscious quality' points to the corresponding excesses.

The Trespasser feels claustrophobic because it adheres so closely to the working out of the relationship between two people, for a moment isolated in a holiday-realm which is not where their ordinary living takes place, where they can concentrate on what is happening within them, and relate it to the magic of their stolen days in high summer. It is like a dream, with a grim awakening into death. If this concentration and the desire to be faithful to the events make the book restricted in its application at first sight, they also make it humanly direct and powerful. No unbiased reader can be totally unmoved by it, or unimpressed – though one may feel it unrelenting, oppressive and lowering. Nor can it be dismissed as the realistic treatment of a sad 'slice of life', like newspaper reports of divorce cases and suicides, for Lawrence has taken care that this shall not be possible. As with *The White Peacock*, the style is the controlling and the interesting thing, taking the reader below the level of event. Where the first book showed an intention to be poetic and to work through repeated emblems or symbols, weakened by survivals of nineteenth-century mannerism or high-flown literary-ness, *The Trespasser* has gone further. Its very tight structure is given by a rapid succession of brief numbered sections, unlike the long and undisciplined chapters of the first book, and more like the method of Tolstoy in *Anna Karenina*. Continuously, the staple of the prose, apart from the simpler conversations, is a carefully worked-out motivic web which is the literary equivalent of Wagner's use of themes in the orchestral music of his operas. It is not surprising that this idea occurred to Lawrence; he was half-way to it in *The White Peacock*, and his friendship with Helen Corke took him into musical and literary circles where Wagner was the dominant influence. The story of a musician first seen leaving the opera house at Covent Garden at the end of the season in which Richter had conducted the *Ring*, it is full of Wagnerian allusions. Lawrence's knowledge of the operas themselves could not be more superficial: but his grasp of the musical method is that of an artist seizing on something he was already intuitively working towards. The motivic structure of the book plays across the rapid sequence of episodes, and their simple basic plot, which has three movements: brief prelude in the present; main action as long reminiscence; postlude back in the present. The underlay of repeated and developed themes gives an orchestral or many-stranded meaning to the clear thread of the action. This accompaniment expands the limited application of the story of two actual people, and is meant to give the book the ambitious implications that had marked *The White Peacock*, but is subject to the same criticisms.

The analysis below displays the coherence of the motivic structure – what Lawrence called its surprising 'steady progressiveness', which he also recognised as making it too 'chargé', too florid, fluid and luscious. The coherence is a virtue, in that it springs from an effort of constructive intelligence. But it would be uncritical to stop at that point, which fails to meet the adverse position 'I can see that it is intentional and coheres: I still think that it is bad.' The adverse critic may admit that the badness, as in *The White Peacock*, is not cliché, inertly derivative, or mere slack writing, but is the product of a kind of originality, yet still fails. The critical task is to find some word less simply dismissive than 'bad' to describe this. The common ground for both critics is that the weaknesses are hard to distinguish from the strengths, since they are worked into the structure.

It emerges from this argument that some of Lawrence's deep preoccupations are present in the book, but that its defects spring from his attempt to deploy them too consciously in an elaborated imagery which goes beyond what comes to him 'unbidden'. The insistent working-out of the poetic structures produces the lusciousness that the reader sometimes winces at, the over-emphatic uses of the motivic material, the extreme intensity of the writer's own involvement, so that in writing about Siegmund and Helena he is overlaying them with his own preoccupations. The raptness and ninetyish mannerism of the style can also overlay the temperamental differences between the two main characters which at other times Lawrence carefully establishes, and so the conflict of personal character tends to have thrown over it the colourful but muffling blanket of a uniformly figurative prose which is too much Lawrence intervening. This criticism is less true of the later pages showing the return from the Isle of Wight to London and Siegmund's death. He comes back from his idyll to face a real family situation in the London suburbs which dissolves mannerism. This section of the book is strong and moving, and original in the treatment of Siegmund's internal movements of thought and emotion; the plot itself – for instance the poignant scenes between Siegmund and his little daughter – is finely imagined and rendered.

The last point the commentator might make is historical: the method or medium of *The Trespasser* is like an experiment in the mode of writing which Lawrence used to better effect in the first part of *The Rainbow*: though even there, criticisms must be made. And if Virginia Woolf used *The Trespasser* as a model for *The Waves*, which is a thought worth considering, then the book has an added interest for the student of the period. The method and the limitation of *The Waves* (there is only one dreamy and self-indulgent poetic voice, which speaks through several mouths) might seem borrowed from *The Trespasser*; but Lawrence manages for more of the time to differentiate his characters, for all that his method works against this; and parts of the book are more painfully real than anything in *The Waves*: the world breaks into the poetic monologue.

The book starts and finishes in a present which is in February and then later in the spring and summer of 1910. We are introduced in the first scene to Helena Verden, the heroine, closely identifiable with Helen Corke – even to her short stature and thick neck. She is a musician, and is first seen being accompanied by her friend Louisa; their audience is the young man Cecil Byrne (like Cyril Beardsall, a persona of Lawrence himself). Rapidly, by means of a motivic transition through the image of the unused violin of a dead player, we are taken back to the previous July, and the last night of the opera season at Covent Garden. 'Siegmund' Macnair,[3] who owned the violin, is seen leaving the theatre with it after the performance, and we embark at once on the main narrative, which takes place in a single week. He joins Helena for a snatched and illicit few days together on the Isle of Wight, to which he escapes from his marriage to a bitter and estranged wife and their resentful children. On the island, the only people they talk to are the landlady of the cottage where they stay, and a strange Doppelgänger called Hampson, also a musician, who surges up from the past to give Siegmund a warning of his fate, a *Todesverkündigung*. He is, like Annable in the previous book, a deliberate insertion, an admonitory figure, made to provide an oracular commentary, which is strangely like the author talking to his invented character Siegmund: an alter ego talking to a third ego. Like Annable, what he has to say is redolent of Lawrence's preoccupations below the level of 'plot'. However unprepared the intrusion may seem, it is not inorganic, since Hampson talks the motivic language of the book.

In their few days together, the lovers manage a kind of ecstasy, but it is flawed. Lawrence conveys with insight how in their passion they sometimes talk past each other to a projection of the other which is not the reality. They are halted by a dismaying awareness of not being 'with' each other at these moments, and fall into separate despairs which emphasise their division. Lawrence also conveys a fatal incompatibility. Like Lettie, Helena wants power over a man but does not want the physical man himself. She can at best yield herself to his passion as a kindness, a sacrifice. The word is used, and is ominous. Siegmund is withered by this experience, a rejection and failure which undermine the idyll, and there strengthens in him the unspoken resolve to cut through his intolerable dilemma by killing himself. She cannot see this resolve forming. The pages describing their journey back to London and parting are poignantly imagined, and the catastrophe is harrowing. Siegmund's solitude with Helena, his search in his own thoughts for consolation; his bitter isolation on his return to his outraged family, his last night of loneliness in the body that only he can love, the last moments of his life: all this is well done both at the level of realism, and at the underlying level. The narrative brings Helena back from a holiday in Cornwall to find that he is dead; and shifts back into the present: first to the self-dramatisations of the egoist, his wife, then to the possible rehabilitation of Helena, who is seen at the end of the book re-exerting her power, this time on Cecil Byrne. The implications of the ending are purely negative: she cannot give to Byrne what she could not give to Siegmund, and Byrne, we suppose, will have to learn this.

Once more, at this synoptic level, this early book is a serious enterprise: a second study of the relationships possible, or not possible, between modern men and women. In *The White Peacock* the direct depiction of sexual love was discreetly avoided: now Lawrence's figurative language enables him to come closer to the kind of encounter which sooner or later he would have to attempt. He is already bold in his willingness to describe an illicit affair with more sympathy for the sufferings of the sinners than of the righteous. The affinities with *The White Peacock* are simple and strong: Siegmund is from the beginning more mature and conscious, but he shares George's robust physicality, his sensitivity, his capacity to be ensnared and to suffer, and his ultimate defeat. Helena shares a good deal with Lettie: it is as if, meeting Helen Corke, Lawrence had thought yes, this was the sort of woman he had been imagining in the first book, and her attraction and her lethal limitation were as he had supposed. The author of *The White Peacock* underwent the spell himself.[4]

There are other affinities, which may seem odd or coincidental at first. But it is not just a random observation that in *The White Peacock*, George, in a state of tension in the presence of Lettie 'smiled painfully. His hand was resting on the table, the thumb tucked tight under the fingers, his knuckles white as he nervously gripped his thumb' (*WP*(C) 25). These instinctive gestures give a hint of the life of the body which we ignore, and in *The Trespasser* the gesture is given a meaning. Siegmund is having his mysterious interview, like a dream, with Hampson, who turns out to be a former acquaintance and in oracular language makes the drift of Siegmund's life clear to him:

> Siegmund pondered a little.
> "You make me feel – as if I were loose, and a long way off from myself," he said slowly.
> The young man smiled, then looked down at the wall, where his own hands lay white and fragile, showing the blue veins.
> "I can scarcely believe they are me," he said. "If they rose up and refuted me, I should not be surprised. But aren't they beautiful?"
> He looked, with a faint smile, at Siegmund.
> Siegmund glanced from the stranger's to his own hands, which lay curved on the sea-wall as if asleep. They were small for a man of his stature, but lying warm in the sun, they looked particularly secure in life. Instinctively, with a wave of self love, he closed his fists over his thumbs. (*T*(C) 113)

The posture of the two people, side by side with their hands on a wall before them, is repeatedly used by Lawrence as emblematic of separateness-with-relationship. It was briefly noted earlier in the book: 'Together they leaned on the wall, warming the four white hands upon the grey bleached stone, as they watched the water playing' (*T*(C) 76). Now, with Hampson, Siegmund is reminded that his hands, which look as if they were out there ('loose, and a long way off', like his essential self), are nonetheless him. Yet it is hard to believe, Hampson says, and he can imagine his hands 'refuting' him, as Lettie's had 'disclaimed' her (see p. 54 above). Then Siegmund makes his mysterious impulsive movement of self-enclosure, as if catching back the straying self.

This instinctive reaction is obsessively repeated as he nears the death he knows he must give himself. On his last evening

> His fists were tightly clenched, his fingers closed over his thumbs, which were pressed bloodless. He lay down on the bed. . . . At eight o'clock he sat up. A cramped pain in this thumbs made him wonder. He looked at them, and

mechanically shut them again under his fingers, into the position they sought after two hours of similar constraint. Siegmund opened his hands again, smiling.

"It is said to be the sign of a weak, deceitful character," he said to himself. (*T*(C) 190)

Later that same evening 'He hurried down the platform, wincing at every stride, from the memory of Helena's last look of mute, heavy yearning. He gripped his fists till they trembled; his thumbs were again closed under his fingers' (*T*(C) 197). The decision to kill himself is never expressed in words. The nearest he comes to it, after having so identified himself with his hands, is to think:

> . . . what remained possible? Why, to depart. 'If thine hand offend thee, cut it off.' He could cut himself off from life. It was plain and straightforward. (*T*(C) 202)

The Biblical injunction (Matthew 5.30) substitutes the part for the whole. One's hands are before one's eyes in a way no other part of the body is. They move as if instinctively, one works most things in the outside world with them, they are as much an intermediary as eyes, ears and tongue. And, as Hampson says, they are us. The statement 'I am I' was to become a basic and central proposition for Lawrence from which all else derived. Here he is approaching that formulation in a characteristic way: not as the Cartesian assertion that I am because I am a thinking centre of consciousness. 'I am I' not because I think, but because I see my hands before my face and know my identity with these prehensile or tendril-like extensions which are in the world and are also me. My tenderness for them is my tenderness for myself; wounded or threatened, they shut in on themselves like flowers. They *know* something, and if I attend to them I learn it: since they are me, the thing they know is about me.

Like George Saxton, Siegmund strips to swim, more than once. There is no Cyril present to admire him, but he is pleased with the body that he sees. Swimming, he hits a rock and cuts himself:

> He glanced at himself, at his handsome, white maturity. As he looked he felt the insidious creeping of blood down his thigh, which was marked with a long red slash. Siegmund watched the blood travel over the bright skin. It wound itself redly round the rise of his knee.

"That is I, that creeping red, and this whiteness I pride myself on is I, and my black hair, and my blue eyes are I. It is a weird thing to be a person. What makes me myself among all these?"

. . .

"I am at my best, at my strongest," he said proudly to himself. "She ought to be rejoiced at me, but she is not, she rejects me as if I were a baboon, under my clothing."

He glanced at his whole handsome maturity, the firm plating of his breasts, the full thighs, creatures proud in themselves. (*T*(C) 74)

Helena wants what Lawrence later called a 'speaking head': a mind and a personality lodged in the top storey, above a suit of clothes. The man who sheds his clothes on the beach in order to enter the sea knows that he is the whole of himself, and feels the rejection of his body not just as a sexual failure but as a rejection of the totality, including the blood which has for once emerged from within the skin.

On his last morning on the island, Siegmund goes for a final swim: a kind of ritual for him, with overtones of worship and sacrifice ('He undressed by his usual altarstone'):

He found great pleasure in this feeling of intimacy with things. A very soft wind, shy as a girl, put its arms round him, and seemed to lay its cheek against his chest. He placed his hands beneath his arms, where the wind was caressing him, and his eyes opened with wondering pleasure.

And afterwards:

He looked at himself, at his limbs and his body in the pride of his maturity. He was very beautiful to himself.

"Nothing, in the place where I am," he said. "Gone like a puff of steam that melts on the sunshine."[5] (*T*(C) 135–7)

By a natural and inevitable symmetry, on the morning when he kills himself his whole body is in a fever, as if in protest; and in an unconscious state he cannot move or break out of this agony. But he finally throws the bedclothes off, sits up, and becomes wakeful:

It seemed to him as if he ought to have endured the heat of his body, and the infernal trickling of the drops of sweat. But at the thought of it he moved his hands gratefully over his sides, which were now dry, and soft, and smooth; slightly chilled on the surface, perhaps, for he felt a sudden tremor of shivering from the warm contact of his hands.

. . . He felt his chest again to make sure it was not clammy: it was smooth as silk. This pleased him very much. (*T*(C) 200)

For the last time the hands which feel are known as part of the body which is felt, and is grateful. We are reminded of George Saxton's gesture as he stands in the field after scything; and behind him we sense the gesture of Lawrence himself, recorded in the letter to Blanche Jennings.

But if you tug any thread in this texture, you see a movement elsewhere in the pattern. Here, for instance:

He sat in the chair beside her, leaning forward, his hands hanging like two scarlet flowers listless in the fireglow, near to her, as she knelt on the hearth, with head bowed down. One of the flowers awoke and spread towards her. It asked for her mutely. She was fascinated, scarcely able to move.[6] (*T*(C) 69)

Or this:

She had peculiar hands, small, with a strange delightful silkiness: often they were cool or cold; generally they lay unmoved within his clasp, but then they were instinct with life, not inert. Sometimes he would feel a peculiar jerking in his pulse, very much like electricity, when he held her hand. Occasionally it was almost painful, and felt as if a little virtue were passing out of his blood. But that he dismissed as nonsense. (*T*(C) 155)

But Lawrence himself would not dismiss it as nonsense. It is a reference to the Gospel story of the healing of the woman with an issue of blood: 'And Jesus, immediately knowing in himself that virtue had gone out of him, turned about him in the press, and said, Who touched my clothes?' (Mark 5.30) Lawrence's thought-world is perfectly in touch with that old world: he knows for instance that the 'virtue' is in the 'blood'.

The hands which can gratifyingly touch one's own sides[7] are also capable of carrying a charge, as of electricity, when two people touch. The Doppelgänger Hampson extends this analogy, as a conscious equation:

> "The best sort of women – the most interesting – are the worst for us. . . . By instinct they aim at suppressing the gross and animal in us. Then they are supersensitive – refined a bit beyond humanity. We who are as little gross as need be, become their instruments. Life is grounded in them, like electricity in the earth; and we take from them the unrealised life, turn it into light or warmth or power for them. The ordinary woman is, alone, a great potential force, an accumulator, if you like, charged from the Source of life. In us her force becomes evident.
>
> She can't live without us, but she destroys us. These deep, interesting women don't want *us*: they want the flowers of the spirit they can gather of us. (*T*(C) 112)

This starts as worked-out intellectual equivalent, but the word 'grounded' acts as a node or function, where the 'electrical' image, which is an intellectual fancy or conceit, links with the flower image, which seems more instinctive. We are reminded of an earlier passage where the same thoughts are entertained, and made rich by the same lapse towards the world of flowers and plants:

> Suddenly she strained madly to him, and, drawing back her head, placed her lips on his, close, till at the mouth they seemed to melt and fuse together. It was the long, supreme kiss, in which man and woman have one being, Two-in-one, the only Hermaphrodite.
>
> When Helena drew away her lips, she was exhausted. She belonged to that class of 'Dreaming Women', with whom passion exhausts itself at the mouth. Her desire was accomplished in a real kiss. The fire, in heavy flames, had poured through her to Siegmund, from Siegmund to her. It sank, and she felt herself flagging. She had not the man's brightness and vividness of blood . . .
>
> He held her close. His dream was melted in his blood, and his blood ran bright for her. His dreams were the flowers of his blood. Hers were more detached and inhuman.[8] (*T*(C) 64)

Here the dangerous notion of fusing is introduced, and the physical concept, from the world of metalworking and industry, therefore inorganic, is from the same realm as the electrical analogy. And once again the thought is transformed into the organic realm, and the 'flowers' become the valuable product, the beautiful developmental growth. The phrase 'sank, and she felt herself flagging' is the node, where the dying flame changes into something like a plant wilting as the sap recedes: the sap is equated with blood, and the flowers of Siegmund's blood are his dreams. So he flowers for her. It is made explicit that his 'flowers' are of the 'blood', where hers are of the 'spirit'.

The idea of flowering is already familiar from *The White Peacock*, and so are some of the extensions; for instance:

"I like the sunshine on me, real and manifest and tangible. I feel like a seed that has been frozen for ages. I want to be bitten by the sunshine". (*T*(C) 79)

Or Hampson's remark to Siegmund:

"You haven't much reserve. You're like a tree that'll flower till it kills itself . . .". (*T*(C) 111)

Or his concluding oracle:

"Fools – the fools, these women," he said. "Either they smash their own crystal, or it revolts, turns opaque, and leaps out of their hands. Look at me, I am whittled down to the quick. But your neck is thick with compressed life: it is a stem so tense with life that it will hold up by itself. I am very sorry". (*T*(C) 113)

That may seem obscure. The 'crystal' is a witch's ball, and almost certainly associated with *The Lady of Shalott*[9] – that is to say with women who are fated to see life magically separated off or safely contained within a sphere or mirror, and who are destroyed by direct contact with it. But again the image reverts into the other mode: Siegmund is a plant or flower, and his throat the stem which holds up the inflorescence, his head. Since he hangs himself in the end, all the references to his throat and Helena's lead towards that breaking of the stem.[10]

The plant-flower-stem-blossom complex is related both to the hands, which can be seen as flowers, and the throat, which holds up that other flower, the head. The sap which flows in the plant is like the blood which is 'vivid' in the body; it is also like the power, the electricity, which is communicated by touch. It is not in itself a weakness that the elements of this imagery are labile or unstable: that the 'dreams' in Siegmund's blood are also 'flowers'. The instability or volatility prevents the system from becoming a mere algebra, where figurative expressions always stand for one thing and so only have one meaning, and the relationship between the elements of the system is logical and therefore deducible. That would be deathly. What we have instead is more like a natural universe, in which the inhabitants relate to each other, but have an independent life, capable of mutation by natural processes of association, so that the relationships are gratuitous yet not arbitrary. Yet the weaknesses of the book are inherent in the same processes: those moments when the reader feels that a natural imaginative movement is prolonged by a deliberate working-out which leaves the original impulse of vision or insight and becomes at best ingenious and at worst insistent.

I analyse below an extended passage – one of the equivalents in *The Trespasser* of the 'poetic' chapters in *The White Peacock*. Here the image-web is being orchestrally deployed, for good and ill. It will be seen that at their best there is a natural logic of association between the motifs, so that, to use the musical analogy, the individual figures or comparisons are like notes on a keyboard; they can become parts of different phrases, and inflected by different key-systems, so that they are freely adaptable, and therefore have different meanings in different contexts, while maintaining themselves as part of the system. For instance, the natural scene of the novel, the Isle of Wight in summer, supplies sun, moon, and sea; the flowers of the land; the birds, the bees. Lawrence can link these as a system from the base provided by the suppressed equivalence sap = blood. Thus the sun fosters or wilts flowers, in which the sap rises or falls. Flowers are visited by bees, which seek pollen. The bee can visit many flowers because of its wings; it is in that respect like birds; also like bats. One surprising intrusion, the bat's wing, with the sun shining through it, is red – because of the blood in it. These properties or constituents can be used to inflect Helena's and Siegmund's wordless states or ecstasy or dread, attraction or hostility; and they enable Lawrence to capture fugitive mental states which are not thinking, but what we loosely call moods: also fundamental aspects of personality. Finally they are used by Siegmund himself to win some comfort out of his tragedy – as a bee wins honey from its incessant to-and-fro.

The whole passage occupies section VIII of the novel (pp. 86–91 of the Cambridge edition). It begins with an overt statement: 'She wanted to sacrifice to him, make herself a burning altar to him: and she wanted to possess him.' The paradox is one Lawrence explored in several early works. He begins to explain:

> That night she met his passion with love. It was not his passion she wanted, actually. But she desired that he should want *her* madly, and that he should have all – everything. It was a wonderful night to him. It restored in him the full "will to live". But she felt it destroyed her. Her soul seemed blasted.

That basic exposition of their dilemma, summary and mental, opens out into the description which follows, and which seems vividly and simply pictorial, but is a fuller exposition of the dilemma at the level of instinctive perception, in which the directly opposed mood or tonality of the characters' minds can be expressed with the same figures of speech, just as musical motives may be tonally transformed. The reader can see in the whole passage a characteristic mixture of lushness and coherence:

> At seven o'clock in the morning Helena lay in the deliciously cool water, while small waves ran up the beach full and clear and foamless, continuing perfectly in their flicker the rhythm of the night's passion. Nothing, she felt, had ever been so delightful as this cool water running over her. She lay and looked out on the shining sea. All, it seemed, was made of sunshine more or less soiled.

The last word represents her mood (an unconscious recollection of her rejection of sexuality, moving towards consciousness) but it is countered or appeased by the continuation:

> The cliffs rose out of the shining waves like clouds of strong, fine texture; and rocks along the shore were the dapplings of a bright dawn. The coarseness was fused out of the world, so that sunlight showed in the veins of the morning cliffs and the rocks.

'Fused' has reappeared, here connoting refinement in the fire, so that the soiling is burnt away, and the coarseness removed. The 'veins' are a node here: they can be veins of mineral in the rock, but also the veins which carry blood. In a sense the metamorphosis below follows naturally, and carries the crucial equivalence, but the reader will flinch at the Biblical opening, and the word 'inefficiency' is a strange choice. The working-out is becoming mechanical, and literary:

> Yea, everything ran with sunshine, as we are full of blood, and plants are tissued from green-gold, glistening sap. Substance and solidity were shadows that the morning cast round itself to make itself tangible: as she herself was a shadow cast by that fragment of sunshine, her soul, over its inefficiency.

Then we move back to an original perception:

> She remembered to have seen the bats flying low over a burnished pool at sunset, and the web of their wings had burned in scarlet flickers as they stretched across the light. Winged momentarily on bits of tissued flame, threaded with blood, the bats had flickered a secret to her.

The word 'flicker', first used to describe the waves, had had a sexual connotation. That 'flicker' was a rhythmic movement of light, caused by the rocking of the waves. As a memory, the rhythm had disturbed her, and produced the idea of being soiled. Now the movement of light on the remembered bat's wings reminds her subliminally that the beating of wings is comparably rhythmic, so again there is an association with Siegmund's lovemaking, which she has to repress or turn into something else. She universalises the perception by transferring it to the white of the chalk cliffs, suffused with pink by the sun:

> Now the cliffs were like wings uplifted, and the morning was coming dimly through them. She felt the wings of all the world upraised against the morning in a flashing, multitudinous flight. The world itself was flying. Sunlight poured on the large round world till she fancied it a heavy bee humming on its iridescent atmosphere across a vast air of sunshine.

Again the working-out has become mechanical. It has also moved into Lawrence's 'Hardy' mode, where the cosmic vision is meant to suggest an Olympian standpoint, but which can easily seem pretentious.

> She lay and rode the fine journey. Sunlight liquid in the water made the waves heavy, golden, and rich with a velvety coolness like cowslips. Her feet fluttered in the shadowy underwater. Her breast came out bright as the breast of a white bird.

The transition has been made. The bat was a disturbing omen, and the bee carried obvious sexual overtones, but the white bird is asexual and indifferent, and her mood of immunity or self-sufficiency is restored. The reader who follows this movement of feeling can be struck both by the subtlety of the mental process and by the luridness of the rendering.

> Where was Siegmund, she wondered. He also was somewhere among the sea and the sunshine, white and playing like a bird, shining like a vivid, restless speck of sunlight. She struck the water, smiling, feeling alone with him. They two were the owners of this morning, as a pair of wild, large birds inhabiting an empty sea.
> Siegmund had found a white cave welling with green water brilliant and full of life as mounting sap. The white rock glimmered through the water, and soon Siegmund shimmered also in the living green of the sea, like pale flowers trembling upward.

So if the bat is disturbingly like Siegmund to Helena, the cave is reassuringly like Helena to Siegmund. He is not disturbed: but he ought to be. He swims into a tiny bay, inaccessible from the land, and the 'significance' now becomes obvious and heavy, indeed crude. He wades on to 'sand that was pure as the shoulders of Helena', and lies on it 'soft and warm as white fur', 'swelling with glad pride at having conquered also this small, inaccessible sea-cave, creeping into it like a white bee into a white, virgin blossom that had waited, how long, for its bee.' It is too easy a transition to the bee-image; yet the simplicity is also the simplicity of Siegmund's self-congratulation at his sexual conquest, and so appropriate, like all the rendering of 'character' in the whole passage. It is then very strikingly qualified. Running the sand through his fingers and saying 'Surely it is like Helena', he too discovers something disturbing and the reader moves back from distaste to a sense of an important reality:

> . . . he laid his hands again on the warm body of the shore, let them wander, discovering, gathering all the warmth, the softness, the strange wonder of smooth, warm pebbles, then shrinking from the deep weight of cold his hand encountered as he burrowed under the surface, wrist-deep. In the end, he found the cold mystery of the deep sand also thrilling. He pushed in his hands again and deeper, enjoying the almost hurt of the dark, heavy coldness. For the sun and the white flower of the bay were breathing and kissing him dry, were holding him in their warm concave, like a bee in a flower, like himself on the bosom of Helena, and flowing like the warmth of her breath in his hair came the sunshine, breathing near and lovingly: yet, under all, was this deep mass of cold, that the softness and warmth merely floated upon.

The crudeness disappears with this remarkable note: Siegmund feels a threat equivalent to the bat's wings, so that his joy is as mysteriously admonished as Helena's. But for the moment he is happy like a child, drying himself on the sand, and getting all dusty. He washes himself clean, his desire for cleansing being the direct opposite of hers (she wants to be cleansed of *him*):

> He must feel perfectly clean and free, fresh, as if he had washed away all the years of soilure in this morning's sea and sun and sand. It was the purification. Siegmund became again a happy priest of the sun.

Heavy as it is, that too is an important note, in this book and others. The sun is the one persistent but mysterious positive; often mentioned; never directly identified. But its priests raise their hands to it, offer themselves to it; these little rituals and sacrifices take place; and meanings are found, as at the end of the section, where Siegmund and Helena are given slightly stagey words for what they have just experienced separately. They do not quite understand what they want to say, nor what the other says:

"I found a little white bay – just like you – a virgin bay – I had to swim there."

"Oh!" she said, very interested in him, not in the fact.

. . .

"I saw the sun through the cliffs and the sea, and you," she said.

He did not understand . . . he found himself saying:

"You know, I felt as if I were the first man to discover things: like Adam when he opened the first eyes in the world."

"I saw the sunshine in you," repeated Helena quietly.

In Lawrence's world, it is one of the highest tributes that that can be paid, and this very positive note must be taken as qualifying Siegmund's tragedy, just as the moment of vision momentarily enlarges Helena's limitation. It is unfortunate that Lawrence cannot give them words and perceptions that are both natural and significant. The significance wins, at the cost of the tone.

The intimation which Siegmund receives from the 'deep mass of cold' is picked up overtly a few pages later:

He himself might play with the delicious warm surface of life, but always he recked of the relentless mass of cold beneath, the mass of life which has no sympathy with the individual, no cognisance of him. (*T*(C) 94)

This Hardyesque perception is transformed by the Doppelgänger, Hampson. Commenting on the beauty of the day – its warmth, brightness, blueness, happiness – he goes off into a flight of fancy:

". . . I call a day like this, 'the blue room'. It's the least draughty apartment in all the confoundedly draughty House of Life" . . .

"I mean," the man explained, "that after all, the great mass of life that washes unidentified, and that we call death, creeps through the blue envelope of the day, and through our white tissue, and we can't stop it, once we've begun to leak."

"What do you mean by 'leak'?" asked Siegmund.

"Goodness knows – I talk through my hat . . .". (*T*(C) 110)

But he is not talking through his hat, he is extending the web. His conversation darts to another part of it, seemingly unconnected:

"A craving for intense life is nearly as deadly as any other craving. You become a 'concentré'; you feed your normal flame with oxygen, and it devours your tissue. The soulful ladies of romance are always semi transparent."

It seems wild talk, at first. Our second thought, it becomes clear that it is Lawrence speaking. The ideas have their place in the system. The soulful ladies are Ladies of Shalott; and the short story 'The Witch à la Mode' explores the whole context of witchcraft, lamplight, and the long kiss which is vampire-like. The idea of a spirituality like a pressure-lamp, which burns so intensely that it consumes the vessel, the person concerned, links this passage with Miriam Leivers, in *Sons and Lovers*. There, too, we encounter the notion of 'leaking' – or a reversal of that process ('as if he had not sufficient sheathing to prevent the night and the space breaking into him').

So, one way or the other, you can become pervious, and space or death can seep into you, as the sea seeps into the sand on the beach: the cold 'mystery' that Siegmund first encountered when he thrust his hands through the sand, the surface or envelope of the earth. It is identified by Hampson as 'the great mass of life that washes unidentified, and that we call death' – paradoxically death is not the negation of life so much as its neutral or unindividuated complement. It negates identity, and receives the individual back to 'the great mass of life'. This is the equivocal and entirely notional comfort that Siegmund has to seek, as his determination grows to rejoin that 'great mass', hoping that it may be, in some form, life.

He manages a moment of prophetic clarity, pervaded with the misery of the thought that his relationship with Helena has been a failure, and that he has no way out of his situation but death. Returning on the ferry from Ryde to Portsmouth, he sees a narrowly averted accident: a small boat is nearly run down by the steamer he is on, and the occupants drowned. But they escape: life is on their side as it is not on his. He has a moment of illumination: seeing the good fortune of these other people, their life asserted, suddenly all his perceptions knit together in a concerted passage. This seems to me less like Lawrence cranking his poetic machine to produce the web of images (one's intermittent uneasiness earlier in the book). Now the web is established as a firm tissue;

there is momentum, and real feeling involved; and the coherence is more passionate and less willed:

"Ah dear Lord!" he was saying to himself. "How bright and whole the day is for them. If God had suddenly put his hand over the sun, and swallowed us up in a shadow, they could not have been more startled. That man, with his fine white-flannelled limbs and his dark head, has no suspicion of the shadow that supports it all. Between the blueness of the sea and the sky he passes easy as a gull, close to the fine white sea-mew of his mate, amid red flowers of flags, and soft birds of ships, and slow moving monsters of steamboats.

For me, the day is transparent and shrivelling. I can see the darkness through its petals. But for him it is a fresh bell-flower, in which he fumbles with delights like a bee.

For me, quivering in the interspaces of the atmosphere is the darkness, the same that fills in my soul. I can see death urging itself into life, the shadow supporting the substance. For my life is burning an invisible flame. The glare of the light of myself, as I burn on the fuel of death, is not enough to hide from me the source and the issue. For what is a life but a flame that bursts off the surface of darkness and tapers into the darkness again. But the death that issues differs from the death that was the source. At least I shall enrich death with a potent shadow, if I do not enrich life." (T(C) 159)

We see how the elements of the network can shift to produce fresh connections. The fortunate strangers are immune, like the gulls that Helena and Siegmund had wanted to identify themselves with. The whiteness, the lazy floating above the earth, imply absence of soiling, easy grace, success, untroubled being. They are in the 'blue room', and for them the 'red flowers of flags' are triumphal. But Siegmund now has the deathly inkling that Helena had had; she saw the red flicker of the bat's wings across the sun, and since it was her unconscious rejection of Siegmund's sexuality, it was also an omen of his death. Now he has the same omen revealed to him: he sees the light – or rather he sees the darkness – through the sun-shrivelled petals of the flower in which he had wanted to be a bee. The bee-image, here as elsewhere, is heavy and clumsy, but is transformed by the light-association.

That negative light is by an image-shift associated with the cold which he had felt seeping through the sand. In this metaphorical chain the level of the sea rising up through the layer of sand becomes the oil level in a lamp, rising up the wick to issue in the flame which is paradoxically his life, is him.

So here the other notion, often entertained in *The White Peacock* as in this book, of the plant which flowers fiercely as it nears death, or is nipped into blossom by a fierce sun, is shown converting itself, by way of the idea of perviousness, into the other Lawrentian image of the lamp-flame or the candle-flame. The node here is the equivalence sap=blood=vital fuel or oil.

The notion of life as a flame coming off the darkness and ending again in the darkness produces another set of images which are central to Lawrence's thought.[11] The vigorous natural man whose life comes off him like a candle-flame tends to take the place of the early perception of the vigorous tree or flower in blossom. Here we are at the point where the two perceptions are linked in the web of imagery which is the main interest of *The Trespasser*. The favoured image of the candle-flame appears shortly after: 'There was a soft vividness of life in their carriage; it reminded Siegmund of the soft swaying and lapping of a poised candle-flame' (*T*(C) 168). The strange but apt word 'lapping' links the flame-movement and its tiny sound with the sea's sound and movement.

The distinctive features of the candle-flame are that it is soft, warm and golden: honey-like, and sun-like. In these respects it fits the tonality which is spread over Siegmund himself, and is also appropriate to the affirmative but limiting and usually too conscious perception that he is like a bee, visiting flowers for honey, and like all male bees a mere insignificant unit doomed to die when this season's sun goes. Before that time comes, he has to lay up his store of honey. He draws the conscious analogy himself; and while it is logical, and the reader's sympathy with Siegmund makes it welcome comfort, it is over-extended and becomes mechanical:

> "Ah, well!" thought Siegmund – he was tired – "– if one bee dies in a swarm, what is it, so long as the hive is all right? Apart from the gold light, and the hum and the colour of day, what was I? – nothing! Apart from these rushings out of the hive, along with the swarm, into the dark meadows of night, gathering God knows what, I was a pebble. Well, the day will swarm in golden

again, with colour on the wings of every bee, and humming in each activity. The gold, and the colour, and sweet smell, and the sound of life, they exist, even if there is no bee: it only happens we see the iridescence on the wings of the bee. It exists, whether or not, bee or no bee. Since the iridescence and the humming of life *are*, always, and since it was they who made me, then I am not lost. At least, I do not care. If the spark goes out, the essence of the fire is there in the darkness. What does it matter! Besides, I *have* burned bright; I have laid up a fine cell of honey somewhere – I wonder where. We can never point to it. But it *is* so – what does it matter, then!" (*T*(C) 165–6)

Returning to London, Siegmund has returned to the hive:

As he leaned on the Embankment parapet the wonder did not fade, but rather increased. The trams, one after another, floated loftily over the bridge. They went like great burning bees in an endless file into a hive, past those which were drifting dreamily out: while below, on the black distorted water, golden serpents flashed and twisted to and fro.

"Ah!" said Siegmund to himself. "It is far too wonderful for me. Here, as well as by the sea, the night is gorgeous and uncouth. Whatever happens, the world is wonderful."[12]

So he went on amid all the vast miracle of movement in the city night, the swirling of water to the sea, the gradual sweep of the stars, the floating of many lofty, luminous cars through the bridged darkness, like an army of angels filing past, on one of God's campaigns; the purring haste of the taxis, the slightly dancing shadows of people: Siegmund went on slowly, like a slow bullet winging into the heart of life.

The last remarkable transformation, from bee to bullet – for this is his last night – is a sinister check to our feelings; it cancels the banal notion of the ecstasy of the sun-drunk bee, and almost justifies its too insistent use before.

In these terms Siegmund's tragedy and his nature are explored. I find him solid and sympathetic: his attempt to find a grain of dignity and some significance, however humble, in the fate to which he acquiesces gives him imaginative strength. His contribution to the complex poetry of the book achieves a distinct note, against the strong tendency of the 'music' to drown personal distinctions.

Helena's limitations are also well expressed. It is not just a matter of overt utterances such as Lawrence's saying that 'her passion is exhausted at the mouth' or Hampson's formula about 'the best sort of women'. It is dramatically conveyed as *her* personal contribution to the poetic complexity. There are two distinct elements. One is a vein of prettifying fancy:

> "That yellow flower hadn't time to be brushed and combed by the fairies, before dawn came. It is towzled . . .," so she thought to herself. The pink convolvuli were fairy horns, or telephones from the day fairies to the night fairies. The rippling sunlight on the sea was the Rhine Maidens spreading their bright hair to sun. That was her favourite form of thinking. The value of all things was in the fancy they evoked. She did not care for people; they were vulgar, ugly, and stupid, as a rule. (*T*(C) 75–6)

That strikes one as apt, but also easy to see and convey, and tending to make her falsely naive, trivial, and not worth attention. The more important element is her capacity to envisage the vulgarity or ugliness of people, including Siegmund, in frightening ways. Physical reality does not just awe her, it repels her. One perception seems at first almost neutral, or even thrilling; but has frightening implications:

> Presently she laid her head on his breast, and remained so, watching the sea and listening to his heart-beats. The throb was strong and deep. It seemed to go through the whole island, and the whole afternoon, and it fascinated her: so deep, unheard, with its great expulsions of life. Had the world a heart? – Was there also deep in the world a great God thudding out waves of life, like a great Heart, unconscious? It frightened her. This was the God she knew not: as she knew not this Siegmund. (*T*(C) 79)

The reader familiar with the later Lawrence notes the early formulation of the idea of the unknown god as personification of the totally other. It is a negative perception here.

The figure is used again in one of those night-scenes in which

Lawrence conveys how the lovers discover that they are talking
past each other to a projection, or fantasising in the presence of a
real person who is not the fantasy. The insight produces a separate
despair in each of them, as here:

> His voice was nothing to her, it was stupid. She felt his arms
> round her, felt her face pressed against the cloth of his coat,
> against the beating of his heart. What was all this? This was not
> comfort or love. . . . She did not want his brute embrace – she
> was most utterly alone, gripped so in his arms. . . . The secret
> thud, thud of his heart, the very self of that animal in him she
> feared and hated, repulsed her. She struggled to escape.
> "What is it? – won't you tell me what is the matter?" he
> pleaded.
> She began to sob dry wild sobs, feeling as if she would go
> mad. He tried to look at her face, for which she hated him. And
> all the time he held her fast, all the time she was imprisoned in
> the embrace of this brute, blind creature, whose heart confessed
> itself in 'thud, thud, thud'. (T(C) 125–6)

The panic state, the hysteria, is not unmotivated: it is based in a
disgust for the realities which will not adapt themselves to her
taste for the pretty, the small – all those things which can be
manipulated because they are known to be a conscious fantasy.

A central element in her poetry is the notion of 'fusing'. This
appeals to her for various reasons. The old ideal of two lovers
fusing into one is her cliché-wish for a relationship in which the
other person, being a rediscovered half of oneself, is not other, and
is therefore known, and can be possessed. The image can also
provide a comforting sense that a refining process is taking place,
and something intricate and pure is produced, which may be
worked into an artistic form.

Siegmund too has moments of feeling this: 'For him, Helena
was a presence. She was ambushed, fused in an aura of his love'
(T(C) 57). When the word recurs, it is as part of a common
aspiration, a shared delusion:

> Suddenly she strained madly to him, and drawing back her
> head, placed her lips on his, close, till at the mouth they seemed
> to melt and fuse together. It was the long, supreme kiss, in which
> man and woman have one being . . . (T(C) 64)

Lawrence then makes the overt comment about the dreaming woman, 'with whom passion exhausts itself at the mouth'. It is a moment in which the passion conceals their incompatibility, the cruelty of her limitation, and her fatal unknowing predatoriness. At a later stage

> He clasped her close, seeming to rock her with his strong panting. She felt his body lifting into her, and sinking away. It seemed to force a rhythm, a new pulse, in her. Gradually, with a fine, keen thrilling, she melted down on him, like metal sinking on a mould. He was sea and sunlight mixed, heaving, warm, deliciously strong. (*T*(C) 84)

The momentary abandonment is conveyed in terms which we learn to read as danger signs. The woman 'melting down on' the man, 'fusing' with him is, time after time in Lawrence, a fatal night-creature, a dangerous will, and a conscious seeker of her own desire. Here the idea is softened by her truthful perception that there is that in him ('sea and sunlight mixed') which she needs, and which she seizes on in a predatory way, in desperation.

As the relationship works itself out, and as each becomes more despairing in separateness, the image becomes more overtly an omen of their disaster:

> "No more sea, no more anything," she thought dazedly, as he sat in the midst of this fierce welter of sunshine. It seemed to her as if all the lightness of her fancy and her hope were being burned away in this tremendous furnace, leaving her, Helena, like a heavy piece of slag seamed with metal. (*T*(C) 119)

Here we have a modification of the notion of fusing, which reflects back on her earlier perception that 'the coarseness was fused out of the world, so that sunlight showed in the veins of the morning cliffs and the rocks.' That happy moment had itself been shadowed by the immediate association with the bat's wing, red against the sun: now it is becoming purely hopeless, and is succeeded some pages later by this:

> The rosiness died out of the sunset as embers fade into thick ash. In herself, too, the ruddy glow sank and went out. The earth was a cold dead heap, coloured drearily, the sky was dark with flocculent grey ash: and she herself, an upright mass of soft ash. (*T*(C) 125)

Siegmund's final perception in this vein is also sad, but more positive:

> And moreover, in the intense joy and suffering of his realised passion, the Island, with its sea and sky, had fused till, like a brilliant bead, all their beauty ran together out of the common ore, and Siegmund saw it naked, saw the beauty of everything naked in the shifting magic of this bead.[13] (*T*(C) 145)

He has won a treasure out of the refining process, analogous with his fine cell of honey: but she is left with – indeed is – the slag, is herself a pillar of ash: an image we shall find again in later books, where the superinduced notion of 'looking back' when one ought to be looking forward into the new phase of life turns the pillar of ash into a pillar of salt: Lot's wife.[14]

Siegmund, the musician, says to Helena:

> ". . . You seem to have knit all things in a piece for me. Things are not separate: they are all in a symphony. They go moving on and on. You are the motive, in everything." (*T*(C) 98–9)

The 'motive' is the musical phrase which carries and complicates the overall design while remaining part of the endless melody; and which is capable of continuous transformation as the composer works out this larger design. In Wagner's music some of the motives express personality; some give a significance to events and can later be used as reminiscences; some have the kind of significance for the whole work which forces commentators to interpret them as formulae with a direct charge of meaning. That interpretation is reductive, since it turns back into the limiting verbal or conceptual currency that the composer or poet had escaped from.

In the image-web of *The Trespasser* it is easy – rather dangerously easy – to see that Siegmund 'is' the bee seeking honey until the end of summer; that he and Helena repeatedly compare themselves to seabirds, and this is a fantasy of purity or freedom; that the flowers represent their passion and its inevitable passing with the end of summer. The intention is also to situate these people in a world which is mysterious as well as colourful, and of which they are part. As in *The White Peacock*, the comparisons, overt or suppressed, are meant to discover a fundamental unity of nature. At the same time, the images are meant to render character. Siegmund is meant to be seen as conveying with weight and dignity a direct perception of what is happening to him – not only thinking – though he does reflect – but feeling. Helena is doing the same thing. This is well conveyed when she is reacting defensively or hysterically, but there is a dangerous affinity between her kind of fanciful prettiness and Lawrence's own lushness, just as in *The White Peacock* the narrator's poetry too often sounded like Lettie's similar vein of fancy.

The overall intention is to produce in the stream of consciousness of the two main characters a reaction-language which is both personal to each, and shared, and with universal implications. The language must be rich enough to do justice to the intense experience, flexible enough to carry the tones of an individual voice and the perceptions of a single character, and powerful enough to carry a wider meaning. As in *The White Peacock*, Lawrence's ambition is remarkable, and it is not surprising that he failed to carry off all these things with complete success.

As an example of the originality, and the failure to convey it neatly, consider four brief passages, which in their insistent pattern are an attempt to convey Siegmund's way of thinking, which is his way of being open to things. He has much of his creator, Lawrence, in him: he can make way for things to happen in him and to crystallise out as perception, conviction, or choice of action. Quite early in the book

> When he seemed to be going to sleep, he woke up to find thoughts labouring over his brain like bees on a hive. Recollections, swift thoughts flew in and alighted on him as wild geese swing down and take possession of a pond. Phrases from the opera tyrannized over him, he played the rhythm with all his blood. (*T*(C) 52)

Or again

> Drowsed by the sun and the white sand and the foam, their thoughts slept like butterflies on the flowers of delight. (*T*(C) 79)

Or again

> . . . his thoughts laboured like ants, in spite of himself, striving towards a conclusion. (*T*(C) 146)

> . . . all his thoughts, like bees, were flown out to sea, and lost. (*T*(C) 148)

The central perception here is something important about the mind, or the consciousness. Siegmund is aware of it as something 'visited' by 'thoughts' which are compared to other creatures, of independent life and different natures. It is not a machine, a computer, generating strings of logicalities; or a control-tower sending out commands to an alien body. It is a place to which figurative messages tentatively come; or where things are felt obscurely and without volition. The processes taking place within Siegmund, and culminating in his death, are not conscious weighings-up of clear options. A settling takes place within him, and it is towards death. When it has happened, a place in his mind realises it, but will not put it into words, other than the Biblical phrase 'if thine hand offend thee . . .'. What is finally achieved in him is announced at the beginning of the book:

> He felt busy within him a strong activity which he could not help. Slowly, the body of his past, the womb which had nourished him in one fashion for so many years, was casting him forth. He was trembling in all his being, though he knew not with what. All he could do now, was to watch the lights go by, and to let the translation of himself continue. (*T*(C) 49)

In this, he is acting like a creature being born. Analogically, a flower pursues the extraordinary evolution of its being from state to state, from seed to seeding, like successive births in which the transformations are so radical that one might almost question the evidence of one's eyes – that this is one creature following the laws of its being. An important difference is the consciousness of self which Siegmund cannot totally suppress, and the awareness of others, particularly Helena. The final value of their passion is that it can link them back into the natural universe. As 'the earth in which his strange flowers grew', she is the influence which causes

him to produce, as 'flowers of his blood', his dreams, which
blossom for their season:

> When Siegmund had Helena near, he lost the ache, the
> yearning towards something, which he always felt otherwise.
> She seemed to connect him with the beauty of things, as if she
> were the nerve through which he received intelligence of the sun
> and wind and sea, and of the moon and the darkness. Beauty
> she never felt herself, came to him through her. It is that, makes
> love. (*T*(C) 76)

Here 'sun and wind and sea', and 'the moon and the darkness'
are enumerated as the largest of the forces which make and move
their world. The sun which they both seek and expose themselves
to, which in places they seem to worship, raising their hands to it
like priests, is the positive force of life which irradiates them, and
in so far as they are flowers or trees fosters their growth and
blossoming, making Siegmund's 'blood' vivid. The moon is a
powerful counter-influence which is constantly felt in the
impressive night-scenes, which provide the occasions when the
lovers feel lost, estranged and negated: where they conflict and fail
to understand each other. It seems especially associated with the
woman's consciousness or will. It provides a sterile glitter which
is naturally associated with the corrosiveness of the sea, and
tends elsewhere in Lawrence to generate the image of the pillar
of salt. It also provides the occasion, even the incentive, to 'fuse'
as here:

> Resting herself on her hands, she kissed him, a long anguished
> kiss, as if she would fuse her soul into his for ever. Then she rose,
> sighing, sighing again deeply. She put her hands to her head
> and looked at the moon. (*T*(C) 103)

Here and in the last and grandest of the night-scenes Helena is
explicitly associated with the Madonna – 'a personification of the
great motherhood of woman': 'all the while, delicately, she
fondled and soothed him, till he was child to her Madonna'
(*T*(C) 103, 129). It is the supreme temptation to woman to
assume this role, and the supreme temptation to man to submit:
this for Lawrence became a kind of doctrine.

The cosmic background to this emotion is given by the scene, as they await the rise of the moon:

> The sea was smoking with darkness under half luminous heavens. The stars, one after another, were catching alight. Siegmund perceived first one, and then another dimmer one flicker out in the darkness over the sea. . . . Gradually he remembered how, in the cathedral, the tapers of the choir-stalls would tremble and set steadily to burn, opening the darkness point after point with yellow drops of flame, as the acolyte touched them, one by one, delicately, with his rod. The night was religious, then, with its proper order of service. Day and night had their ritual, and passed in uncouth worship.
>
> Siegmund found himself in an abbey. He looked up the nave of the night, where the sky came down on the sea like arches, and he watched the stars catch fire. At least it was all sacred, whatever the God might be. Helena herself, the bitter bread, was stuff of the ceremony, which he touched with his lips, as part of the service. (*T*(C) 127–8)

After the first two sentences, this may seem willed and conscious analogy-seeking. The climax of the scene is different: with the moon, something unsought bursts in, though I also think that at 'Then the night took up this drinking-cup' in the passage below, Lawrence is again extending by strength of will and intelligence what first came to him from deeper down:

> In the midst of their passion of fear, the moon rose. Siegmund started, to see the rim appear ruddily beyond the sea. His struggling suddenly ceased, and he watched, spell-bound, the oval horn of fiery gold come up, resolve itself. Some golden liquor dripped and spilled upon the far waves, where it shook in ruddy splashes. The gold-red cup rose higher, looming before him very large, yet still not all discovered. By degrees the horn of gold detached itself from the darkness at back of the waves. It was immense and terrible. When would the tip be placed upon the table of the sea?
>
> It stood at last, whole and calm, before him. Then the night took up this drinking-cup of fiery gold, lifting it with majestic movement overhead, letting stream forth the wonderful unwasted liquor of gold over the sea, a libation.

Siegmund looked at the shaking flood of gold and paling gold spread wider as the night upraised the blanching crystal, poured out further and further the immense libation from the whitening cup, till at last the moon looked frail and empty.

And there exhaustless in the night the white light shook on the floor of the sea. He wondered how it would be gathered up. "I gather it up into myself," he said. And the stars and the cliffs and a few trees were watching, too. "If I have spilled my life," he thought, "the unfamiliar eyes of the land and sky will gather it up again."

Turning to Helena, he found her face white and shining as the empty moon. (*T*(C) 133)

It is a bold imagining; as elsewhere in the book, the boldness and the originality can overcome the weaknesses. The colours are emblematic: the moon starts as 'ruddy' and becomes 'golden'. Indeed the words gold or golden are used eight times; but the transition from the colour of blood through the colour of the sun proceeds with the pouring out until the final emptying produces blanching, whitening, a white light. It is as if the libation were a communion, a draining of blood, until the moon is 'frail and empty'. The associations of 'horn' are active, I think (all of them; so that this is an ejaculation as well as a sacrifice and a libation. What is poured out is first wine, then blood and subliminally seed). In all senses, Siegmund has spilled his life; but sees the sacrifice, or the waste, as in the order of things. But it is an appalling perception that is conveyed in the last sentence, where the whole weight comes to bear on the phrase 'empty moon'. The Madonna who in pictures stands upon the crescent moon is also the 'bitter bread' of the ritual: bitter because she is salt and corrosive like the sea. The ruddy horn has been poured out before her, and the red has turned to gold and then to white; but she remains 'white and shining as the empty moon', as if she were some vampire or enchantress, always avid and never restored.

This other long set-piece, like the morning bathing-scene, is important for the general tonal drive of the whole book, and it too displays the characteristic mixture of weakness and strength. Again it shows that an original strong imagining – one of the things which come 'unbidden to the pen' – is prolonged, elaborated and worked into the whole structure by a skilful deployment of related images. These we feel to be partly willed, and they give themselves away as such by being lush, emphatic, even corny. It is easy to slip into saying that Lawrence should have stopped short where his spontaneity gave out. No writer can do that and achieve a connected structure. In any case the working-out is fulfilling intentions which are related to the spontaneity, and not totally conscious, so that the easy dichotomy cannot be sustained. It is not an evasion but a statement of the difficulty to say that the weaknesses and strengths of this book are inseparable, and I take it that in the passages I have quoted in this chapter the reader has been struck by both.

Siegmund, the trespasser of the title, is in a limited sense a sinner against his wife and family: he has trespassed against them. These are the trespasses which we forgive and hope to be forgiven for. But at privileged moments in the book he has also gone beyond into regions of illumination. When the sun shines on him he has a feeling that the world is good. On his last morning on the island, he can feel 'it is all enchanted'; and later on the same day 'whatever happens, the world is wonderful' (T(C) 169). But he is not supported by Helena. There is one moment when she has a similar illumination:

> She stood still in the archway, astounded. The sea was blazing with white fire, and glowing with azure as coals glow red with heat below the flames. The sea was transfused with white burning, while over it hung the blue sky in a glory, like the blue smoke of the fire of God. Helena stood still and worshipped. It was a moment of astonishment, when she stood breathless and blinded, involuntarily offering herself for a thank offering. She felt herself confronting God at home in his white incandescence, his fire settling on her like the Holy Spirit. Her lips were parted in a woman's joy of adoration. (T(C) 138)

The language is rich with overtones, though the reader may not yet know what to make of them. The notion of sacrifice is present. 'The blue smoke of the fire of God' suggests that the world is forever being offered up, as if its activity were a perpetual adoration. But knowledge of the later Lawrence, especially the great short stories, leads me to suggest that Helena unconsciously yet characteristically becomes the Virgin, who said 'Behold the handmaid of the Lord', and who remained intact after a purely spiritual impregnation.

And in the night-scene her Madonna-role is confirmed; it is sterile, turning what was ruddy into something blanched, leaving everything empty. Her power is negative, and so she cancels out Siegmund's passion, earthing it as lightning is earthed. It is as if there is played out between them a conflict of polar opposites, in which the masculine sun is defeated by a feminine moon. Warmth is drained by the cold; the land invaded or undermined by the sea. At the end of the book Cecil Byrne, feeling his kinship with the dead Siegmund, becomes aware 'how much he was filling the place of a ghost with warmth'. Helena's last words are 'I want rest and warmth.' It is as if she had drawn it all out of Siegmund and is now turning to the younger man with the same demand. In her way, she is deathly. As in *The White Peacock*, there is a suggestion that women are designed to negate and destroy men, and it is part of the universal process.

5 Short Stories I

The chronological relationship between Lawrence's stories and the other early writings is complicated. One quickly finds that each work can be given at least three dates. The date of publication is not in itself significant, since some stories were collected late or even posthumously, and others were published in two forms – an early periodical publication followed by collection in a volume in revised form. At the beginning of the time-scheme is another date: that of the personal experience which Lawrence embodies, transmuted, in the fiction. Between experience and publication there are the stages of first writing and subsequent, often radical, redrafting. These three or four significant dates are interwoven with the dates of other stories[1] and the novels being written at the same period.

The White Peacock was rewritten more than once between 1906 and 1909, and published in 1911. The first version of *The Trespasser* was written in 1910; in the same year the first version of *Sons and Lovers* was started, the final version being published in 1913. Between 1907 and 1914, when the volume of collected short stories *The Prussian Officer* was published, Lawrence wrote, published in magazines, and later rewrote the stories in that volume and others which were collected later or published after his death. I deal with those which seem to me most important in four chapters, one placed before *Sons and Lovers* and three after. The arrangement is partly thematic, partly chronological.

The first story he ever wrote, 'A Prelude', like 'A Modern Lover', and 'The Shades of Spring', has obvious affinities with *The White Peacock* and *Sons and Lovers*. They are all set at the Haggs Farm and use the Chambers family as characters, or touch on Lawrence's relationship with Jessie. Two later stories, 'Love Among the Haystacks' and 'Second Best', offer a different standpoint or a more mature insight. 'The Witch à la Mode' is set in the Croydon of Lawrence's teaching days, and has a character

111

obviously based on Helen Corke. 'Daughters of the Vicar' and 'Odour of Chrysanthemums' form a natural pair, not only because they deal with the mining community in or near Eastwood.

The four stories dealt with in later chapters come from a new world. 'The Prussian Officer' and 'The Thorn in the Flesh' are set in Germany, and draw on the military life which Frieda Lawrence's parents knew, and which Lawrence glimpsed in Metz, Trier, and near Munich in 1913. 'The White Stocking' (among the first stories Lawrence ever started, but radically rewritten later) in one sense belongs to the Nottingham period, but now looked back on with affection from a distance. 'New Eve and Old Adam' is decisively from a new phase, because it is about being married to someone like Frieda, and because Lawrence is therefore embarked on his main life's work.

In *The White Peacock* the Haggs is used as setting for a plot which places the interest not on the Lawrence-figure but on George Saxton. In *Sons and Lovers* the centre of interest becomes the Lawrence-figure Paul Morel, and the important person at the Haggs becomes Miriam Leivers, the daughter. Three other early stories are also set at the Haggs: 'Love Among the Haystacks', drafted in 1910 or 1911, perhaps, but so revised in 1913 that it strikes us as a mature piece; 'A Modern Lover', written in 1909-10; and 'The Shades of Spring', drafted in 1911.

The interest of 'A Modern Lover' and 'The Shades of Spring' is that they show Lawrence circling round his own experience, which baffled him. He searches for ways out of his own emotional block by imagining an alter ego, a Lawrence-figure, returning from working in London to Eastwood, older, more mature, and meeting again an older Jessie Chambers.[2] In 'A Modern Lover' he is at last able to make a frank sexual approach to her. In 'The Shades of Spring' he imagines renewing the acquaintance as an older married man, but imagines also that she has replaced him with a lover, a gamekeeper. In both stories the attempt at a new approach fails – as if Lawrence in honesty could not imagine a way forward, and reverts into bafflement. But in both cases he has also imagined a second alter ego in the same story, a more successful if limited lover. In 'A Modern Lover' it is Tom Vickers, an electrical engineer at the mine; in 'The Shades of Spring' it is Arthur Pilbeam, the gamekeeper. These two men have succeeded with the Jessie-figure, who seems willing to settle for them as second best, as the character Frances settles for another Tom in the story actually called 'Second Best'.

The Lawrence-figure who is imagined returning home in these stories is more mature as well as older than Cyril Beardsall in *The White Peacock*. He has ceased to be the unfocused 'I' who tells that story yet cannot present himself from outside. He now becomes a 'he', though he remains the principal centre of consciousness. He has worked in the metropolitan south, where Cyril also went; while he was there some maturing process has taken place which makes him want to come back to square accounts. The maturing is not only a process of meeting other people, especially women, and becoming involved with them; it is also a matter of recognising a special fate or vocation.

We have an insight into this when we see the young school teacher of the sketch 'A Lesson on a Tortoise' on Friday afternoon, taking the last lesson of the week, and wanting to keep his boys passively quiet yet occupied. He brings in a tortoise for them to draw. Then this happens (it is not an external event, but it is evidently real and important to him):

> I wanted peace for myself. They began to sketch diligently. I stood and looked across at the sunset, which I could see facing me through my window, a great gold sunset, very large and magnificent, rising up in immense gold beauty beyond the town, that was become a low dark strip of nothingness under the wonderful upbuilding of the western sky. The light, the thick, heavy golden sunlight which is only seen in its full dripping splendour in town, spread on the desks and the floor like gold lacquer. I lifted my hands, to take the sunlight on them, smiling faintly to myself, trying to shut my fingers over its tangible richness.
> "Please Sir!" – I was interrupted, "Please Sir, can we have rubbers?' (*P*II 25)

The mundane interruption leads into the gist of the story, which is that one boy has abused the teacher's trust by stealing rubbers. He is detected, and the teacher is sickened to discover the abject irremediable baseness of many people. The same lesson is learnt in the other tiny sketch 'The Fly in the Ointment': an intruder is found in the lodgings of (we suppose) the same teacher. Facing the would-be burglar 'my blood seemed to change its quality. It went cool and sharp with disgust. I was accustomed to displays of the kind in school, and I felt again the old misery of contempt and disgust'. As an experience which can be conceptualised as social wisdom, it is summed up at the end of the sketch: 'He could affect and alter me, I could not affect nor alter him.'

But the paragraph about the sunlight, with its repeated use of the word 'gold', shows the teacher recognising, or invoking, an influence which is more than an atmospheric effect. This is the sun which Cyril Beardsall in his poignant aside in *The White Peacock* had described as 'all my father to me', in the 'ceiling of the valley' where he spent his childhood. Now it looks in on him in the sordid metropolis, which is momentarily cancelled out. The light is 'thick, heavy, golden', and those who, recollecting Siegmund Macnair, think of his cell of honey, are not surprised when the description records its 'full dripping splendour'. There follows the now familiar priestly gesture, the lifting of the hands.

A very similar young man is imagined as the central character Cyril Mersham who in 'A Modern Lover' returns from 'the large city in the south' to a farm which is again recognisable as the Haggs. The story begins with a page or two of formal scene-setting prelude, like the opening of a novel by Hardy. The lone walker, at the end of day, is making a difficult way over a muddy country road. We begin with three paragraphs of Lawrence's unforced visual accuracy and freshness. There then follows something much more ambitious, which the reader may dismiss as faded and dated. Certainly it is 'poetic': Mersham sits down and contemplates the evening landscape, and what passes before the mind's eye (Lawrence's, Mersham's, the reader's) is an overlaying of the actual by the symbolic: and as in *The White Peacock* and *The Trespasser* strength and weakness stand together. The trigger is the evening-star, one of Lawrence's favourite omens:[3]

> It was all very wonderful and glamorous, here, in the old places that had seemed so ordinary. Three-quarters of the scarlet sun was settling among the branches of the elm in front, right ahead where he would come soon. But when he arrived at the brow where the hill swooped downwards, where the broad road ended suddenly, the sun had vanished from the space before him, and the evening star was white where the night urged up against the retreating, rose-coloured billow of day.

That last strong phrase is the node which turns the landscape into a seascape, with the level mist becoming the sea's surface:

> Between him and the spaces of Leicestershire and the hills of Derbyshire, between him and all the South-Country which he had fled, was the splendid rose-red strand of sunset, and the white star keeping guard.
> Here, on the lee-shore of day, was only the purple showing of the woods. . . . Unreal, like a dream which wastes a sleep with unrest, was the South and its hurrying to and fro.

The striking scene, and the apt transformation, is then pushed into a too-overt and lush prefiguring of the imagery of *The Trespasser*:

> Here, on the further shore of the sunset, with the flushed tide at his feet, and the large star flashing with strange laughter, did he himself walk naked with lifted arms into the quiet flood of life.

It is characteristic early Lawrence: powerful and weak at the same time. The power lies in the note of ritual laving, or self-dedication. The passage goes on in the same mode:

> What was it he wanted, sought in the slowly lapsing tide of days. Two years he had been in the large city in the south. There always his soul had moved among the faces that swayed on the thousand currents in that node of tides, hovering and wheeling and flying low over the faces of the multitude like a sea-gull over the waters, stooping now and again, and taking a fragment of life – a look, a contour, a movement – to feed upon.

This is the complex of images which Siegmund invokes as he returns from the Isle to London. But without a second natural node or vector, the imagery moves uncomfortably and lushly into a third vein, which we learn to associate with the original of Helena. It becomes more like frank bad writing:

> Of many people, his friends, he had asked that they would kindle again the smouldering embers of their experience; he had blown the low fires gently with his breath, and had leaned his faced towards their glow, and had breathed in the words that

rose like fumes from the revived embers, till he was sick with the strong drug of sufferings and ecstasies and sensations, and the dreams that ensued. But most folk had choked out the fires of their fiercer experience with rubble of sentimentality and stupid fear, and rarely could he feel the hot destruction of Life fighting out its way.

Here an experience like that of reviving Helen Corke's feelings and reliving her experience is given a tinge of witchcraft. The fumes inhaled from the tripod are linked with the frequent theme of life as fire working itself out, either in fierce flame or damped-down by caution. All three elements, witchcraft, starlight and sea, are mingled in the powerfully lush peroration:

> Surely, surely somebody would give him enough of the philtre of life to stop the craving which tortured him hither and thither, enough to satisfy for a while, to intoxicate him till he could laugh the crystalline laughter of the star, and bathe in the retreating flood of twilight like a naked boy in the surf, clasping the waves and beating them and answering their wild clawings with laughter sometimes, and sometimes gasps of pain.

The modern reader is embarrassed by that ninetyish purple manner. But Lawrence, as always, is ambitious. Abruptly he switches from being somewhere in the wake of Symonds and Pater, and becomes first Milton at the end of *Lycidas*, and then himself:

> He rose and stretched himself. The mist was lying in the valley like a flock of folded sheep; Orion had strode into the sky, and the Twins were playing towards the west. He shivered, stumbled down the path, and crossed the orchard, passing among the dark trees as if among people he knew. (*P/H SS* I 1–3)

This prelude is a remarkable, or at least an interesting piece of writing. It is not gratuitous. The implication is that Cyril Mersham in his two years in the south has glimpsed a priestly role which makes him a mediator in other lives, and which is part of a larger process in which the stars are implicated.

We might use our modern terminology and say that Orion, the evening star, the sun are Lawrence's totem; or we might use the classical term tutelary deity. Lawrence escapes the banality of such terms by making the presences active and implying a kinship. Certainly it is beyond popular horoscopy – yet he is appealing to the vague inkling which underlies the debased use in popular journalism. Entirely characteristic is the compulsive or obsessional image of the naked worshipper, raising his hands to the sun, and gladly entering the cleansing sea.

The succeeding sections of the story are in another mode: much more realistic, though interrupted by remarkable figures of speech. For instance, as Mersham enters the farm his exaltation is doused by the sense that he is no longer welcome as he had once been:

> His disappointment rose as water suddenly heaves up the side of a ship.

Or again:

> His heart closed tight like a fir-cone, which had been open and full of naked seeds when he came to them. (*P/H SS* I 4)

And later, he falls into his characteristic pose: we recognise it in *Sons and Lovers*, but here it has the gamekeeper imagery of *The White Peacock*:

> Mersham sprawled his length in the chair, his eyelids almost shut, his fine white hands hanging over the arms of the chair like dead-white stoats from a bough.[4] (*P/H SS* I 13)

The plot is not a matter of happenings, but of aroused feelings. Mersham exerts himself to work his old spell over the family, but is now conscious of himself doing it. He wants to re-exert his hold over Muriel, because he now knows that he wants her physically. He makes his claim in the presence of her new young man, Tom Vickers, the electrician from the mine. He demonstrates to her that Tom is limited, and that he, Mersham, is the finer spirit that she wants. Vickers leaves, Mersham having felt a more powerful attraction towards him than Muriel seems to feel; but having seen Vickers off in a kind of tenderness, he goes outside with Muriel and challenges her to become his lover. She hesitates: his

exaltation vanishes again, and the story ends with a baffled
leave-taking.

The exchange with Muriel is one of the first of those
conversations in Lawrence where the verbal give-and-take carries
pressures of relationship beyond the words. There is no tip to the
reader about the interior fluctuations going on in the speakers:
only their words, their minute physical adjustments of pose, their
sense that a third party is listening and must be implicated or
excluded. Lawrence is developing his notations for this kind of
exchange. Mersham is also ready to instruct, to offer opinions.
About change for instance: gathering that the family is about to
leave the farm, he says:

> "So you ought to say to yourself 'What a treat – I'm going to say
> goodbye directly to the most painful phase of my life!' – You
> make up your mind that it shall be the most painful, by refusing
> to be hurt so much in the future."

It is a key-doctrine for Lawrence, but here it comes out as an
assertion, a thought. More suggestive, because more figurative, is
this:

> "You see, . . . – thought – that's not life. It's like washing and
> combing and carding and weaving the fleece that the year of life
> has produced." (*P/H SS* I 8–9)

But this is still, however strikingly, a thought. Life itself, the
unconscious forward-moving process, is characteristically
imagined as a fire:

> "Life," he said, and he was always urging this on Muriel in
> one form or another, "Life is beautiful, so long as it is
> consuming you. When it is rushing through you, destroying
> you, life is glorious. It is best to roar away, like a fire with a great
> draught, white hot to the last bit. It's when you burn a slow fire
> and save fuel that life's not worth having."
> "You believe in a short life and a merry," said the father.
> "Needn't be either short or merry. Grief is part of the fire of
> life – and suffering – they're the root of the flame of joy, as they
> say."

That too is a key-doctrine, naturally associated with the thought of change; and the thought about 'thought'. Lastly there is an ingenious remark about communication through speech. Throughout the conversation Mersham is signalling meanings to Muriel, which she receives, though they are beyond the overt meaning of what he says. Because the two are attuned to each other, they can understand each other over the head of the prosaic Tom Vickers. Once when Muriel wants Mersham to be explicit, he refuses what he calls the 'arithmetic' of speech, offering instead an 'algebra'. The moment follows the thought about 'thought'.

". . . Now I think – we've carded and woven to the end of our bundle – nearly. We've got to begin again – you and me – living together – see? – Not speculating and poetising together – see?"

She did not cease to gaze absorbedly at him.

"Yes – ?" she whispered, urging him on.

"You see – I've come back to you – to you – ,"

He waited for her.

"But," she said huskily, "I don't understand."

He looked at her with aggressive frankness, putting aside all her confusions.

"Fibber!" – he said gently.

"But – " she turned in her chair from him, "but not clearly!"

He frowned slightly:

"Nay, you should be able by now to use the algebra of speech. Must I count up on your fingers for you what I mean, unit by unit, in bald arithmetic?"

"No – no!" she cried justifying herself, "but how can I understand – the change in you? You used to say – you couldn't. – Quite opposite."

He lifted his head as if taking in her meaning.

"Ah, yes, I have changed. I forget. I suppose I must have changed in myself. I'm older – I'm twenty-six. I used to shrink from the thought of having to kiss you, didn't I?" He smiled very brightly, and added in a soft voice: "Well – I don't, now."

She flushed darkly and hid her face from him.

"Not," he continued, with slow brutal candour – "not that I know any more than I did then – what love is – as you know it – but – I think you're beautiful – and we know each other so well – as we know nobody else – don't we? And so we . . .".
(*P/H SS* I 9–10)

'Living' is offered as the antithesis of 'speculating and poetising' which (we assume) is now Lawrence's way of describing the relationship he and Jessie had had. 'Living' is also going to mean a sexual relationship, though it is striking that Mersham offers this as something he has *decided* to embark on as a conscious act of will, now that he no longer 'shrinks from the thought of having to kiss you'. This too is a remarkably frank confession, though we may reflect that his previous shrinking, though unnatural, was at least instinctive. Now he is being 'natural' by choice. Would the later Lawrence have called this 'sex in the head'?

Meanwhile Muriel's natural and justified reluctance to take this changed person at his new word (can he really mean *that*, after so long?) is brushed aside as literalism – the arithmetic of overt propositions is displaced by the algebra of implication. Algebra was what Miriam Leivers wanted to learn in *Sons and Lovers*, and Paul had difficulty in teaching her. There it was the symbol of the world of the intellect that she feared she was going to be debarred from as an under-educated girl. Here it is a sign of something else. Tom Vickers is

among the men of handsome, healthy animalism, and good intelligence, who are children in simplicity, who can add two and two, but never xy and yx. (*P/H SS* I 13)

Mersham, however, has a greater power ("I can make her sad and set her wondering"). This is a poetic, an interpretative gift ("you think I'm a wonderful, magical person"). It is not the gift of teaching algebra, where x equals a fixed quality; but that of poetry, where the equivalences are neither exact nor fixed. It is more like magic.

When Vickers has gone, Mersham asks Muriel to come out into the starlit night:

The fields were open, and the night went up to the magnificent stars. The wood was very dark, and wet; they leaned forward and stepped stealthily, and gripped each other's hands fast with a delightful sense of adventure. When they stood and looked up for a moment, they did not know how the stars were scattered among the tree-tops till he found the three jewels of Orion right in front.

It is the magic of the youthful experience recovered; with the assurance of his own personal constellation.

But the attempted rapprochement fails. Again in his now direct and bald way, he asks her to become his lover: thinks that her reluctance is fear of pregnancy; implies that he will take care of that; becomes scornful and then angry at her mistrust. But finally she rejects him because it would be surreptitious, stolen and shamefaced.

> This stung him; – at once, it was as if the glamour went out of life. It was as if she had tipped over the frail vessel that held the wine of his desire, and had emptied him of all his vitality.

The image here prefigures the night-scene of sacrifice and libation in *The Trespasser*. This symbolic perception, of the emptying, the waste of the sacramental wine in his crystal goblet, so that when it is emptied *he* is emptied, terminates the story, and the relationship. He has been offering reasons and reassurances; but she offers only a negation, and he is left once more (that is to say Lawrence is left once more) contemplating a negative polarity, which 'earths' him. Indeed a complementary electrical image immediately follows:

> He had played a difficult, deeply-moving part all night, and now the lights suddenly switched out, and there was left only weariness.

The remarkable descriptive prelude, long and over-ambitious, is balanced by a brief postlude:

> At parting also he had not kissed her. He stood a moment and looked at her. The water in a little brook under the hedge was running, chuckling with extraordinary loudness: away on Nethermere they heard the sad haunting cry of the wild-fowl from the North. The stars still twinkled intensely. He was too spent to think of anything to say; she was too overcome with grief and fear and a little resentment. He looked down at the pale blotch of her face upturned from the low meadow beyond the fence. The thorn boughs tangled above her, drooping behind her like the roof of a hut. Beyond was the great width of the darkness. (*P/H SS* I 22)

'The great width of the darkness' is echoed in the last two sentences 'He saw her white uplifted face vanish, and her dark form bend under the boughs of the tree, and go out into the great darkness. She did not say goodbye.' The same 'great darkness' threatens to swallow Paul Morel at the end of *Sons and Lovers*; it is an annihilating engulfment of the threatened identity not supported by a woman's love.

'The Shades of Spring' is a companion piece. Another Lawrence-figure called John Adderley Syson, a name based on that of John Addington Symonds, returns to another Jessie-figure, and finds she has taken a gamekeeper as lover. Hilda Millership gave herself to Arthur Pilbeam on the night that Syson got married. Syson's marriage (perhaps Lawrence's contemplated marriage to Louie Burrows) is not described, but something must be implied by the fact that he is now returning to see Hilda: the drift of the story is that he has some unsatisfied need which he wants to press on her. He is rejected by Hilda, as Mersham is by Muriel; again he feels the attraction of the rival; and again, the woman is made to feel once more the superior attraction – the magic power – of the Lawrence-figure compared with the limited man she has actually chosen.

In *Son of Woman* Murry pointed out that the sudden intrusion of Annable in *The White Peacock* was Lawrence's attempt to imagine an alternative more masculine self. Annable the gamekeeper foreshadows Mellors the gamekeeper in *Lady Chatterley's Lover*, as all readers recognise: but a similar figure is also found in this story drafted in 1911. Murry also noticed that in his bitter narrative of his life Annable essentially concluded it at the age of 26 – Lawrence's age in 1911. Mrs Lawrence died in December 1910; Lawrence ended the relationship with Jessie Chambers; and just after the end of 1911 he broke off his engagement to Louie Burrows; he was desperately ill at the end of the year; his ambiguous or blocked relationship with Helen Corke reached no conclusion. So 1911 was a year of death, illness, solitude and defeat. Some underlying feeling about this year explains why, though Annable continues a posthumous existence after his failure, twenty-six was the age at which he retired from his emotional life. For similar reasons, Siegmund Macnair, who is actually thirty-eight, on his last night says sadly of his body 'I look as young as twenty-six.' Cyril Mersham also takes care to remind

Muriel that he is twenty-six, and doesn't now shrink from the thought of having to kiss her. In 'The Shades of Spring', on the other hand, Lawrence is trying to look ahead one or two years, to imagine what that might be like, and so he makes Hilda Millership twenty-nine, and Syson the same age. But the jump in time does not take him to a point where the problem is solved. Hilda has merely made another choice.

Readers of the early stories also become aware of this tendency to be attracted towards a rival, who is threatening because he also wants, or has won, the chosen girl, and yet is somehow very winning as a male: indeed he is seen as through a girl's eyes. An extreme variant of the motif is seen in 'The Old Adam', where the hero, Edward Severn, is like Lawrence living in Croydon with the Jones family, who gave him lodging. Severn is briefly attracted by the landlady[5] – there is a moment of wordless magnetism activated by a thunderstorm. But the actual physical contact is an unexpected fight with the vulgar husband. Both men are shocked when they have to recognise the hatred which has burst out of them, and yet the actual contact[6] like a rite of passage transmutes their antagonism into a bond; the story ends with them 'close friends, with a gentleness in their bearing, one towards the other. On the other hand, Mrs Thomas was only polite and formal with Severn, treating him as if he were a stranger'.

It is natural to deduce, as Murry did, that Lawrence in these years 1910–12 was attempting to imagine and to dramatise various possible issues – which turned, when fully imagined, into non-issues – from his own isolation and sense of failure. It is also striking how frequently he imagines a relationship with a woman which is subverted and turns into a relationship with a manly man, or the fleeting fantasy of such a relationship. In this group of early stories, sexual success can only be imagined when the central figure is *not* Lawrence, and indeed where Lawrence is nowhere in the story, as in 'Love Among the Haystacks', which is an idyll, and in 'Second-Best', a sardonic little fable in which a woman transfers her allegiance from a possibly unsatisfactory gentleman and intellectual to a possibly more satisfactory farmer.

At the start of 'The Shades of Spring' John Adderley Syson, on the way to renew his relationship with Hilda, finds his way blocked by the keeper, Arthur Pilbeam:

It was a young man of four or five and twenty, ruddy, and well
favoured. His dark blue eyes now stared aggressively at the
intruder. His black moustache, very thick, was cropped short
over a small, rather soft mouth. In every other respect the fellow
was manly and good-looking. He stood just above middle
height; the strong forward thrust of his chest, and the perfect
ease of his erect, self-sufficient body, gave one the feeling that he
was taut with animal life, like the thick jet of a fountain
balanced in itself. (*PO*(C) 99)

He is an amalgam of George Saxton and Annable, with more
than a hint of an idealised young Lawrence. The culminating
image is a guarantee of approval: but the man is limited
nonetheless.

Nothing is said about Syson's marriage, though he laughs
unhappily when admitting it; he has gone on writing to Hilda; and
here he is trying to visit her, as if to renew something. Now
twenty-nine like Syson, she is 'very womanly'. So while the
younger gamekeeper has something of the Lawrence of two or
three years ago, before he left Eastwood, Syson and Hilda are now
imagined two or three years in the future, and Syson has married
somebody and may be already regretting it and looking for a way
back to his childhood sweetheart. What kind of relationship could
they re-establish? The story is a little leap of the imagination,
which quickly comes to the conclusion that things would have
changed – because *they* would have changed.

One crucial recognition comes quickly. They begin to warm to
each other in the old mode:

"You are quite splendid here," he said, and their eyes met.
"Do you like it?" she asked. It was the old, low, husky tone of
intimacy. He felt a quick change beginning in his blood. It was
the old delicious sublimation, the thinning, almost the
vaporising of himself, as if his spirit were to be liberated.
(*PO*(C) 103–4)

That is *his* old reaction, and we recognise it as characteristic,
and, in him, dangerous. It starts in the 'blood'; it is now leading
him back again into the heady realm of the spirit, and *he* had not
wanted it, previously, to lead to the realm of the body. Now he is

older, more conscious, and as they go out together a crucial recognition begins in him:

> "Shall we go out awhile?" she asked.
> "Yes!" he answered. But the predominant emotion, that troubled the excitement and perplexity of his heart, was fear, fear of that which he saw. There was about her the same manner, the same intonation in her voice, now as then, but she was not what he had known her to be. He knew quite well what she had been for him. And gradually he was realising that she was something quite other, and always had been. (*PO*(C) 104)

This is a recognition made by other characters in the short stories: notably the wife in *Odour of Chrysanthemums*. Both this story and 'A Modern Lover' show that Lawrence could move from the blind certainty of *Sons and Lovers*, where Paul Morel's perception of Miriam is the truth about her, and not the product of his own limitation.[7]

Hilda has a complementary feeling, accompanied by a characteristically humble perception of what his view of her had been:

> Watching his face, her eyes went hard. She saw the scales were fallen from him, and at last he was going to see her as she was. It was the thing she had most dreaded in the past. . . . But he would give her her due – she would have her due from him. (*PO*(C) 104–5)

This is rather stated. Lawrence knew that these are things people feel rather than say to themselves in so many words. But for the moment he is prepared to say it, since the thought itself is new to him, and he has not learnt to present it otherwise.

They then repeat moments and gestures of *The White Peacock* and *Sons and Lovers*: she shows him the birds' nests and flowers which are emblems of the whole and direct life they both worship. She reveals that she has a lover, and he knows that it must be the gamekeeper:

> "I think I met him. He is good-looking – also in Arcady."
> Without answering, she turned into a dark path that led uphill, where the trees and undergrowth were very thick.

"They did well," she said at length, "to have various altars to various gods, in old days."

"Ah yes!" he agreed. "To whom is the new one?"

"There are no old ones," she said. "I was always looking for this."

"And whose is it?" he asked.

"I don't know," she said, looking full at him.

"I'm very glad, for your sake," he said, "that you are satisfied."

"Ay – but the man doesn't matter so much," she said. There was a pause.

"No!" he exclaimed, astonished, yet recognizing her as her real self.

"It is one's self that matters," she said.

"Whether one is being one's own self and serving one's own God." (*PO*(C) 105–6)

Lawrence has given her his own thoughts and ideas, and especially the notion of the unknown God who must be found and served. Again, it is rather explicit, as an idea: and yet such things might be said, by people who are exploring in this direction.

Syson goes on learning. Of the gamekeeper Hilda says that though she has a sense of his limitations "Here, among his things, I love him" – partly because he does not, like Syson "make me to be not myself".

"I am like a plant," she replied. "I can only grow in my own soil."

They came to a place where the undergrowth shrank away, leaving a bare, brown space. . . . In the midst of the bare space stood a keeper's log hut. Pheasant coops were lying about. . . . It was a bare wooden place with a carpenter's bench and form, carpenter's tools, an axe, snares, traps, some skins pegged down, everything in order. Hilda closed the door. Syson examined the weird flat coats of wild animals, that were pegged down to be cured. She turned some knotch in the side wall, and disclosed a second, small apartment. . . . The apartment was occupied almost entirely by a large couch of heather and bracken, on which was spread an ample rabbit-skin rug. On the floor were patch-work rugs of cat-skin, and a red calf-skin, while hanging from the wall were other furs. Hilda took down one, which she put on. It was a cloak of rabbit-skin and of white fur, with a hood, apparently of the skins of stoats. She laughed at Syson from out of this barbaric mantle. (*PO*(C) 106–7)

This is the place where, like Connie Chatterley in the last novel, Hilda goes in order to be out of the world with the man she loves. The circus-panoply may remind us also of Alvina Houghton's theatricality with the mock Red Indians of *The Lost Girl*: it may even remind us of 'The Woman who Rode Away'. Of the keeper, one notices that he has the usual function – killing a great many animals – but to unusual effect. His limitation is expressed in a pithy few sentences:

"The stars aren't the same with him," she said. "You could make them flash and quiver, and the forget-me-nots come up at me like phosphorescence. You could make things *wonderful*. I have found it out – it is true. But I have them all for myself, now." (*PO*(C) 107)

Yet she can turn Syson's gift against him, and show him *his* limitation too: "You plucked a thing and looked at it till you had found out all you wanted to know about it, then you threw it away." That could be a self-reference, in that *she* was among the flowers he plucked, as Paul Morel chewed the pink and spat it out (below, p. 182).

An actual antagonism is now stirred between them. "You took me away from myself" she says to him, and he confesses to himself 'He knew that he had mistaken her, had taken her for something she was not. That was his fault, not hers.' Yet he reminds her that she had in some sense *made* him: she had wanted him to be well educated, to get on. But she counters this by saying "you always wanted change, change, like a child." (So much for Mersham's urge to get into the next phase of one's life.)

They see finally that they have come to the end of their relationship, and he makes his little ritual gesture:

"Then I give you 'To our vast and varying fortunes'". He lifted his hand in pledge.

But she will not make the gesture, only repeating the words. He leaves, both enlightened and dispirited, and the characteristic rapprochement of the two men is hinted at:

> At the bottom of the path she left him. He went along with the keeper, towards the open, towards the gate that closed on the wood. The two men walked almost like friends. They did not broach the subject of their thoughts.

There is a postlude. Syson's creator shows that he too has the gift of making things wonderful:

> Instead of going straight to the high-road gate, Syson went along the wood's-edge, where the brook spread out in a little bog, and under the alder trees, among the reeds, great yellow stools and bosses of marigolds shone. Threads of brown water trickled by, touched with gold from the flowers. Suddenly, there was a blue flash in the air, as a kingfisher passed.
> Syson was extraordinarily moved. He climbed the bank to the gorse bushes, whose sparks of blossom had not yet gathered into a flame. Lying on the dry brown turf, he discovered sprigs of tiny purple milkwort and pink spots of lousewort. What a wonderful world it was – marvellous, for ever new. He felt as if it were underground, like the fields of monotone hell, notwithstanding.[8] Inside his breast was a pain like a wound. He remembered the poem of William Morris, where in the Chapel of Lyonesse a knight lay wounded, with the truncheon of a spear deep in his breast, lying always as dead, yet did not die, while day after day the coloured sunlight dipped from the painted window across the chancel, and passed away. He knew now it never had been true, that which was between him and her, not for a moment. The truth had stood apart all the time.
> Syson turned over. The air was full of the sound of larks, as if the sunshine above were condensing and falling in a shower. (*PO*(C) 110)

It is a characteristic blend of elements in Lawrence. As so often in *The White Peacock*, there is close observation, including the homely names of actual flowers. There is the brilliant imaginative stroke at the end. And there is the strange element of nineteenth-century literary melancholy which one is about to dismiss as ninetyish when one wonders whether the myth of the wounded knight is not saying something elaborate but true about a deep element in Lawrence himself: something which draws him to, and links him with witches, priestesses, enchantresses, and Ladies of Shalott.[9]

The final glimpse of Hilda shows her to be such an enchantress, and the reader feels that we have now moved away entirely from the remembered Jessie to some much more dangerous person. Syson imagines 'her will among the brightness of the larks', and from his concealment sees her manipulating the simple keeper: Lady Chrystabel to his Annable. His 'fine, bright arm' is stung by a bee: she sucks the poison out:

> As she looked at the red mark her mouth had made, and at his arm, she said, laughing:
> "That is the reddest kiss you'll ever have." When Syson next looked up, at the sound of voices, he saw in the shadow the keeper with his mouth on the throat of his beloved, whose head was thrown back, and whose hair had fallen, so that one rough rope of dark brown hair hung across his bare arm. (*PO*(C) 111)

It is a variant on the theme of Greiffenhagen's *Idyll*,[10] the painting that so caught Lawrence's imagination that he copied it for his friends: but it also reminds the reader of the end of 'The Witch à la Mode', the first draft of which had been written six or eight months earlier.

The ending is willed and inorganic, because it has veered into another world, that of Helen Corke, the dreaming woman of *The Trespasser*. What Lawrence has more solidly won out of the imagined re-encounter is the genuine and painful recognition that like Syson he was capable of having 'mistaken' the woman, and that 'the truth had stood apart all the time'. It gives him the thought that forms the tragic recognition in 'Odour of Chrysanthemums', which he had in a second draft in 1911, and which he drastically revised later.

The Lawrence-figure in 'The Witch à la Mode' is called Bernard Coutts; and the links here are with the young teacher in 'Lesson on the Tortoise', and with Cyril Mersham. But the woman is based on Helen Corke, and a whole set of themes is derived from that relationship.

The link with Mersham and 'A Modern Lover' – and also with *The Trespasser* – comes within a few paragraphs from the start. It is the moment between day and night which was mysterious and precious to Lawrence:

> The day was dying out. One by one the arc lamps fluttered or leaped alight, the strand of copper overhead glistened against the dark sky that now was deepening to the colour of monkshood. The tram-car dipped as it ran, seeming to exult. As it came clear of the houses, the young man, looking west, saw the evening star advance, a bright thing approaching from a long way off, as if it had been bathing in the surf of the daylight, and now was walking shorewards to the night. He greeted the naked star, with a bow of the head, his heart surging as the car leaped.
>
> "It seems to be greeting me across the sky – the star," he said, amused by his own vanity. (*P/H SS*I 54)

But it is not just vanity; the self-deprecation hides the feeling of kinship, the search for meanings. The elements of the scene here are the ones Mersham contemplated at length in 'A Modern Lover', as preparation for meeting the fictional equivalent of Jessie. But here the man is going to meet, against his conscience (for he is engaged to the equivalent of Louie Burrows), the fictional representation of Helen Corke, and that produces an immediate addition to the heavens. There was no moon in 'A Modern Lover', but here

> Above the colouring of the afterglow the blade of the new moon hung sharp and keen. Something recoiled in him.
>
> "It is like a knife to be used at a sacrifice," he said, to himself. Then secretly: "I wonder for whom?"
>
> He refused to answer this question, but he had the sense of Constance, his betrothed, waiting for him in the Vicarage in the north. He closed his eyes.

The girl's name is ironically chosen, like that of Lady Chatterley. It emerges in the story that she is an ordinary nice girl, and Coutts fears that once married to her he will be bored. Meanwhile he flutters round Winifred Varley, the Helen-Corke-figure, who has been prefigured here as a druid priestess or witch.

The story tells how her spell is broken, but first shows it being exercised.

Winifred and Coutts talk to each other as Cyril Mersham talks to Muriel, and John Adderley Syson talks to Hilda Millership: in a language of hints which reveals under-thoughts but shrinks away from statement until the man finally makes clear his demand. Here too Coutts wants the woman, or thinks he does; but what she wants of him is a strange parasitic relationship which he finally identifies and rejects. Their communication is not the 'algebra' Mersham wants to use with Muriel, but a fully fledged symbolism which is a medium, or a weapon, or a defence. So, for instance, when she says it is a beautiful night he proposes his talisman:

> "The moon has set, and the evening star," he answered. "Both were out as I came down."
> She glanced swiftly at him to see if this speech was a bit of symbolism. He was looking across the valley with a set face.

Then the rather overt talk about 'change' which had been exchanged with Muriel and Hilda is transformed:

> At that moment a train across the valley threaded the opposite darkness with its gold thread. The valley re-echoed with vague throat. The two watched the express, like a gold-and-black snake, curve and dive seawards into the night. He turned, saw her full fine face tilted up to him. It showed pale, distinct and firm, very near to him. He shut his eyes and shivered.

We know by now that what is gold is good; and this snake could be good. But it is threatened by something, and we infer that the face near him 'full', 'pale, distinct and firm' is like the moon, and so a negation. The passage continues, with a curious psychological veracity:

> "I hate trains," he said, impulsively.
> "Why?" she asked, with a curious, tender little smile that caressed, as it were, his emotion towards her.
> "I don't know; they pitch one about here and there . . ."

"I thought," she said, with faint irony, "that you preferred change."

"I do like life. But now I should like to be nailed to something, if it was only a cross."

She laughed sharply, and said, with keen sarcasm:

"Is it so difficult, then, to let yourself be nailed to a cross? I thought the difficulty lay in getting free."

He ignored the sarcasm on his engagement.

This is strange. The notion of crucifixion and sacrifice, linked to the idea of a willed stability, including that of marriage, will re-surface in various ways and various places, most notably in the Tirol, among the crucifixes that reminded Lawrence of Ernest Weekley. But Lawrence will not again propose himself as the willing victim. The implication of the story is that he is torn between this sacrifice and another, the one presided over by the priestess or witch.

Meanwhile the two characters fence dangerously with each other; she turning his own weapon, figurative speech, against him. He resents it in her as an unwillingness to be honest about their love:

"Your foggy weather of symbolism as usual," he said.

"The fog is not of symbols," she replied in her metallic voice of displeasure. "It may be symbols are candles in a fog – –."

"I prefer my fog without candles. I'm the fog, eh? Then I'll blow out your candles, and you'll see me better . . .

". . . If I breathe outwards, in a positive movement towards you, you move off. If I draw in a vacant sigh of soulfulness, you flow nearly to my lips."

"This is a very interesting symbol," she said, with sharp sarcasm. (*P/H SS*I 62–3)

And indeed they are evolving a set of symbols which finally make everything clear to him, so that he can perform the instinctive action which frees him from her. So it is not talk leading to thought and thence to decision; it is an interchange of poetry which produces clarity, and liberation. It is in this sense that we often say 'Ah, now I *see*.' So, exchanging their news, he tells her what he has been doing, and says his activity seems meaningless:

"And you?" he said at length.
"With me it is different," she said quietly.
"You sit with your crystal," he laughed.
"While you tilt –" she hung on her ending. (*P/H SS*I 65)

They have not just exchanged a literary allusion in which she is the Lady of Shalott, who cannot act in the world, but sees it reflected in her mirror or crystal ball, while he is Lancelot, questing for love and spiritual adventure, and necessary to her parasitism, (or Don Quixote tilting at windmills). In tossing the tag to her, and having it instantly understood and tossed back, he has moved a stage in understanding what they both are, and the danger she is to him.

The stage of insight then brings out a startling Lawrentian complexity:

"I've got such a skinful of heavy visions, they come sweating through my dreams," he said.
"Whom have you read?" she smiled.
"Meredith – very healthy," he laughed. (*P/H SS*I 66)

The insouciance conceals an agonising self-doubt. The thought of being pervious to the world, or – in reverse – of finding that one's inner dreads are uncontainable and leaking out, was one of the extreme perceptions of Siegmund Macnair at the point where he was trespassing across more than one borderline; and it is felt too by Paul Morel. It is a mode of disintegration. This may explain why in one mood Coutts (like Lawrence, perhaps) clings to the idea of an ordinary marriage which will ballast and stabilise him, even if it also bores him. It is one risk that such a marriage would turn into a crucifixion. The other risk, epitomised in the attraction to Winifred Varley, is that he will turn instead to some vampire leaching away his vitality, indeed his life. Lawrence at this stage of his life seemed (to himself at any rate) to be offered intolerable dualities, summed up as a day-to-day physicality, limited and ultimately stultifying, set against a heady spirituality which left the soil of the body, and went off into the unbreathable air. The most powerful of the attractions was this second one: generated in the relationship with the mother, refined and intellectualised in the relationship with Jessie, and brought to a new point of frustration in the relationship with Helen Corke, who like his mother wanted power over him, and could neither marry him nor free him. The power over him, the fascination, seemed like a supernatural thing. It is summed up here:

> This was their battle-field: she could not understand how he could marry: it seemed almost monstrous to her; she fought against his marriage. She looked up at him, witch-like, from under bent brows. Her eyes were dark blue and heavy. He shivered, shrank with pain. She was so cruel to that other, common, everyday part of him.

He has now used the word: she is a witch. And in the last few pages of the story, the climax, she uses her strange power on him in a final effort to win him over to her, and he breaks the spell.

Three times she raises her arms to him, in a variation of the Lawrentian ritual gesture:

> She raised her arms, stretched them above her head, in a weary gesture. They were fine, strong arms . . . white, round arms, long arms. The lifting of her arms lifted her breasts.

And again:

> She lifted her arms towards him, hiding her face between them, looking up through the white closure with dark uncanny eyes like an invocation. His breast lifted towards her up-tilted arms. He shuddered, shut his eyes, held his throat rigid. He heard her drop her arms heavily.
>
> "I must go," he said in a dull voice.

Between these two invocations there falls a further fragment of revealing conversation. She says to him 'You snatch things from the Kobolds for me.' Muriel and Hilda had said something similar: he made things wonderful for them, made things come magically alive. He is able to bring back treasure from the fairy world. (Kobolds are sprites from the world of German folktale):

> "Exactly," he said in a biting tone. "Exactly! That's what you want me for. I am to be your crystal, your 'genius'. My length of blood and bone you don't care a rap for. Ah yes, you

like me for a crystal-glass, to see things in: to hold up to the light. I'm a blessed Lady-of-Shalott-looking-glass for you."

"You talk to *me*," she said, dashing his fervour, "of my fog of symbols!"

The apt retort does not conceal the fact that he is confirming his earlier insight – a knowledge of her that will bring freedom from the spell. Nonetheless she attempts to exert her power over him, and her third ritual gesture brings the climax:

"Yes," she assented gravely; "you must go."
He turned to her. Again looking up darkly, from under her lowered brows, she lifted her hands like small white orchids towards him.

Hands as flowers we are now familiar with; but orchids are not ordinary flowers. The long passage which follows finally brings the two into the posture which Syson had glimpsed when he looked back at Hilda and Arthur Pilbeam: but now it is the Lawrence-figure who has his mouth on the woman's throat – as if she, the enchantress, were offering some kind of sustenance:

"Good-bye," he said, looking down at her. She made a small, moaning sound in her throat, lifting her face, so that it came open and near to him like a suddenly-risen flower, borne on a strong white stalk. She seemed to extend, to fill the world, to become atmosphere and all. He did not know what he was doing. He was bending forward, his mouth on hers, her arms round his neck, and his own hands, still fastened onto her wrists, almost bursting the blood under his nails with the intensity of their grip. . . . She turned her face, offered him her throat, white, hard, and rich, below the ear. Stooping still lower . . . he laid his mouth to the kiss. In the intense silence, he heard the deep, dull pulsing of her blood, and the minute click of a spark within the lamp.

Some of the implications are worth bringing out. It is a night-scene, in the circle of lamplight. The 'minute click' which reminds him of the lamp is like the click which the orderly hears when the Prussian officer opens his tankard-lid, and offers his drinking throat to a murderous attack (p. 219). Here no murder

takes place, but the spell is broken, and precisely by the equally
instinctive movement which Coutts makes – he kicks over the
lamp. But first he draws her to her feet, so that they are standing in
a parody of the 'Idyll' posture:

> Then he drew her from the chair up to him. She came, arms
> always round his neck, till at last she lay along his breast as he
> stood, feet planted wide, clasping her tight, his mouth on her
> neck. She turned suddenly to meet his full red mouth in a kiss.
> He felt his moustache prick back into his lips. It was the first
> kiss she had genuinely given. . .
>   The hurt became so great it brought him out of the reeling
> stage to distinct consciousness. She clipped her lips, drew them
> away, leaving him her throat. Already she had had enough. . . .
> He saw her thus, knew that she wanted no more of him than
> that kiss. And the heavy body of this woman hung upon him . . .
> His whole body ached like a swollen vein, with heavy intensity,
> while his heart grew dead with misery and despair. This woman
> gave him anguish and a cutting-short like death; to the other
> woman he was false. As he shivered with suffering, he opened
> his eyes again, and caught sight of the pure ivory of the lamp.
> His heart flashed with rage.
>   A sudden involuntary blow of his foot, and he sent the
> lamp-stand spinning. The lamp leaped off, . . .

She is threatened by the flame, but he beats it out with his
hands. The story ends:

> In another instant he was gone, running with burning-red
> hands held out blindly down the street. (*P/H SS*I 69–70)

One may say, obviously enough, that here is a link with the
theorising in *The Trespasser* about dreaming women, for whom
passion is 'exhausted at the mouth'. The notion is made more
actual here, and more dangerous. It is as if Coutts has narrowly
escaped becoming a victim by managing to negate the magic. His
instinctive act is like the gesture of a hero in a romance, who at the
moment of greatest danger undoes the spell by uttering a magic
word or performing the right ritual action. Singed by the flame,
Coutts is nevertheless free in a way that no explanation, no actual
agreement to part, could make him free.

Love Among the Haystacks immediately strikes the reader as mature: neat, controlled, indeed subtle, and without over-writing. Written in 1913 or 1914, the basic experience belongs to the year 1908 when Lawrence was working in the fields, haymaking with Alan Chambers and writing his confiding letters to Blanche Jennings. The two brothers, Geoffrey and Maurice Wookey, may be based on the Chamberses; but Geoffrey is twenty-three, he tells us; Lawrence's age in 1908. Other experiences recounted in the story may come from 1910 and the Croydon period – especially the perception that the husband of the woman Geoffrey finally makes his own, 'the seedy, slinking fellow, with a tang of horsey braggadocio about him', is 'a mean crawl of a man', with 'something debased, parasitic about him', and that

> He was exactly the worst foe of the hypersensitive: insolence without sensibility, preying on sensibility.

That is the shocked reaction of the teacher in 'A Lesson on a Tortoise' and 'The Fly in the Ointment'. Further elements point us to an even later period: the girl whom Maurice takes as his mate, Paula Jablonowsky, called 'the Fräulein', has something of Frieda in her appearance and style: but reminds the reader also of the Polish woman Lydia Lensky whom Tom Brangwen recognises as his mate early in *The Rainbow*. There is the same appeal of the foreign, which is aristocratic because it is strange.

One interest of the story is that it links the world of *The White Peacock* with that of *The Rainbow*. Lawrence is securely handling, even dominating, his native inherited material; and the sign of mastery is that he is not present. The only trace of him is that Geoffrey is his age, and that both Geoffrey and Maurice have this other Lawrentian thumbprint:

> The two brothers were both fiercely shy of women, and until this hay harvest, the whole feminine sex had been represented by their mother, in presence of any other women they were dumb louts. Moreover, brought up by a proud mother, a stranger in the country, they held the common girls as beneath them, because beneath their mother, who spoke pure English, and was very quiet. Loud-mouthed and broad tongued, the common girls were. So the two young men had grown up virgin but tormented. (*P/H SNI* 5)

The story tells how, with that handicap or spur, they both manage to find the right woman. Maurice takes the strange foreign girl, who escapes the taint of commonness. He is able to do this because of his natural ease and outgoingness. Geoffrey is jealous, having been attracted, but being too slow. The first section of the story modulates into a skilful deployment of Lawrence's rivalry-rising-to-violence theme, with the familiar countercurrent that the rivals are attached to each other, being in this case brothers, and genuinely if inarticulately fond of each other. Jealousy over Paula leads the two to engage in a wordless and barely conscious contest high up on the haystack they are making: Geoffrey actually pushes Maurice over the edge, and for a moment half-hopes he has killed him.

Nothing here is at the level of thought: there is scarcely even speech. The physical process of haymaking allows the one to toss the hay too fast and too awkwardly for the other to keep up with him; and the other to send his fork against his brother's boot. Their few angry words lead to outright wrestling, and Maurice goes over the side.

He is not hurt, but winded; and Paula comes to tend him, so declaring *her* allegiance. As the whole farming group then eat their meal in the field, the tramp arrives and cadges a meal. Geoffrey 'loathed him, longed to exterminate him' as he had been tempted to exterminate his brother. The tramp's wife appears, and he feels a kinship with her because they both seem at odds with the world.

All this is skilful introduction of the characters, setting of the scene, and posing the problem which has to be solved: these two men have to establish a relationship with these two women. Maurice is well on the way, but Geoffrey is handicapped: he is inarticulate and self-thwarting, and the woman is strange, and married. No portentous note has been struck; but it is said, as if in an aside, of the two men working up on the stack, 'small and inefficacious the brothers looked, half-submerged in the great loose trough, lifted high up as if on an altar reared to the sun'.

On that 'altar', that night, Maurice makes love to Paula, and it is essentially their wedding night. But the solemnity is subtly countered by humour: the ladder they go up falls down, so they *have* to stay up there, until Geoffrey comes by and tactfully replaces it so that they can get down again. Even then, Paula thinks at first that Maurice has tricked her into staying with him until it is equally tactfully conveyed to her that the ladder did really fall. What takes place up there is a glad rite which reinforces the note hinted at in the use of the word 'altar', and the beautiful night scene which precedes it is tender and poetic.

Maurice wondered what to do. He wandered round the deserted stacks restlessly. Heat came in wafts, in thick strands. The evening was a long time cooling. He thought he would go and wash himself. There was a trough of pure water in the hedge bottom. It was filled by a tiny spring that filtered over the brim of the trough down the lush hedge bottom of the lower field. All round the trough, in the upper field, the land was marshy, and there the meadow-sweet stood like clots of mist, very sickly smelling in the twilight. The night did not darken, for the moon was in the sky, so that as the tawny colour drew off the heavens they remained pallid with a dimmed moon. The purple bell-flowers in the hedge went black, the ragged robin turned its pink to a faded white, the meadow-sweet gathered light as if it were phosphorescent, and it made the air ache with scent.

Maurice kneeled on the slab of stone bathing his hands and arms, then his face. The water was deliciously cool. He had still an hour before Paula would come: she was not due till nine. So he decided to take his bath at night instead of waiting till morning. Was he not sticky, and was not Paula coming to talk to him? He was delighted the thought had occurred to him. As he soused his head in the trough, he wondered what the little creatures that lived in the velvetty silt at the bottom would think of the taste of soap. Laughing to himself, he squeezed his cloth into the water. He washed himself from head to foot, standing in the fresh, forsaken corner of the field, where no one could see him by daylight, so that now, in the veiled grey tinge of moonlight, he was no more noticeable than the crowded flowers. The night had on a new look: he never remembered to have seen the lustrous grey sheen of it before, nor to have noticed how vital the lights looked, with live folk inhabiting the silvery spaces. And the tall trees, wrapped obscurely in their mantles, would not have surprised him had they begun to move in converse. As he dried himself, he discovered little wanderings in the air, felt on his sides soft touches and caresses that were particularly delicious: sometimes they startled him, and he laughed as if he were not alone. The flowers, the meadow-sweet particularly haunted him. He reached to put his hand over their

fleeciness. They touched his thighs. Laughing, he gathered
them and dusted himself all over with their cream dust and
fragrance. For a moment he hesitated in wonder at himself:
but the subtle glow in the hoary and black night reassured him.
Things never had looked so personal and full of beauty, he had
never known the wonder in himself before.

At nine o'clock he was waiting under the elderbush, in a state
of high trepidation, but feeling that he was worthy, having a
sense of his own wonder. (*P/H SN*I 21–2)

The washing is a preparation, a laving which precedes the more
important rite. We recognise again what Lawrence was trying to
convey to Blanche Jennings about his own pleasure in himself;
and we hear transmuted into the major key the sad self-sympathy
of Siegmund Macnair, both on the beach (where he had covered
himself with dust from the sand) and on his last night. Now that
the theme is reworked in this way, the goodness of the man's body
is given its kinship with the flowers about him. We even remember
the trough as the one that George Saxton knew, and the little
creatures which he spilled on the ground are here given a share of
the surprise and gratification. The main element is a happiness
which seems totally new in Lawrence. There was always wonder,
but before it was intense, questioning and troubled. Now it is
relaxed and sure, because it is going to be shared.

When he comes to the base of the stack where Maurice and
Paula are lying, Geoffrey feels shut out and unsure of his own
worth. At this point the wife of the tramp re-enters in the dark,
seeking shelter, and looking for her husband. The long exchange
which follows starts as between thwarted, unfulfilled and
embittered people, who have only that and their age in common.
The link between them is made almost by accident, and by
physical touch. He gives her a drink: "When he gave her a cup of
water, her hand touched his and he felt her fingers hot and glossy.
She trembled so she spilled the water." She is weary and cold and
wet; and the further contact follows naturally from his natural
kindness – he wants to warm her. He offers to hold her feet in his
hands, and at first she shrinks from the proximity:

"Let me warm them with my hands," he asked her. "I'm hot
enough."

"No thank you," she said coldly. Then, in the darkness, she

felt she had wounded him. He was writhing under her rebuff, for his offer had been pure kindness.

"They're 'appen dirty," she said, half mocking.

He has the wit, the persistence, to renew the offer, and she consents:

. . . She was afraid. But her feet ached so, and the impulse drove her on, so she placed her soles lightly on the two blotches of smoke. His large hands clasped over her instep, warm and hard.

"They're like ice!" he said, in deep concern.

He warmed her feet as best he could, putting them close against him. Now and then convulsive tremors ran over her. She felt his warm breath on the balls of her toes, that were bunched up in his hands. Leaning forward she touched his hair delicately with her fingers. He thrilled. She fell to gently stroking the hair, with timid, pleading finger-tips.

"Do they feel any better?" he asked, in a low voice, suddenly lifting his face to her. This sent her hand sliding softly over his face, and her fingertips caught on his mouth. She drew quickly away. He put his hand out to find hers, in his other palm holding both her feet. His wandering hand met her face. He touched it curiously. It was wet. He put his big finger cautiously on her eyes, into two little pools of tears. (*P/H SN*I 33)

In its way, this meeting is as beautiful as, and more touching than, that between Maurice and Paula. The two have managed to cross the barrier and the mute ambassadors have been their hands: his have ministered to her, and hers have pleaded with him, and thanked him. So the inadequacy of words is pieced out. He becomes aware first of her physical extremity – the cold of the homeless wanderer – and then of her spiritual misery. She becomes aware of the kindness under the self-defeating awkwardness and shyness.

They make love, and sleep together, and the physical gestures follow naturally from, are an expression of, the meeting and the discovery. It emerges that she is called Lydia, Lawrence's mother's name, and the name he gave to the Polish woman whom Tom Brangwen discovers, thaws and marries in *The Rainbow*.

'Second Best' comes from the same world of the country and of farming. It is not actually set at the Haggs, but may be coloured by Lawrence's memories of haymaking there in 1908. It is a small thing, but a marked success – though the ending is ambiguous or cryptic, and thinking about it may make the reader revise too-easy assumptions about the background of the story, and the hint conveyed by the title, which may itself come to seem ironical. Lawrence is not in the story, as he was not in 'Love Among the Haystacks', where freedom from involvement made it possible for him to enter with joy into the self-discovery of the characters and their discovery of each other. In 'Second Best' it is not easy to discern his attitude, but the title may be too easily accepted as a hint. Does the second best turn out to be a wiser choice, entered into for bad reasons (a girl on the rebound from a jilting) but producing a strange discovery? Just conceivably the absent Lawrence is sardonically identified with the 'first best', Jimmy Barrass, who is a 'doctor of chemistry' and therefore presumably an intellectual and a gentleman. Frances has loved him, or at any rate wanted him for five years, and he (rather like Lawrence with Jessie Chambers or Syson with Hilda) has given her half-measures and suddenly got engaged to someone else. Like Hilda, she therefore turns, deliberately, to the second best of the title, Tom Smedley the farmer, and the story makes us wonder if she isn't wiser in doing this than she knows. There is something of Lettie Beardsall in this tall twenty-three-year-old; and there is something of a simplified George Saxton in Tom Smedley. So the choice of *The White Peacock* is being reversed. He is also like Tom Vickers and Arthur Pilbeam in that Frances might come to value his vigour and his manliness, and his way of being at home in his world, which may make the choice a wise one after all. Tom has a good deal of Geoffrey Wookey in him as well:

> Tom was of medium stature, energetic in build. His smooth, fair skinned face was burned red, not brown, by the sun, and this ruddiness enhanced his appearance of good-humour and easiness. Being a year older than Frances, he would have courted her long ago had she been so inclined. As it was, he had gone his uneventful way amiably, chatting with many a girl, but remaining unattached, free of trouble for the most part. Only he knew he wanted a woman. He hitched his trousers just a trifle self-consciously as the girls approached. Frances was a rare,

delicate kind of being, whom he realised with a queer and delicious stimulation in his veins. She gave him a slight sense of suffocation: somehow, this morning she affected him more than usual. She was dressed in white. He however, being matter-of-fact in his mind, did not realise. His feelings had never become conscious, purposive. (*PO*(C) 118)

Lawrence is here, to use his own word, 'realising' the rival, whom he had presented, 'unrealised', as Tom Vickers or Arthur Pilbeam.

The unexpected issue which at one level divides these two and at another unites them is the willed killing of another creature. This too links the story to *The White Peacock*. Tom as farmer regards moles as vermin; they have to be killed. In the first part of the story Frances and her sister Anne see a mole and catch it, and are then at first unable to kill it, either because they are intellectuals, and so on principle against killing; or because they have no good reason to kill it, not being farmers; or because they are tenderhearted. But that last reason doesn't hold for long: the mole bites Anne, and she kills it in a reflex of anger.

Lawrence conveys with his characteristic genius the life of the mole, its very mole-ness, and its imagined joy of living:

> She [Frances] watched the little brute paddling, snuffing, touching things to discover them, running in blindness, delighted to ecstasy by the sunlight and the hot, strange things that caressed its belly and its nose.
> She felt a keen pity for the little creature. (*PO*(C) 115)

But Anne has a hunter's instinct:

> In an instant Anne put her foot upon it, not too heavily. Frances could see the struggling, swimming movement of the little pink hands of the brute, the twisting and twitching of its pointed nose, as it wrestled under the sole of the boot.
> "It *does* wriggle!" said the bonny girl, knitting her brows in a frown at the eerie sensation. Then she bent down to look at her trap. Frances could now see, beyond the edge of the boot-sole, the heaving of the velvet shoulders, the pitiful turning of the sightless face, the frantic rowing of the flat, pink hands.
> "Kill the thing," she said, turning away her face.
> "Oo – I'm not," laughed Anne, shrinking. "You can if you like".

"I *don't* like," said Frances, with quiet intensity. (*PO*(C) 115)

But when it bites her, Anne kills it:

> One ruby drop of blood hung on the small snout, ready to fall. Anne shook it off onto some harebells. Frances suddenly became calm; in that moment, grown-up.
>
> "I suppose they *have* to be killed," she said, and a certain rather dreary indifference succeeded to her grief. The twinkling crab-apples, the glitter of brilliant willows now seemed to her trifling, scarcely worth the notice. Something had died in her, so that things lost their poignancy. She was calm, indifference overlying her quiet sadness. (*PO*(C) 117)

The change of feeling is rendered not as a thought, but as a projection, a change of tonality in the surroundings. The girls then approach Tom, to show him the mole; and the necessity of killing moles becomes an issue between them, even though Frances has already reached this strange acquiescence; which is like a revulsion from her previous love, and even her previous life.

> "You're not so good at knockin' 'em?" he said, turning to her.
> "I don't know, if I'm cross," she said, decisively.
> "No?" he replied, with alert attentiveness.
> "I could," she added, harder, "if it was necessary." He was slow to feel her difference.
> "And don't you consider it *is* necessary?" he asked, with misgiving.
> "We-ell – is it?" she replied, looking at him steadily, coldly.
> "I reckon it is," he replied, looking away, but standing stubborn.
> She laughed quickly.
> "But it isn't necessary for *me*" she said, with slight contempt.
> "Yes, that's quite true," he answered. She laughed in a shaky fashion.
> "*I know it is*," she said; and there was an awkward pause.
> "Why, would you *like* me to kill moles then?" she asked, tentatively, after a while.
> "They do do us a lot of damage," he said, standing firm on his own ground, angered.
> "Well, I'll see the next time I come across one," she promised, defiantly. Their eyes met, and she sank before him,

her pride troubled. He felt uneasy and triumphant and baffled, as if fate had gripped him. She smiled as she departed. (*PO*(C) 119–20)

The next day 'after a secret, persistent hunt, she found another mole playing in the heat. She killed it'. She takes it to Tom.

What is this mole, deliberately killed, and offered to propitiate the chosen male? Might one call it a sacrifice? The whole idea of killing, natural predation, and the conscious lordship over life ran through *The White Peacock*. Cyril Beardsall and Annable felt a natural affinity when the older man found the younger gazing at the corpse of a rabbit being tidied away by maggots in the cleanly economy of nature: but Cyril could not kill a rabbit when the chance arose. Obsessed by the necessity of death, he could not deal it out – though George Saxton could. In the mature 'Second Best', these themes are handled more subtly and calmly. Frances turns from her first love, who bears the mental burden of being a 'doctor of chemistry' and who might be shocked, mentally, at the idea of deliberate killing. She turns to the inarticulate man, the farmer, who insists on the need to kill. Her offering may hint that there is something of the god in him. At any rate, he is in touch with something which he knows as reality, the order of life. The exchange she has with him is not the exchange of ideas, but the contact of two beings, in an opposition at the end of which 'she sank before him, her pride troubled'. She has admitted a superiority: his certainty against her uncertainty, where her assumption of conscious social superiority, or intellectual superiority, drops away. Nothing is as simply stated as that; and the last words, deeply thematic, are not a conventional happy ending:

"We s'll have to tell your mother," he said. And he stood, suffering, resisting his passion for her.
"Yes," she replied, in a dead voice. But there was a thrill of pleasure in this death.

Once more, the necessary gesture has been made, and the gap crossed.

The reader is challenged by the story, which is like a riddle or test. The title invites the simple response: 'this superior girl, intelligent and spirited and lively, has thrown herself away. The 'death' of the last sentence is the death of her prospects in life, and 'the thrill of pleasure' is a perverse self-punishment'. But all that has gone before may be an invitation to respond at a deeper level, to think that what has died is instead a false social attitude, snobbishness, and shallow mentalism. The reader has to decide; and the main clues are the death of the mole itself, and the extraordinary perception that at one moment certain objects in her surroundings 'had a peculiar, unfriendly look about them: the weight of greenish elderberries on their purpling stalks; the twinkling of the yellowing crab-apples that clustered high up in the hedge, against the sky; the exhausted, limp leaves of the primroses lying flat in the hedge-bottom: all looked strange to her'. That is her alienation, her feeling of being jilted, projected on to the world before she sees the first mole. When it is killed 'The twinkling crab-apples, the glitter of brilliant willows now seemed to her trifling, scarcely worth the notice. Something had died in her so that things lost their poignancy. She was calm, indifference overlying her quiet sadness.' In that changed mood, she walks straight to Tom; and it is either the victory of something or a defeat. The last word 'death' is not necessarily a negative word for Lawrence: he thought it necessary at certain points in the unfolding of an existence for the old form of life to die, and give way to the new.

The main link between these stories is that all of them make some use of Lawrence's own early life: especially the farm-life at the Haggs, which is recreated in 'A Prelude', 'The Shades of Spring', 'A Modern Lover', 'Love Among the Haystacks', and distantly in 'Second Best'. 'The Witch à la Mode', 'The Old Adam', 'A Lesson on the Tortoise', 'The Fly in the Ointment' all refer to the teaching years in Croydon, the lodging at the Joneses, the relationship with Helen Corke. The stories in which the Lawrence-figure occurs show that figure circling round the blocked relationships, with Jessie (Hilda, Muriel), with Helen Corke (Winifred Varley). In several of the stories there is a solid-seeming rival, who is limited but successful. The rivalry may border on violence, but it also borders on love. In 'Love Among the Haystacks' the two rivals are brothers, and both win through to love, crossing the mysterious gap. In 'Second Best' one rival has been dismissed from the action before the story starts, and the woman makes a propitiatory offering to the other, the country youth, or to the god in him which

Hilda has also divined in her gamekeeper ('the man doesn't matter so much' she had said).

Another link between the stories is the sense in all of them of a crucial encounter, in which the course of a life may be decided. In the cases where a Lawrence-figure is involved, the attempt at a meeting, a commitment, is thwarted. In all of them what is said matters, but the issue is not decided by discussion, by argument. Much more it is a matter of a gesture being made, an offer across a gulf. A movement of the hands, or what Lawrence calls a 'lifting of the breast' conveys an offer, an appetency. With Geoffrey Wookey it is the actual touch, and the returned touch, which bridge the divide. With Frances it is the offer of a sacrifice. Between Bernard Coutts and Winifred Varley an embrace has to be broken as if the man, a column of blood, has to shake off a leech or vampire, and only a quite exceptional gesture can do it.

What sharply distinguishes the stories is the maturing process which took place in the years 1910–1914, so that we pass from the elements of lushness, mannerism, and general over-ambitiousness in 'A Modern Lover' to the ease and neatness of 'Second Best'. In particular there is a sardonic note, a reticence, a light touch, in the last story which we associate with the Lawrence of the post-war period. This much more 'realist' manner converts into the merest hints or undertones things which had been almost overwhelmingly overt in the period and the manner of *The White Peacock* and *The Trespasser*. But the heavy emphases of that period in their very directness serve a useful purpose. They make us familiar with the themes which in the later manner are so subdued that they might pass unnoticed. The theme of sacrifice for instance, is so discreetly handled in 'Second Best' that the reader might fail to recognise it, but it is there, and 'The Shades of Spring', and 'The Witch à la Mode' are evidence for its significance. Other themes are already familiar: the naked boy entering the sea, raising his hands to the tutelary star; the rite of laving the male body;[11] hands as the agency of greeting, of meeting, of worship; hands or faces as flowers; hands as murdered animals; the sun as golden benediction; life as consuming fire or as banked-up fire; thwarted desire as spilled wine; the witch's mirror-ball; the posture of the two figures in Greiffenhagen's 'Idyll'.

These properties, gestures, actions, poses, come naturally and are used unselfconsciously by the young Lawrence. Their recurrence in the stories, as in the first novels, relates the fictional characters to their universe in a way which is unlike that of other writers of the time,[12] and implies a sense of human life and nature such as neither Wells nor Bennett nor Galsworthy – no, nor Conrad nor James – could conceive. The only analogy is with Hardy. But if we link these properties with another note which recurs in these stories, the originality, the strangeness is increased. Consider three sentences which have been quoted in passing in this chapter:

> Then my blood seemed to change its quality. It went cool and sharp with disgust.

> He felt a quick change beginning in his blood. It was the old delicious sublimation, the thinning, almost the vaporizing of himself . . .

> Frances was a rare, delicate kind of being, whom he realised with a queer and delicious stimulation in his veins.

In that last sentence, Lawrence wrote 'felt' in 1911, and changed it to 'realised' in 1914. What is implied here is a reception of others, a way of 'realising' them which self-conscious readers will recognise as instinctive, but which, before Lawrence, was not put into words. Finding words for something wordless is evidently one of his enterprises; with the associated paradox that he is therefore making conscious, in the head, what is actually felt somewhere else. From the beginning, Lawrence's word for it is the 'blood'. These three examples show Lawrence at the crucial stage of his development, first stating the idea rather baldly, then finding a more subtle formulation, and then managing not to use what is in danger of becoming a technical term, and therefore a mentalised counter, a cliché. Only the use of the word 'veins' guides us back to his formulation.

However the thought I would like to leave in the reader's mind at this point is that the young writer of 1908 to 1911 is, despite his 'literariness' or mannerism, to be entirely distinguished from all other writers using the language of the period 1890–1910. Many of them gestured towards some quality of feeling about the world which they located in Renaissance Italy or Greek myth, or medieval romance. Lawrence feels as direct intuitions those significances and relationships which in others had been literary borrowing, esotericism, nostalgia, or playacting. As esotericist one might talk about the relationship between the macrocosm and the microcosm. Without needing to reflect, Lawrence *knows* his kinship with the sun, the evening star, Orion, who are friends and protectors; and the moon, who is a threat. Other living creatures are in the world with him in a way that they are not for ordinary people. That is why the women in two of these stories can say the Lawrence-figure makes things wonderful for them. They see and feel through him. He for his part is so at home that he can, like Maurice Wookey, feel 'no more noticeable than the crowded flowers' among which he stands naked in the evening warmth, 'feeling soft touches and caresses that were particularly delicious'. Maurice, or the imagined boy entering the sea in the prelude to 'A Modern Lover', can laugh 'as if he were not alone'. But he, Lawrence, is alone, and that is his trouble.

Though he has that place in the great non-human world, he has not found his place in the human world because of some block in himself. He is able by 1913 to imagine Geoffrey and Maurice Wookey secure in both worlds, and Frances moving from his kind of failure to a possible success with a totally other kind of man. The relationship between his kind of man and that other kind is a rivalry in which the man with spiritual power envies the other who by nature and situation simply and securely *is*, 'taut with animal life, like the thick jet of a fountain balanced in itself'.

6   Sons and Lovers

Critics slight *Sons and Lovers* at the moment, but it seems to me that the book will always be popular. It was Lawrence's greatest success in his lifetime, so that publishers were always urging him to write another book like it. It is still usually the first book of his that people read, and most enjoy it. It is a classic in the original sense: one of the books that live because people go on reading them with pleasure. This is something that critics in their turn must pay attention to.

One does not have to look far for reasons for this popularity. The story itself is – to most people – only incidentally interesting because it is so closely related to Lawrence's own experience. What they prize is the consequence: the vividness, the actuality of so much of the writing. Most of it feels as if it is simply veracious, even literal. It often starts from a literal base:

> In convalescence he would sit up in bed, see the fluffy horses feeding at the troughs in the field, scattering their hay on the trodden yellow snow;

Why 'fluffy'? one asks. Oh yes, winter coat. Why 'yellow' snow? Oh yes, I see. It goes on:

> . . . watch the miners troop home – small, black figures trailing slowly in gangs across the white field. Then the night came up in dark blue vapour from the snow.

Is that last sentence 'realistic' or 'poetic'? Meaningless question. The words go on to realise the wonder:

> In convalescence everything was wonderful. The snowflakes, suddenly arriving on the window-pane, clung there a moment like swallows, then were gone, and a drop of water was crawling down the glass. The snowflakes whirled round the corner of the

150

house, like pigeons dashing by. Away across the valley the little black train crawled doubtfully over the great whiteness. (*S & L*(P) 107)

The whole book has this effortless lucid aptness, which seems like realism but, examined, is poetry. Lawrence later deprecated the style as 'hard, violent', and too full of 'presentation', and in his next major fiction moved back into a mode more like that of *The White Peacock* and *The Trespasser*. Many readers regret this.

There are, nonetheless, passages in *Sons and Lovers* which strike the reader as suddenly moving into a different vein reminiscent of the two first novels. They are usually taken as isolated pieces of injected symbolism and are rather schematically interpreted in consequence. They seem like intrusions or outcrops, and most readers are, though impressed, also disconcerted by them, being used to the seeming literalness of the staple narrative prose.

Moreover, the book has now acquired the nostalgic attraction of a period flavour, while the regional setting always seemed important, and so did the 'class' atmosphere. We are in the northern Midlands at the turn of the century, seeing the daily life of the mining community through the eyes of one of its children, and seen with such intensity and clarity, especially in the first of the three parts, that the reader feels in direct contact with life. The very grimness, the meanness of the industrial setting is fixed with such a penetrating eye that it is like being in love: the world comes alive again, and everyday things seem blessed. This is no accident; in that first Part Lawrence is writing as one in love with what he tells: it is his own childhood that he is re-creating. We have only to think of the weary and despairing eye which he cast over the same landscape in *Lady Chatterley's Lover*: the same place is seen by an ageing and defeated man, where once he had been young and hopeful.

The common reader's reaction to *Sons and Lovers* is that he or she is responding to an essential veracity, tinged with natural nostalgic love: the glow of affection which most people reflect back on their very early childhood, followed by an account of the pains of growing up. Even though it quickly becomes clear that these pains are intense, the sort of case Lawrence presents is by no means uncommon. It might seem that the book has no elaborate designs on the reader, or that Lawrence has no concealed motives or bias. That is not so, however, and it is in sensing motive and

bias that critics have in recent years developed their doubts. They
have questioned aspects of the veracity: it was not that they felt an
autobiographical novel or Bildungsroman must adhere with total
fidelity to every fact of the writer's life, but rather that the way in
which the facts are presented, together with the departures from
fact, may spring not just from the writer's art, but also from an
inner bias that the author has not mastered, or is unaware of.
There might therefore be a deep unfairness of a betraying kind.
This matters in a book which is undertaken as a clearing of
accounts, a way of getting things straight with oneself.

The White Peacock and some of the earliest short stories –
especially those in which a Lawrence-figure is present – have
shown a succession of attempts by Lawrence to confront through
fictional characters his own emotional life, and specifically his
failure to love successfully. These stories are of blocked
relationships; of a love presented to a woman who cannot meet it;
or a love offered by a woman which is of a dangerous kind; so that
the men and women are not 'there' for each other (an expression
which Lawrence uses in *Sons and Lovers*, and repeats in the short
stories of the period after 1912[1]). This repeated bafflement is a
sign that Lawrence is circling round his own trouble, approaching
it through his imagined people. It is a mark of his truthfulness that
he cannot imagine for his fictional representatives a happy ending
that he can't see for himself. It is an indication also of his chosen
main topic – a fundamentally re-thought and re-felt approach to
love between the sexes. Unromanticised, love has become a
difficult enterprise, not at all the story-book stereotype of
inclination, passion and the happy-ever-after.

If Lawrence felt at some point 'There is something *in me* which
blocks my own intentions, the good progress of my life. I must get
this clear to myself as a condition of finding a way out', then the
writing of *Sons and Lovers* becomes diagnostic, therapeutic, and a
necessary preliminary to anything further. As he said in a letter to
Arthur McLeod, his schoolteacher friend from the Croydon years,
'one sheds ones sicknesses in books – repeats and presents again
ones emotions, to be master of them.' (*Letters II* 90). That was
certainly the intention, but is he fully the master yet? (And was he
ever? Murry would have added). We remember also that Jessie
Chambers, who is given a central role in the book as Miriam
Leivers, read the early version *Paul Morel*, which was much more
'fictional', indeed melodramatically imagined, then the final

version. With her habitual percipience, she thought the fictive
elements were weaknesses, and that Lawrence could only do what
he wanted by getting more of himself and his relationship with his
parents into the book; so she pressed him to make it more
veracious in that sense. When she read the final version she was
deeply hurt because she felt that he had not been fair to her: had
not recognised what she had done for *him* intellectually (there is
much in the book about what he did for her: Miriam is presented
as an almost idiot pupil). He had been unable to represent
something central in their love (his own ingrown virginity), and
had finally taken his mother's side against her.

She was a remarkable woman: it was a miracle that in that
corner of provincial England these two exceptional people should
have grown up together and done so much for each other in
unpropitious surroundings.[2] She is an important witness, and the
reader who is trying to assess the truth of the book must read what
she says. But looking for any absolute truth is a vain endeavour:
no outsider can reach it, especially now. Both witnesses are dead,
and both were so deeply involved that they can have no
impartiality. We are driven back to the book, *Sons and Lovers*,
which must be read and judged like any other. Perhaps Lawrence
was not fair to Jessie, in his presentation of their love and what she
did for him, but she has left her own record of their relationship
and her book will always be a classic too. One is left making a
mental distinction between the real Jessie Chambers and the
character of Miriam Leivers in *Sons and Lovers*;[3] left thinking also
that any unfairness basically springs from the virtual identity of
viewpoint which the author shares with his central character Paul
Morel. Fairness is hardly possible for that reason.

There is final fundamental point to be made about this element
of autobiography, and about Lawrence's standard practice of
including in his fictions large elements of actual experience,
usually his own. A moment's thought shows that it can never have
been his aim simply to write disguised autobiography. The use of
'real life' is meant to ground what he writes in actuality, and to
make it a grappling with what he knew at first hand. But he is
always using this material for some purpose beyond reportage,
and that use will produce departures from fact. It is surprising
that Jessie did not take more account of this – though it is also true
that the use and the departures can themselves be the subject of
diagnosis.

Lawrence sent a synopsis of *Sons and Lovers* to his publisher's reader Edward Garnett. Garnett was going to be his first and most influential reader, so Lawrence wanted to anticipate and trump his responses – to lead him away from his prejudices about Flaubertian 'form', and to make him see the new form in the new art being offered to him. If it covered a feeling that the book tended in places to ramble and repeat itself, the synopsis did not succeed; for Garnett stuck to his own ideas about form, and cut the text a certain amount. Even so, Part Two still seems to move slowly and uncertainly. The ordinary reader doesn't mind that, and may not even notice, because on a first reading the vividness of the writing carries one without much effort or illwill over the parts of the plot which might otherwise seem redundant. Lawrence wrote:

> . . . I want to defend it, quick. I wrote it again, pruning it and shaping it and filling it in. I tell you it has got form – *form*: haven't I made it patiently, out of sweat as well as blood. It follows this idea: a woman of character and refinement goes into the lower class, and has no satisfaction in her own life. She has had a passion for her husband, so the children are born of passion, and have heaps of vitality. But as her sons grow up she selects them as lovers – first the eldest, then the second. These sons are *urged* into life by their reciprocal love of their mother – urged on and on. But when they come to manhood, they can't love, because the mother is the strongest power in their lives, and holds them. As soon as the young men come into contact with women, there's a split. William [the eldest son] gives his sex to a fribble, and his mother holds his soul. But the split kills him, because he doesn't know where he is. The next son [Paul] gets a woman [Miriam] who fights for his soul – fights his mother – all the sons hate and are jealous of the father. The battle goes on between the mother and the girl, with the son as object. The mother gradually proves stronger, because of the tie of blood. The son decides to leave his soul in his mother's hands, and like his elder brother, go for passion. He gets passion [with Clara Dawes]. Then the split begins to tell again. But, almost unconsciously, the mother realises what is the matter, and begins to die. The son casts off his mistress, attends to his mother dying. He is left in the end naked of everything, with the drift towards death.
>
> It is a great tragedy, and I tell you I've written a great book.

It's the tragedy of thousands of young men in England. . . . Now tell me if I haven't worked out my theme, like life, but always my theme. Read my novel – it's a great novel. If *you* can't see the development – which is slow like growth – I can. (19 November 1912, in *Letters I* 476–7)

Lawrence's synopsis emphasises that the book is a tragedy, and ends with the phrase 'the drift towards death'. It is a valuable corrective to the easily-held notion that Lawrence's evident delight in a great deal of the early story, his sense of life, will carry him and the reader through the difficult times (we all lose our parents, and growing up is usually hard): once that is all over, Paul Morel can walk 'towards the faintly humming, glowing town, quickly'. If that is taken as a happy ending, a cinematic fade with the colour getting warmer and the music louder and more triumphant, it is a misreading. It is Lawrence's intention that Paul should show 'he would not give in': but the whole force of the preceding book suggests that at the end of the book he is very close to defeat and collapse; and to pull himself back from a carefully established impulse just to die,[4] so resolving his difficulties and rejoining the loved and sustaining mother – to do that may be the task of a lifetime, and will cost an effort of will and intelligence such as few people can manage.

If the book is not a total tragedy, the two principal characters Paul and Miriam are left at the end of it, alone, estranged, and damaged by all that has gone before. Mrs Morel's death has been a defeat for her and no victory for anyone else; it is the negative consummation of a will-driven and baffled life. Walter Morel, the miner-father, has lost his youthful glamour and become a paltry ruin. The elder brother, William, dies early in the story, and (like Annable's in *The White Peacock*) his failure and death are an admonitory portent to Paul, who inherits from him the relationship with the mother. There has been much family strife, including violence and threatened violence. And none of the main characters has successfully managed to love anybody else, unless it is contended that the deep love between Paul and his mother is a good. But how can that be entirely so, when it has crippled him emotionally?

A keynote or moral can be found in a letter to Else Jaffe written only a month after the letter to Garnett. The subject is Lawrence's relationship with Frieda, Else's sister. Lawrence and Frieda, in love and living together, had to contemplate the hurt they were doing to Frieda's husband, and especially her children, whom she grieved for, and who were grieving for her. Else had presumably been saying 'renounce your love for the sake of these others'. Lawrence, replying, has his own life behind him, and the recent painful experience of living it over again in writing *Sons and Lovers*. He writes:

> I think you ask us to throw away a real apple for a gilt one. Nowadays it costs more courage to assert ones desire and need, than it does to renounce.
>
> If Frieda and the children could live happily together, I should say 'Go' – because the happiness of two out of three is sufficient. But if she would only be sacrificing her life, I would not let her go if I could keep her. Because if she brings to the children a sacrifice, that is a curse to them. If I had a prayer, I think it would be 'Lord, let no one ever sacrifice living stuff to me – because I'm burdened enough.' . . . The worst of sacrifice is that we have to pay back. It is like somebody giving a present that was never asked for, and putting the recipient under the obligation of making restitution, often more than he could afford. (14 December 1912, in *Letters I* 486)

This is hard-won wisdom; he is replying to Else's rule-book morality with something real. One thinks how much Paul Morel in *Sons and Lovers* is living for his mother, to pay her back for something she has missed.

The word 'sacrifice' and powerful feelings associated with it are familiar in the earlier writing, but now come into sharper focus associated with a judgement which is firmly against it. The word is often used in *Sons and Lovers*, and to think about the course of the events is to see how much gets sacrificed – though to whom and for what is sometimes a difficult question. What is certain is that all the women and most of the men either make sacrifices of themselves or are sacrificed: sometimes they know it, and sometimes not. The sum of the sacrifices is the 'tragedy' of Lawrence's claim to Garnett.

The theme is announced quietly and mysteriously, in a tonality which seems positive. All readers must have been struck by the scene in which Mrs Morel holds the baby Paul up to the sun (one of the outcrops or intrusions I mentioned). She seems to be merely

asking him to look; but something else is implied. The overt action
follows a series of thoughts in which Mrs Morel forms a kind of
solemn vow: 'With all her force, with all her soul she would make
up to it [the child] for having brought it into the world unloved.' A
vow to make up to someone for something is often a determination
to enforce a will, with harmful direct or side-effects – so common
experience tells us. The object of the devotion can be made to
suffer through this determined love. The afterthought is
reinforced by the action which follows:

> Once more she was aware of the sun lying red on the rim of the
> hill opposite. She suddenly held up the child in her hands.
>   "Look!" she said. "Look, my pretty!"
>   She thrust the infant forward to the crimson, throbbing sun,
> almost with relief. She saw him lift his little fist. Then she put
> him to her bosom again, ashamed almost of her impulse to give
> him back again whence he came. (*S & L*(P) 74)

It strikes us as like a solemn dedication, in which the child too,
raising its fist, recognises a paternity or allegiance or source:
'whence he came' is a strong claim. Yet the gesture is ambiguous:
the holding out is like an offering in another sense – a willingness
to give back, to sacrifice.
    There are echoes or ramifications of this scene throughout the
book. One which repeats the notion that Paul 'belongs to the sun'
occurs in the chapter 'Lad-and-Girl-Love'. Paul and Miriam are
returning from an outing with friends:

> He remained concentrated in the middle of the road. Beyond,
> one rift of rich gold in that colourless grey evening seemed to
> make him stand out in dark relief. She saw him, slender and
> firm, as if the setting sun had given him to her. A deep pain took
> hold of her, and she knew she must love him. And she had
> discovered him, discovered in him a rare potentiality,
> discovered his loneliness. Quivering as at some 'annunciation',
> she went slowly forward. (*S & L*(P) 216)

Again, the implications are ambiguous. If 'the setting sun had
given him to her', does that make her possessive, too sure of her
title to him? And the implications of 'annunciation' may mean
that she is like Mary, and is to become a mother of the loved one,

rivalling his own mother; or that as virgin she is to have a sexless love. In either case, if she is saying 'Behold the handmaid of the Lord', that is an impulse to sacrifice her own individual will.

He, to whom his mother sacrifices herself,[5] towards whom in due course Miriam sacrifices herself, and Clara Dawes also, learns to demand or accept sacrifices; yet discovers that in the end he too has been an offering. He starts on the course of sacrificing others very young, with the doll Arabella, which belongs to his sister Annie. He breaks it by accident. Annie, whom he loves, is grief-stricken, and as long as she mourns he is profoundly upset – that is, he feels guilt. But 'her grief wore itself out' and something strange then shows itself in him. He wants to be rid of the guilt, along with the object of it:

> "Let's make a sacrifice of Arabella," he said. "Let's burn her."
> She was horrified, yet rather fascinated. She wanted to see what the boy would do. He made an altar of bricks . . .

He burns the doll, carefully and with great pleasure and some vengeful violence:

> So long as the stupid big doll burned he rejoiced in silence. At the end he poked among the embers with a stick, fished out the arms and legs, all blackened, and smashed them under stones.
> "That's the sacrifice of Missis Arabella", he said. "An' I'm glad there's nothing left of her."
> Which disturbed Annie inwardly, although she could say nothing. He seemed to hate the doll so intensely, because he had broken it. (*S & L*(P) 96–7)

So an impulse to sacrifice may spring from an intolerable guilt; but the guilt can go up in the smoke of the sacrifice. It is a useful psychic mechanism and may be used against people one has injured. You purge your guilt by taking revenge on the thing or person who makes you feel guilty, and their annihilation frees you. This fierce morality, which seems immoral, is the ethical residue of the book: offer up your guilt and be free of it; do not accept even a loving bondage. Essentially, become free. Others will make you what they need you to be: refuse, and become yourself. Only by an assertion which is at times cruel can Paul Morel escape the traps that love has set for him. At the end of the book he is perhaps emerging from a near-mortal sickness into convalescence. One implication of his walking 'quickly' to the humming town is that though solitary he is back in life, and free.

The idea of sacrifice is most obviously associated with Mrs Morel and Miriam. Their opposition conceals – or conveys – what they have in common: their intensity, their spirituality, and their love for Paul, which is both noble and subtly possessive. They sacrifice him in the sense that at the end of the book he, their joint creation, is incapable of a free self-giving to a woman who is not either all mind and spirit, or all passion and sensuality, but who loves him and is loved by him in both ways. So, for all their love, they have damaged him. They sacrifice themselves in that the struggle between them leaves them both lonely and defeated; and Mrs Morel dies of her defeat as much as of cancer. But Clara Dawes is also made a sacrifice, in that she is used to meet a need, and then left because the need is only one need. Walter Morel too is slighted, ignored and left out of account. People are as much hurt by a love which offers itself as self-denying as by the seemingly self-seeking way in which Paul uses Miriam and Clara. So it is potentially a disheartening book – or it would be if the sense of life in the writing were not constantly working against the tragedy of the human actions.

With Miriam in particular, the word 'sacrifice' recurs with monotonous frequency, as if to enforce the thought that some are willing victims, and seem to want their own harm, to glory in it. The instances begin to pile up in the chapter 'Lad-and-Girl-Love': to give just one example:

> . . . Then she fell into that rapture of self-sacrifice, identifying herself with a God who was sacrificed, which gives to so many human souls their deepest bliss. (*S & L*(P) 223)

The word recurs in 'The defeat of Miriam':

> . . . The old feeling that she was to be a sacrifice to this love. . . . She saw tragedy, sorrow, and sacrifice ahead. And in sacrifice she was proud, in renunciation she was strong . . . (*S & L*(P) 271)

The recurrences reach a natural development in the later chapter 'The Test on Miriam'; she gives herself physically to Paul entirely in a spirit of self-sacrifice:

> . . . There was something divine in it; then she should submit, religiously, to the sacrifice. He should have her. And at the thought her whole body clenched itself involuntarily, hard, as if against something; but Life forced her through this gate of suffering too, and she would submit. (*S & L*(P) 345)

The use of the word threatens to become willed and automatic. At the crucial moment the act of love is more fully described as a rite. And here it is associated with the revelation of the body, that epiphany which in the previous novels and in the short stories had always been the reverent beholding of the male body. Here for once the woman's body is disclosed for the same kind of worship. The difference is that it is the body of a victim, and the gesture which we recognise, the lifting of the hands, is deeply ambiguous – both a plea for mercy and a gesture of propitiation and assent:

> He never forgot seeing her as she lay on the bed, when he was unfastening his collar. First he saw only her beauty, and was blind with it. She had the most beautiful body he had ever imagined. He stood unable to move or speak, looking at her, his face half smiling with wonder. And then he wanted her, but as he went forward to her, her hands lifted in a little pleading movement, and he looked at her face, and stopped. Her big brown eyes were watching him, still and resigned and loving; she lay as if she had given herself up to sacrifice: there was her body for him; but the look at the back of her eyes, like a creature awaiting immolation, arrested him, and all his blood fell back
> . . .
> . . . She lay to be sacrificed for him because she loved him so much. And he had to sacrifice her. (*S & L*(P) 351)

The summating comment later is 'As he rode home he felt that he was finally initiated': it is a word with ritual connotations. And also 'there remained afterwards always the sense of failure and of death. If he were really with her, he had to put aside himself and his desire. If he would have her, he had to put her aside' (352).

The little phrase 'with her' is the equivalent of being 'there';[6]

and it echoes the remark 'Now he realised that she had not been with him all the time, that her soul had stood apart, in a sort of horror.' This self-renunciation, this sacrifice, is contrasted with the kind of self-transcendence which he really wants:

> 'To be rid of our individuality, which is our will, which is our effort – to live effortless, a kind of conscious sleep – that is very beautiful, I think; that is our after-life – our immortality.' (*S & L*(P) 349)

So it is as if the smoke of Miriam's sacrifice had not gone up to Heaven, was not acceptable to the Lord, because her self-sacrifice was an effect of the will, a self-clenching which preserved the consciousness, kept it operating, and in opposition to the act.

This is an important point about Miriam's own nature, and about what she seeks, both in the relationship with Paul, and in her experience of the outside world. It is a matter of the consciousness being always awake and focused, so that she may the more intensely (indeed religiously) feel what is at any moment before her. Part of Paul's attraction for her is his capacity to 'realise' things in this way for her. It is as if he becomes an intermediary, constantly intensifying things for her. We remember Hilda in the short story 'The Shades of Spring' saying to the Lawrence-figure Syson that he had made things magical for her. Miriam feels that

> till he had seen it, she felt it had not come into her soul. Only he could make it her own, immortal. (*S & L*(P) 209)

When they are lovers, the physical relationship itself is affected:

> Not for an instant would she let him forget. Back again he had to torture himself into a sense of his responsibility and hers. Never any relaxing, never any leaving himself to the great hunger and impersonality of passion; he must be brought back to a deliberate reflective creature. As if from a swoon of passion she called him back to the littleness, the personal relationship. He could not bear it. 'Leave me alone – leave me alone!' he wanted to cry; but she wanted him to look at her with eyes full of love. His eyes, full of the dark, impersonal fire of desire, did not belong to her. (*S & L*(P) 346)

So two elements in Miriam are related: the shrinking of self-sacrifice is the complement, the accompaniment, of the clenching of consciousness. The victim traps the person sacrificing her.

Or so it is claimed in the novel, by the narrator. It is possible that one 'unfairness' to Miriam consists of regularly transferring to her aspects of Lawrence's own difficulties, and only hinting how much like *him* she is. We do however notice that her shrinking unwillingness to relinquish her virginity is first expressed by Paul himself:

> "I know," he cried, "you never will [understand]! You'll never believe that I can't – can't physically, any more than I can fly up like a skylark –"
>
> "What?" she murmured. Now she dreaded.
>
> "Love you." (*S & L*(P) 277)

This is like Lettie's momentary confession to Leslie Tempest that she cannot be 'flesh of his flesh'.

And Miriam's desperate wish to be always conscious is also Paul's: indeed it is a condition of his art:

> He was conscious only when stimulated. A sketch finished, he always wanted to take it to Miriam. Then he was stimulated into knowledge of the work he had produced unconsciously. In contact with Miriam he gained insight; his vision went deeper. From his mother he drew the life-warmth, the strength to produce; Miriam urged this warmth into intensity, like a white light. (*S & L*(P) 208)

The relationship with Miriam is vital to him, for reasons which this passage suggests; but another part of him (and it would be hard to say that it was less conscious, less a matter of the will) wants the 'impersonality' of passion. The crucial comparison with 'a white light' is a recurrent image which links Miriam with his mother, so that one questions the statement here that it is from his mother that he receives 'the life-warmth'. What Lawrence cannot see is that this comes, or should have come, from his father.

It follows that the relationship with Clara Dawes, where the impersonality of passion is deliberately sought and created, is more willed than real. Clara too has her moment of epiphany, of

revelation as a desirable body, in the scene at her house after the
night at the theatre. Paul creeps downstairs to find her kneeling
naked in the firelight:

> Then he stood, arrested. Clara was kneeling on a pile of white
> underclothing on the hearthrug, her back towards him,
> warming herself. She did not look around, but sat crouching on
> her heels, and her rounded, beautiful back was towards him,
> and her face was hidden. She was warming her body at the fire
> for consolation. The glow was rosy at one side, the shadow was
> dark and warm on the other. (S & L(P) 403–4)

The description is like that of a heavenly body in partial eclipse.
The words 'rosy' and 'warm' suggest a polar opposition to what is
'blanched' and cool in Miriam. The revelation of the available
and desirable body has none of the Christian-religious overtones
associated with Miriam: this adoration is purely pagan: 'She
stood letting him adore her and tremble with joy of her'.

But this love too is crippled by its one-sidedness. Paul goes to
Clara for the satisfaction of a need ('I don't know anything. Be
with me now, will you, no matter what is is?'). Being 'with' him is
responding to his demand, and turns out to be too much like
mothering a demanding child: it is not the same as being 'there'
with him. So it is a failure too, in the end.

> ... Clara was not there for him, only a woman, warm,
> something he loved and almost worshipped, there in the dark.
> But it was not Clara, and she submitted to him. (S & L(P) 420)

There again is the element of sacrifice: she is denied something,
and in the end she expresses a justified grievance in terms not
unlike Miriam's.

Yet the experience is not a small thing. Indeed, in describing it,
Lawrence moves into the language-range familiar later in *The
Rainbow*:

> All the while the peewits were screaming in the field. When
> he came to, he wondered what was near his eyes, curving and
> strong with life in the dark, and what voice it was speaking.
> Then he realised it was the grass, and the peewit was calling.
> The warmth was Clara's breathing heaving. He lifted his head,

and looked into her eyes. They were dark and shining and strange, life wild at the source staring into his life, stranger to him, yet meeting him; and he put his face down on her throat, afraid. What was she? A strong, strange, wild life, that breathed with his in the darkness through this hour. It was all so much bigger than themselves that he was hushed. They had met, and included in their meeting the thrust of the manifold grass-stems, the cry of the peewit, the wheel of the stars . . .

And after such an evening they both were very still, having known the immensity of passion. They felt small, half afraid, childish and wondering, like Adam and Eve when they lost their innocence and realised the magnificence of the power which drove them out of Paradise and across the great night and the great day of humanity. It was for each of them an initiation and a satisfaction. To know their own nothingness, to know the tremendous living flood which carried them always, gave them rest within themselves. If so great a magnificent power could overwhelm them, identify them altogether with itself, so that they knew they were only grains in the tremendous heave that lifted every grass-blade its little height, and every tree, and living thing, then why fret about themselves? They could let themselves be carried by life, and they felt a sort of peace each in the other. (*S & L*(P) 421)

This is impressive, as it is meant to be. Lawrence is deliberately trying to establish something as important, but it also seems a shade portentous. The device, like a reverse camera-zoom, of making his characters suddenly seem like 'grains' because the viewpoint is, in a flash, infinitely distant and it is the whole universe that we are looking at was tried occasionally in *The Trespasser* and recurs in *Sons and Lovers* – most notably in the last paragraphs of the whole book, where the word 'grains' is met again.[7] But because the feeling is willed the expression becomes overemphatic. Lawrence wants to present a positive experience (despite the limitation), and needs to make it real, as a polar opposite of the experience with Miriam. It is needed for the symmetry of the novel: Clara has to represent an attitude which is not Miriam's – reckless, mindless even, in her passion. Yet she cannot give Paul what he needs as much or more, what he can only get from Miriam. The overall pattern is touching, if a little too neat, but the imagined part, however grandly it is written up (as here), is never as real in its splendour as the real part is convincing in its bafflement and sadness.

Some justice is done to Clara. Like Miriam, she casts in Paul's teeth his ultimate inability to love. She says

> "You've never come near to me. You can't come out of yourself, you can't . . .".
> "I feel . . . as if I hadn't got you, as if all of you weren't there, and as if it weren't me you were taking. . . . You've never given me yourself." (*S & L*(P) 430–1)

The charge is justified: it was something Lawrence had heard from his own women. So the affair with Clara dies as Mrs Morel dies. It is suggested that Clara has won something out of the defeat: it has been for her, as having Miriam was for Paul, an 'initiation', and she has through the affair 'gained herself' – she has grown into the next phase of her existence as a more maturely developed or solidly based self: so it has been a 'baptism of life'.

It remains for Paul simply to give her up, so that Clara may return to her husband Baxter Dawes, who has been lurking in the background as a rival (the word is used half-a-dozen times). He and Paul at one moment have a climactic fight which both releases their antagonism and also links them in a curious bond.[8] The reader will remember the idea as present in several of the short stories, and more mysteriously in *The White Peacock*. Annable was the first alter ego: fatherly to Paul, but dangerous because of his thwarted maleness. A similar but younger figure, in direct competition for a loved woman had been introduced in 'The Shades of Spring' and 'A Modern Lover'. There had been an actual struggle with a husband in 'The Old Adam'. This passage in the fight between Paul and Dawes anticipates something similar in 'The Prussian Officer', where the wordless opposition of a strange rivalry reaches a consummation in the death of both combatants:

> . . . his knuckles dug in the throat of the other man. He was a pure instinct, without reason or feeling. His body, hard and wonderful in itself, cleaved against the struggling body of the other man; not a muscle in him relaxed. He was quite unconscious, only his body had taken upon itself to kill this other man. For himself, he had neither feeling nor reason. He

lay pressed hard against his adversary, his body adjusting itself to its one pure purpose of choking the other man, resisting at exactly the right moment, with exactly the right amount of strength, the struggles of the other, silent, intent, unchanging, gradually pressing its knuckles deeper, feeling the struggles of the other body become wilder and more frenzied. Tighter and tighter grew his body, like a screw that is gradually increasing in pressure, till something breaks. (*S & L*(P) 434)

Once the 'bond' has been in this strange way cemented, it is easier for Paul to relinquish Clara to her husband as a natural solution, a disembarrassment. But that is an imagined solution. With Miriam, Lawrence was writing about a painful actuality. So the reader finds Paul repeatedly breaking off the relationship with Miriam, and then coming back to her. This is one aspect of the less sure progress of the Second Part of the book: one feels that Lawrence like Paul, is looking for a way forward, and not finding one: so the imagined Clara is brought in to provide a way out.

We see the long painful process mostly through Paul's eyes – especially his exasperated perception of Miriam's submissive nature, which both shrinks and clenches itself to take things in, like a sea-anemone. Paul and his mother fear and hate this capacity of Miriam's to absorb him in a spiritual banquet. It is well conveyed in vivid little scenes: how she cannot let the hens peck food from her fingers, jump from a stile into Paul's arms (Clara can, and is shown doing it), cannot let herself go on the swing. Yet she feels intensities of adoration in the presence of flowers, birds' nests and all the things into which she can pour herself. But that is the wrong phrase: rather she drinks them up, and it is characteristic that she brings things up to her lips, taking them as nearly into herself as she can.

The intensity with which that is conveyed verges on dislike. Paul is irritated into bullying her in the lessons he gives her: her capacity, shrinking, to take punishment arouses his capacity to abuse her. He wants to fling his pencil in her face. We are perhaps in the presence of a potential murderer and murderee – at any rate, the profound if hidden desire to be abused arouses the corresponding willingness to tyrannise. A whole aspect of sacrifice is explored here – and what it does to both parties. In a way, it turns him into a butcher, even a monster.

The second (or is it the third?) time that they break off is after she has given herself to him in the passage described above. In conventional moral terms, he has slighted her sacrifice and exploited her monstrously. Yet it is still seen through his eyes, until one moment when we are suddenly forward in the world of 'New Eve and Old Adam'.

She bit her finger moodily. She thought over their whole affair. She had known it would come to this; she had seen it all along. It chimed with her bitter expectation.

"Always – it has always been so!" she cried. "It has been one long battle between us – you fighting away from me."

It came from her unawares, like a flash of lightning. The man's heart stood still. Was this how she saw it?

"But we've had *some* perfect hours, *some* perfect times, when we were together!" he pleaded.

"Never!" she cried; "Never! It has always been you fighting me off."

"Not always – not at first!" he pleaded.

"Always, from the very beginning – always the same!"

She had finished, but she had done enough. He sat aghast. He had wanted to say, 'It has been good, but it is at an end'. And she – she whose love he had believed in when he had despised himself – denied that their love had ever been love. 'He had always fought away from her?' Then it had been monstrous. There had never been anything really between them; all the time he had been imagining something where there was nothing. And she had known. She had known so much, and had told him so little. She had known all the time. All the time this was at the bottom of her!

He sat silent in bitterness. At last the whole affair appeared in a cynical aspect to him. She had really played with him, not he with her. (*S & L*(P) 359–60)

The moment is finely caught. She is given her flash of just indignation. But because she exaggerates, allowing nothing to have been good (and the reader has seen much that was good) Paul is given grounds for his self-justifying compensatory bitterness. It shows a littleness in him, but people have such moments. The trouble is not that Lawrence can't give his fictional representative a weakness, as that he so persistently adopts his point of view, and his mother's, and so rarely Miriam's – except in her self-abasing sacrificial mood.

At the very end, in the chapter 'Derelict', Paul has lost his mother and Clara and is indeed derelict. He sees Miriam, and they have a last conversation. She offers him marriage, presented as her way of mothering him. He contemplates the idea, and turns the offer back to her.

This seems to have been a crucial scene for Lawrence and perhaps it echoes something that actually happened. Both 'A Modern Lover' and 'The Shades of Spring' dramatise such a last encounter, and while the second is imagined, the first seems real. In it Mersham lies in the armchair in what seems to have been Lawrence's characteristic posture, 'his fine white hands hanging over the arms of the chair like dead-white stoats from a bough'. In *Sons and Lovers*

> His hands lay quite inert on the arms of his chair. She was aware of them. She felt that now he lay at her mercy. If she could rise, take him, put her arms round him, and say, 'You are mine', then he would leave himself to her. But dare she? She could easily sacrifice herself. But dare she assert herself?

This was a question which preoccupied the Lawrence of *The White Peacock*, in a diffuse way. And of course the capacity to assert oneself, to take what one really wants, is a central postulate of all his work.[9] The ability, the courage, to come forward and make one's claim, if only in a gesture, is also explored in the short stories. He continues:

> She was aware of his dark-clothed slender body, that seemed one stroke of life, sprawled in the chair close to her. But no; she dared not put her arms around it, take it up, and say, 'It is mine, this body. Leave it to me'. And she wanted to. It called to all her woman's instinct. But she crouched, and dared not. She was afraid he would not let her.

For a moment the 'dark-clothed slender body, that seemed one stroke of life' is seen as an inversion of those other male bodies, unclothed, which make a mute appeal to Louisa Lindley in 'Daughters of the Vicar', to the widow Elizabeth in 'Odour of Chrysanthemums', and elsewhere. It seems to require a proprietorial claim – but that gesture Lawrence tended to repudiate. Here in any case Miriam cannot make the gesture, and her inability, expressed characteristically as a gesture of the hands, makes a silent appeal to Paul, who shows that *he* can cross the divide, make the gesture, and also make her appeal for her in words:

> Her impotence before him, before the strong demand of some unknown thing in him, was her extremity. Her hands fluttered; she half-lifted her head. Her eyes, shuddering, appealing, gone almost distracted, pleaded to him suddenly. His heart caught with pity. He took her hands, drew her to him and comforted her.
> "Will you have me, to marry me?" he said very low. (*S & L*(P) 489)

The physical gesture, of kindness and kinship, repeats the gesture made in the short stories, and prefigures a crucial moment in 'New Eve and Old Adam'. It expresses warmth and tenderness, but Paul has to admit, from his consciousness, that he does not want this marriage. It is the final wound. Miriam's response is maternal, and of course it is not another mother that he wants:

> . . . raising herself with dignity, she took his head to her bosom, and rocked him softly. She was not to have him then! So she could comfort him. She put her fingers through his hair. For her, the anguished sweetness of self-sacrifice. For him, the hate and misery of another failure . . .
> It was the end then between them. She could not take him and relieve him of the responsibility of himself. She could only sacrifice herself to him – sacrifice herself every day, gladly. And that he did not want. He wanted her to hold him, and say, with joy and authority: 'Stop all this restlessness and beating against death. You are mine for a mate'. She had not the strength. Or was it a mate she wanted? Or did she want a Christ in him?

That passing thought is not amplified or explained.[10] But the inner process goes on:

> He felt in leaving her, he was defrauding her of life. But he knew that, in staying, stifling the inner, desperate man, he was denying his own life. And he did not hope to give life to her by denying his own. (*S & L*(P) 490)

Perhaps that *is* a reflection of the Christ-reference. Did Christ give life to people by denying his own? But essentially it is a rejection of the whole idea of sacrifice.

As for him, with his mother dead and Clara and Miriam both dismissed as not adequate to his need, he is left in a void which is physically felt – an emptiness which radiates from him. The final lines of the book are a climactic utterance of great intensity and depth of meaning. Here coincide some of Lawrence's most deeply instinctive feelings. They are like mental gestures at the boundary of consciousness, trying to get the largest meanings into focus:

> When he turned away [from Miriam] he felt the last hold for him had gone. The town . . . stretched away over the bay of railway, a level fume of lights. Beyond the town the country, little smouldering spots for more towns – the sea – the night – on and on! And he had no place in it!

Earlier in the book Lawrence had once or twice used the Hardy-like trick of imagining an immensely distant viewpoint so that the characters look minute. Here for a moment we have the natural perspective of a wide view: that viewpoint can be giddily turned into the cosmic one. This is about to happen. But it is also made intensely Lawrence's personal vision by an idiosyncrasy:

> Whatever point he stood on, there he stood alone. From his breast, from his mouth, sprang the endless space, and it was there behind him everywhere. (*S & L*(P) 491)

For a paragraph or two, I must digress, and bring to bear the other loci which give these two sentences their force. For instance, this vertiginous solitude, as of the unsupported centre of a strange empty world, reminds us of what had seemed an odd chance remark to Clara. Looking at some bluebells straying beyond the boundary of a wood, Paul had said:

> "It makes me think of the wild men of the woods, how terrified they would be when they got breast to breast with the open space."
>
> "Do you think they were?" she asked.
>
> "I wonder which was more frightened among old tribes – those bursting out of their darkness of woods upon all the space of light, or those from the open tiptoeing into the forests."

"I should think the second," she answered.

"Yes, you *do* feel like one of the open space sort, trying to force yourself into the dark, don't you?" (*S & L*(P) 296)

That gives us the notion of being 'breast to breast', and of straying into or out of a circle, and into light or into darkness. But the idea of being alone, unsupported, perhaps unreal in consequence, is an inversion of his feelings about his mother:

> There was one place in the world that stood solid and did not melt into unreality: the place where his mother was. Everybody else could grow shadowy, almost non-existent to him, but she could not. It was as if the pivot and pole of his life, from which he could not escape, was his mother. (*S & L*(P) 278)

One part of this complex feeling is his inability to escape. But another part is the substantial self-sufficiency which Mrs Morel herself feels: it carries her through her married life, and she senses it in related terms from very early in the book:

> Mrs Morel was alone, but she was used to it. Her son and her little girl slept upstairs; so, it seemed, her home was there behind her, fixed and stable. (*S & L*(P) 39)

Having something known and solid behind you, and feeling safe, is a universal need. But Paul has imported into the feeling the characteristic notion of the pole, the pivot at the centre of the circle of consciousness. What is behind you, in good circumstances, is known and stable. What is in front of you is unknown and may be dangerous. At the centre is something erect, fixed and solitary.

The idea is given a powerful extension in the description of Paul's childhood games at night. Whenever he left his house as a child 'the whole great night opened out, in a hollow, with a little tangle of lights below. . . . The farthest tiny lights seemed to stretch out the darkness for ever'. We are approaching the cosmic dread of the end of the book. What mitigates it here is the lamp-post:

> The children looked anxiously down the road at the one lamp-post, which stood at the end of the field-path. If the little, luminous space were deserted, the two boys felt genuine desolation . . .

There was only this one lamp-post. Behind was the great scoop of darkness, as if all the night were there. In front another wide dark way opened over the hill brow. Occasionally somebody came out of this way and went into the field down the path. In a dozen yards the night had swallowed them. The children played on . . .

They would also fight between themselves, leading to a strange sequel:

Paul never forgot, after one of these fierce internecine fights, seeing a big red moon lift itself up, slowly between the waste road over the hill-top, steadily like a great bird. And he thought of the Bible, that the moon should be turned to blood.[11] And the next day he made haste to be friends with Billy Pillins. And then the wild, intense games went on again under the lamp-post, surrounded by so much darkness. Mrs Morel, going into the parlour, would hear the children singing away . . . they had the feel of wild creatures singing. It stirred the mother: and she understood when they came in at eight o'clock, ruddy, with brilliant eyes, and quick, passionate speech. (*S & L*(P) 116–17)

We begin to make the associative links which led from point to point in this mental world. The circle of safe lamplight is related to, and guaranteed by, the nearby home itself, and the mother in the lighted home. Out there in the night the children can be like the wild creatures which haunt around outside the circle;[12] but it is essential that they are able to return, and always to feel the stability provided by the mother. That in turn explains the earlier passage which links the noise of the wind in the great ashtree in front of the house, the equally frightening sound of their parent's violent quarrels, and the intensely wished-for restoration of security:

Having such a great space in front of the house gave the children a feeling of night, of vastness and of terror. This terror came in from the shrieking of the tree and the anguish of the home discord. . . . He [their father] might hit their mother again. There was a feeling of horror, a kind of bristling in the darkness and a sense of blood . . .
. . . Then at last, if the wind allowed, they heard the water of the

tap drumming into the kettle, which their mother was filling for morning, and they could go to sleep in peace.

So they were happy in the morning – happy, very happy playing, dancing at night round the lonely lamp-post in the midst of the darkness. (*S & L*(P) 98–9)

The central perception here is of the pivot, focus, or pole – the lamp-post which sheds its kindly light, and reminds one of the home that is waiting in the dark, and the mother in the home. The light gives a circle of safety; or, if you stand at the centre as if you *were* the lamp-post, a semi-circle which is the area of your vision. This goes beyond the light into the limitless dark. All that space starts at the breast, and the hands go out into it. By a natural but dreaded inversion, the circle of light can be a circle of darkness: the wood,[13] out of which the bluebells flow, or out of which the savage tribes burst. These are amazed to find themselves 'breast to breast' with a world of light. The idea of being 'breast to breast with the universe' is a constant in Lawrence, recurring for the last time in his very last work, *Apocalypse*.[14] How you feel about being breast to breast with it depends on your feeling of being in your element, or being supported. Support comes from behind, and in Lawrence's case meant having a woman at his back. In Paul Morel's case the pivot, the support, has been removed with his mother's death. Since she has gone from behind him there is emptiness and darkness behind him as well as in front, and it threatens to invade his circle of light. This is a danger which Siegmund had felt in *The Trespasser*: you can become as if pervious; and space and death can seep into you, as if you were leaking in reverse. That too is expressed in *Sons and Lovers*, in the passage which begins

There was a great hollow of darkness fronting him, and on the black upslopes patches of tiny lights, and in the lowest trough of the light, a flare of the pit.

It goes on

If Miriam caused his mother suffering, then he hated her – and he easily hated her. Why did she make him feel as if he were uncertain of himself, insecure, an indefinite thing, as if he had not sufficient sheathing to prevent the night and the space breaking into him? (*S & L*(P) 246)

Because she would displace his mother, she is this threat. We see that Miriam could never hope to win.

To return to the conclusion of the whole book: the passage continues:

> The people hurrying along the streets offered no obstruction to the void in which he found himself. There were small shadows whose footsteps and voices could be heard, but in each of them the same night, the same silence. He got off the car. In the country all was dead still. Little stars shone high up; little stars spread far away in the flood-waters, a firmament below. Everywhere the vastness and terror of the immense night which is roused and stirred for a brief while by the day, but which returns, and will remain at last eternal, holding everything in its silence, and its living gloom.

From its immensely distant viewpoint, the passage begins to take off into the Hardy-like cosmic vision. But the feeling is not determined by any Schopenhauerian or Darwinian sense of the neutrality of the universe or the deadness of God: rather by the deadness of the mother who had sustained the universe for him. So it is a movement towards death, because she is dead and has taken all sense of life with her. If he is to survive he has to counter this sense of eternality in his loss. A new movement of the mind begins:

> There was no Time, only Space. Who could say his mother had lived and did not live? She had been in one place, and was in another, that was all.

This is a dubious rationalising self-consolation, but shows an effort towards an acceptance which will also comfort him:

> And his soul could not leave her, wherever she was. Now she was gone abroad into the night, and he was with her still. They were together . . .

So, having been the light, when he was in the light, she is now the dark in which he also stands. I use that word deliberately, since the sense of *his* being now (in the course of nature, since she has gone) the upright figure which must stand alone at the centre of his own circle, whether light or dark – this has to become an acceptance too, a firm resolve. His mind moves on in this direction:

> But yet there was his body, his chest, that leaned against the stile, his hands on the wooden bar. They seemed something. Where was he? – One tiny upright speck of flesh, less than an ear of wheat lost in the field.

The chest, pressed against the stile, reminds him by that pressure that he exists, that he is solid, and 'breast to breast' with the universe. The hands are 'something' because they are him, and because they are his most immediate and instinctive intermediary with the whole outside world into which they reach.[15] As for the tiny upright speck, which is himself, the fact that it is 'upright' has to be set against the fact that it is also infinitely small. The 'ear of wheat' turns gold when it is ripe, and at the back of Lawrence's mind, I think, is the Biblical text which had an abiding significance for him: 'Verily, verily I say unto you, Except a corn of wheat fall into the ground and die, it abideth alone: but if it die, it bringeth forth much fruit'. (John 12.24). The beginnings of a firm stance which are struggling into being in him are almost swept away by his own sense of limitation:

> He could not bear it. On every side the immense dark silence seemed pressing him, so tiny a spark, into extinction, and yet, almost nothing, he could not be extinct. Night, in which everything was lost, went reaching out, beyond stars and sun. Stars and sun, a few bright grains, went spinning round for terror, and holding each other in embrace, there in a darkness that outpassed them all and left them tiny and daunted. So much, and himself, infinitesimal, at the core a nothingness, and yet not nothing.

The will to go on is being formed, even in the heart of this terror of nothingness. He is a 'spark', and so a source of light; he is therefore linked with the sun and the stars. He had been 'an ear of wheat' just before, and sun and stars are also 'bright grains'. From the point of view of the universe they are as minute, within their system, as he is, one grain in the field of wheat. But they give light, and he is on their side: indeed the association with the sun, almost suppressed here, but just volunteered as an inkling of hope, is Lawrence's way out of his impasse. For the whole of the book enforces the impression that while the mother is a 'light' to him, she is a light in the dark. When she goes out, it is therefore night. What he needs is day, the sun. The passage ends:

> "Mother!" he whimpered – "mother!"
> She was the only thing that held him up, himself, amid all this. And she was gone, intermingled herself. He wanted her to touch him, have him alongside with her.
> But no, he would not give in. Turning sharply, he walked towards the city's gold phosphorescence. His fists were shut, his mouth set fast. He would not take that direction to the darkness, to follow her. He walked towards the faintly humming, glowing town, quickly. (*S & L*(P) 491–2)

The last impulse towards her and death is resisted. He has to leave her. As he sets off 'quickly' for the town, for the world of human activity which has during this process offered him its prospect of a 'fume' of lights, his fists are clenched: the gesture of self-enclosure, self-support and determination which Siegmund had developed and then noticed as he went to his entirely different fate. We can safely assume that Lawrence has moved away from Siegmund's impulse to suicide as entire negation, defeat and collapse.

In later life Lawrence thought he had been unfair to his father, had taken too much his mother's side. Yet he was the man who also said 'Never trust the artist. Trust the tale'. Most readers feel that something like justice has been done: that the father, who is shown being snapped at, snubbed, patronised and ignored by his family is shown also to have his qualities. We remember in particular the little gestures of love that he makes to Paul (getting none in return), the courtliness that he shows to his sons' young women, the frequent moments of respect for his wife (even his anger is that of an inferior), the grief at the older son's death and the scarcely comprehending pride in the younger son's success. Other critics have pointed to the gaiety which he spreads around him as he does his little household tasks, and the careful description of his working day – especially his getting up in the silent house, eating his breakfast and setting off for the pit. His work is a discipline, almost a vocation, and the life is in its way fulfilling. His limitations are clearly described: grasped at a very deep level – the fear of the unknown or the incomprehensible outside world that is felt by a totally instinctual being locked in a very small circle of experience and unable mentally to reach outside it: comforting himself with drink and sociability at the pub because it is secure, unthinking, familiar and warm, and gives him what he does not get at home.

Most readers end the book with a warm feeling for Walter Morel, for all his limitations, and his moments of contemptible violence. If at the end he is a ruin, and diminished in esteem, it is inevitable that a man whose whole being depended on physical strength and youthful glow should lose that strength and that glow. But that is sad, not reprehensible. And that he married a 'conscious' woman capable quickly of discounting the charm and the glow, but never of forgiving the limitations – that is a tragedy, for both of them. It means that much of their married life was a conflict; but it is stupid to think that conflict is avoidable, or totally wasted energy, and there is a grim point of view which says that they fought their fight out, and did not run away from it.[16]

Thinking about Lawrence himself, one feels that it was always likely that he would manage, despite himself, to do his father some kind of justice, because his father was the first and original representative of the kind of man who mattered vitally to Lawrence. He could only imagine how his father had been before he was born, or even before the marriage, so the unmistakable glamour which is given in the early pages to the young Walter Morel could only come either from his mother's account (in which case she retained a soft spot for the man she married) or from Lawrence's own imagination. The choice of crucial words and images establishes things which no later conceptual analysis can dissolve:

> He danced well, as if it were natural and joyous in him to dance. . . . Gertrude Coppard watched the young miner as he danced, a certain subtle exultation like glamour in his movement, and his face the flower of his body, ruddy, with tumbled black hair, and laughing alike whatever partner he bowed above. (*S & L*(P) 44)

George Saxton dances well too, so do Elsie Whiston and Sam Adams in 'The White Stocking': it is the poetry of the body and the blood, and expresses, better than words and thought can, vigour and joy and an unclenching of the self. The almost incidental but

inevitable remark about the face being the flower of the body puts
Walter among Lawrence's elect. Only the noble are flowers:
most of us are cabbages, or at best cauliflowers. At the end of the
same paragraph, other crucial words establish a network of
correspondences which spreads through the whole book:

> She was a puritan, like her father, high-minded and really stern.
> Therefore the dusky, golden softness of this man's sensuous
> flame of life, that flowed off his flesh like the flame from a candle,
> not baffled and gripped into incandescence by thought and
> spirit as her life was, seemed to her something wonderful,
> beyond her. (*S & L*(P) 45)

That is a moment of awe and self-transcendence that Mrs
Morel does not often repeat, and it is *her* limitation that she
doesn't. She here feels something essential to Lawrence's
universe, which, since it is a feeling, can only be represented in
analogies. But the candle-flame which rises straight up off the
body of the candle by a natural and invisible upward movement of
the melting wax, always stands, for Lawrence, as a representation
of the unforced flow of life at its best; the soft golden light has both
gentleness and warmth. It is contrasted here with the pressure-
lamp, where air and spirit-vapour are pumped up under
piston-pressure to hiss through a mantle and produce a fierce
white light. This figure represents the action of the will, of
thought, of conscience, morality and social pressures, to produce a
forced mental illumination.

So Morel offers – or he does as a young man, as a remembered
or imagined ideal – an implicit standard by which others are
judged, and notably the inversions of the standard: Miriam and
Gertrude Morel herself. It is an odd business, since the source of
the standard is never acknowledged as such. One has to feel for the
metaphors and then go down to their roots. We are much more
conscious of the adverse judgement that is being made: of Miriam,
for instance, who is well caught by a single sentence of Paul's: 'But
even your joy is a flame coming off of sadness.' And a paragraph or
two later, it is said of her:

> All the life of Miriam's body was in her eyes, which were usually
> dark as a dark church, but could flame with light like a
> conflagration.

And again:

> There was no looseness or abandon about her. Everything was gripped stiff with intensity, and her effort, overcharged, closed in on itself. (*S & L*(P) 203)

So in so far as she is a candle, it is a sad or paradoxically dark one; and if she bursts into flame it is a disaster. The word 'gripped', used of Miriam several times, may remind us of gestures of the hands, especially of Siegmund's hands clenched over his thumbs. It also links back with the phrase 'gripped into incandescence' used of Mrs Morel, so that there is a carrying-forward of the basic light-image used of both women. It is the pressure-lamp again, as 'overcharged' suggests; and this is made evident in the passage already discussed, where it is said in passing that 'From his mother he drew the life-warmth, the strength to produce; Miriam urged this warmth into intensity, like a white light.' The white light links both women: so that, although they fight each other for Paul they are actually of the same kind, wanting to do the same things for him. Was that thought the one which most wounded Jessie Chambers? Was it an unfairness, or a deep insight she could not face? The implicit contrast is with Walter Morel, who alone in the book (unless Clara Dawes is allowed to have something of his nature) represents the other polarity.

One striking element in the description of his 'light' was that it had 'a dusky golden softness'. This in him which is soft and golden and ruddy is contrasted with something hard and white in them: something warm with something cold, something sun-like with something moon-like. A few pages after this passage, and in the same chapter, occurs the strange night-scene (one of the 'outcrops') where Mrs Morel, pregnant, has been locked out in the night by the drunken Morel after a bitter quarrel. He falls asleep and she cannot get back into the house. Without any warning we are suddenly in an atmosphere of strange intensity, where what is noticed and represented is obviously carrying a high charge of significance. The symbols (to use the convenient word) are ones that Lawrence resorted to repeatedly – though he could not always have said what they mean, and nor can we. They appear at their hours like the sun and moon themselves. And indeed, sun and moon[17] are chief among them.

The moon was high and magnificent in the August night. Mrs Morel, seared with passion, shivered to find herself out there in a great white light, that fell cold on her, and gave a shock to her inflamed soul.

The great white light that fell cold on her is related to the white light that the conscious women try to 'grip into incandescence'. Yet here it is an outside influence, from the feminine heavenly body.

Mrs Morel is obsessively gripped round her resentment of the scene that has just passed – almost delirious with it. It is some time before 'the presence of the night came again to her'. Conscious again

She hurried out of the side garden to the front, where she could stand as if in an immense gulf of white light, the moon streaming high in face of her, the moonlight standing up from the hills in front, and filling the valley where the Bottoms crouched, almost blindingly.

Then there is another movement of consciousness:

She became aware of something about her. With an effort she roused herself to see what it was that penetrated her consciousness. The tall white lilies were reeling in the moonlight, and the air was charged with their perfume, as with a presence. Mrs Morel gasped slightly in fear. She touched the big pallid flowers on their petals, then shivered. They seemed to be stretching in the moonlight. . . . She bent down to look at the binful of yellow pollen, but it only appeared dusky. Then she drank a deep draught of the scent. It almost made her dizzy.

When finally she gets back inside and is going to bed 'As she unfastened her brooch at the mirror, she smiled faintly to see her face all smeared with the yellow dust of lilies. She brushed it off, and at last lay down'. (*S & L*(P) 59–62)

Once more this is not algebra. One can't just say that the moon 'stands for' a will-driven feminine dominance which is cold; nor that the lilies 'stand for' a remembered passion now passing away; nor that the pollen on her face, easily brushed off, is her own participation in that passion. That association is enforced by the

word 'yellow', which reminds us of Walter. And the other word
'dusky' was used of Walter's soft golden light, like a yellow candle
flame; so some opposition between the cold white light and his
warm golden light, but more complicated, is being implied. It is
complicated because of the associations (for instance) of the lilies
themselves. They are the flowers presented by the angel to the
Virgin at the Annunciation, and Mrs Morel is here carrying Paul.
They imply a virginity in the woman which has survived the
passion and the impregnation – perhaps not been touched by it.

The same set of notations recurs in the chapter 'The Test on
Miriam'. Paul has taken Miriam, but felt it was a sacrifice. He is
being impelled, without knowing it, away from this violation of a
constant virginity towards a frank self-giving in passion – that is,
toward Clara. There is between him and Miriam a suppressed
conflict not very far from that between his father and his mother.
He has a kind of annunciation of his own, clearly related to his
mother's strange experience before his birth:

> Through the open door, stealthily, came the scent of
> madonna lilies, almost as if it were prowling abroad. Suddenly
> he got up and went out of doors.
> The beauty of the night made him want to shout. A
> half-moon, dusky gold, was sinking behind the black sycamore
> at the end of the garden, making the sky dull purple with its
> glow. Nearer, a dim white fence of lilies went across the garden,
> and the air all round seemed to stir with scent, as if it were alive.
> He went across the bed of pinks, whose keen perfume came
> sharply across the rocking, heavy scent of the lilies, and stood
> alongside the white barrier of flowers. They flagged all loose, as
> if they were panting. The scent made him drunk. He went down
> to the field to watch the moon sink under.
> A corncrake in the hay-close called insistently. The moon slid
> quite quickly downwards, growing more flushed. Behind him
> the great flowers leaned as if they were calling. And then, like a
> shock, he caught another perfume, something raw and coarse.
> Hunting round, he found the purple iris, touched their fleshy
> throats and their dark grasping hands. At any rate, he had found
> something. They stood stiff in the darkness. Their scent was
> brutal. The moon was melting down upon the crest of the hill. It
> was gone, all was dark. The corncrake called still.
> Breaking off a pink, he suddenly went indoors.

"Come, my boy," said his mother. "I'm sure it's time you went to bed".

He stood with the pink against his lips.

"I shall break off with Miriam, mother," he answered calmly . . . .

"On Sunday I break off," he said, smelling the pink. He put the flower in his mouth. Unthinking, he bared his teeth, closed them on the blossom slowly, and had a mouthful of petals. These he spat into the fire, kissed his mother, and went to bed. (*S & L*(P) 355–6)

The symbolism is not as obvious as it seems. The moon is once more the agent of annunciations of feminine influence and power. But here it is 'dusky gold' and that is a 'good' colour, borrowed from the sun. The lilies, identified as Madonna lilies, have the equivocal mixture of the virginal and the sexual. One can hardly say that they 'stand', simply, for Miriam: rather for something which both she, and more powerfully Paul's mother share: something which Paul needs and is intoxicated by. At any rate their whiteness is like the white light of the incandescent consciousness. The coarse raw scent which strikes across that more spiritual scent is more obviously that of passion, of frank sexuality. It is characteristic that Paul should 'touch their fleshy throats and their dark grasping hands': the throat here as elsewhere is the juncture between face and body, and Lawrence focuses on it obsessively: the hands have time and again been seen as the necessary wordless instrument of direct contact, of possession.

The unexpected element is the pink; and one might with some plausibility guess that it stands for that in Miriam which he has taken and gobbled up, greedily, and is now about to spit out. Paul is given to eating flowers at crucial moments:[18] earlier in the same chapter, out in the fields with Miriam and Clara, picking cowslips

He kneeled on one knee, quickly gathering the best blossoms, moving from tuft to tuft restlessly, talking softly all the time. Miriam plucked the flowers lovingly, lingering over them. He always seemed to her too quick and almost scientific. Yet his bunches had a natural beauty more than hers. He loved them, but as if they were his and he had a right to them. She had more reverence for them: they held something she had not.

The flowers were very fresh and sweet. He wanted to drink
them. As he gathered them, he ate the little trumpets.
(*S & L*(P) 294)

Miriam, we remember, brought things to her mouth, as if to kiss
them, or to draw them into her, and was criticised for it. But Paul
is destructive, almost cannibalistic.

Something important is implied about Miriam and Paul here.
Her reverence is contrasted with his predatoriness; and for a
moment too one thinks of the passage about 'being the sons of
mothers whose husbands had blundered rather brutally through
their feminine sanctities, they were themselves too diffident and
shy. They could easier deny themselves than incur any reproach
from a woman'. This is true only of his long hesitation: Paul does
finally 'blunder rather brutally' through Miriam's feminine
sanctities, and Clara's too: there is more of his father in him than
he could bear to admit – or Lawrence either, but his images do it
for him.

The other related passage, which stands out with the same
intensity, is also concerned with flowers, and has the same
symbolic force, is the episode where Miriam is eager to show Paul
the rose bush in the woods. She has seen it, and wondered at it, but
she needs him to see it. The passage runs:

The tree was tall and straggling. It had thrown its briars over
a hawthorn bush, and its long streamers trailed thick, right
down to the grass, splashing the darkness everywhere with
great split stars, pure white. In bosses of ivory and in large
splashed stars the roses gleamed on the darkness of foliage and
stems and grass. Paul and Miriam stood close together, silent,
and watched. Point after point the steady roses shone out to
them, seeming to kindle something in their souls. The dusk
came like smoke around, and still did not put out the roses.

Paul looked into Miriam's eyes. She was pale and expectant
with wonder, her lips were parted, and her dark eyes lay open to
him. His look seemed to travel down into her. Her soul
answered. It was the communion she wanted. He turned aside
as if pained. He turned to the bush.

"They seem as if they walk like butterflies, and shake
themselves," he said.

She looked at her roses. They were white, some incurved and
holy, others expanded in ecstasy. The tree was dark as a

shadow. She lifted her hand impulsively to the flowers; she went forward and touched them in worship.

"Let us go," he said.

There was a cool scent of ivory roses – a white virgin scent. Something made him feel anxious and imprisoned. (*S & L*(P) 210)

The overtones here are very rich. It is a kind of annunciation again. At the point where 'the dusk . . . still did not put out the roses' I am reminded that 'the light shineth in darkness; and the darkness comprehended it not'. Miriam's ecstasy is essentially chaste, as the whiteness and coolness and the 'virgin scent' insist; yet she is 'open' to Paul and his 'look seemed to travel down into her' – as if he were the angel, or even the Holy Ghost. But this spiritual impregnation, which is what she wants so that things become 'immortal' for her, is evidently not what he wants. Or not only that: there is no doubt that the moment touches him deeply, yet the mystic communion and the spiritual union are not enough; and it is only Miriam who lifts her hand, and goes forward to touch the flowers. Indeed this intensity is what irritates him and makes him cruel to her.

In these culminating passages, which for all readers stand out as particularly rich and impressive, Lawrence is knitting together his various themes. What holds them together is a set of polarities: the white of lilies and roses; the gold of candle flame and pollen; the contrasting scents. Behind the heraldic white and gold stand the sun and the moon. It is the man, Walter Morel, who has in him at the start of the book the dusky gold flame of life. It is the woman, Gertrude Morel, who is associated first with lilies and the moonlight. In the next generation, the girl Miriam, who at the surface level is in conflict with the mother, shares the mother's intensity, and is associated with the worship of the virginal. She is a priestess; she has vowed herself as if to an essential chastity, and in that spirit she sacrifices herself to Paul.

If there is this fundamental opposition or polarity, on what side does Paul himself stand? He is held up by his mother to the sun, from which he came, as if she wanted to offer him back, another sacrifice. He is seen by Miriam in the light of the setting sun. He is at one moment associated with the sunflowers which grow in his mother's garden, and which she tends with special pleasure. But he is not very firmly in the sun's realm, because that is also his father's. He is felt to be, in the symbolism as in the life-situation, torn between the whiteness, the 'blanched and chaste' intimacy of his mother and Miriam, which fosters his intensity and his spiritual knowledge and power, and the 'life' which was at a single early point in the novel so effectively represented by his father. Yet he hates and despises his father.

It is very striking that in *Sons and Lovers* Walter Morel, the archetype of all Lawrence's miners, is never given the reverent ritual washing that in 'Daughters of the Vicar' Alfred Durant receives from his ministering Louisa. Like all miners, Morel has to wash; he is seen doing it once: he is already in decline, but

> He had still a wonderfully young body, muscular, without any fat. His skin was smooth and clear. It might have been the body of a man of twenty-eight

One stops there. Why twenty-eight, in particular? Was Lawrence twenty-eight when he wrote those words? Not quite, as it happens. But he shrinks, as always, from the identification with his father:

> . . . except that there were, perhaps, too many blue scars, like tattoo-marks, where the coal dust remained under the skin, and that his chest was too hairy. But he put his hand on his sides ruefully . . .
>
> Paul looked at his father's thick, brownish hands all scarred, with broken nails, rubbing the fine smoothess of his sides, and the incongruity struck him. It seemed strange they were the same flesh.

The gesture of rubbing the sides we know, from Lawrence's own letter, from the previous fiction; from elsewhere in this book. 'The same flesh' has also been turned into a charged phrase.

Paul half wonders at, half-patronises his father, in his uneasy way ("I suppose," he said to his father, "you had a good figure once.") Mrs Morel allows herself a flash of retrospective pride:

> "You should have seen him as a young man", she cried suddenly to Paul, drawing herself up to imitate her husband's once handsome bearing.
>
> Morel watched her shyly. He saw again the passion she had had for him. It blazed upon her for a moment. He was shy, rather scared, and humble. Yet again he felt his old glow. (*S & L*(P) 250–1)

The 'old glow' is given this brief faint showing, and it may be that this brevity represents the main unfairness of the story. Yet it is also clear from the crucial passages that we have been examining that the 'glow' is one of the poles on which the whole universe of the book rotates. It is another consequence of the unfairness that the other pole – the night-side, of the moon, of lilies, of blanched roses, of spiritual passion, as embodied in Miriam and Mrs Morel – is so constantly turned towards us and so lovingly, so intensely conveyed. Here Lawrence was being faithful to his own experience: these were the main influences on him, his mother and Jessie, and if he had to fight his way out of their embrace as if it were a death, they were nonetheless the people who made him what he was. It was his tragedy that he was alienated from his father, who should have represented the other claim on him – and who is represented in the imagery of the book as the opposite, the good polarity, which cannot be fully recognised.

We come back to the theme of sacrifice. His mother and Miriam are like priestesses, making sacrifices. What they sacrifice first of all is themselves, and one ought to do full justice to their heroic self-denial. Lawrence conveys this, again partly against his conscious intention. But they also, inexorably, want to sacrifice him, Paul Morel, without necessarily knowing or meaning it. They want him to be a particular something, and they want to *know* him fully as that kind of person; they want therefore to own him; and the girl as much as the mother wants to mother him. This is like eating him up in a spiritual communion: or it is like laying a hand on him and saying 'be mine' (flesh of my flesh) in a way which is not that of a wife, but a progenitor. It is inevitable that his mother can only release him by dying. With Miriam he has to act as he does with the pink; first he eats her up and then he spits her out. That must seem a terrible injustice and an almost wanton cruelty; but it comes instinctively from the deepest level, as the only way to survive, to be free; which means being free of guilt as well. At the end of the book he has only just survived, but what he walks toward, with his fists shut, is 'a gold phosphorescence'; the town is 'faintly humming' (like a hive, perhaps); and it is 'glowing'.

Even there, we must have an afterthought. The end of *Sons and Lovers*, like the end of *The Rainbow*, is positive because Lawrence wants it to be. But the breakdown, the despair, the near-madness of Ursula Brangwen just before the end of *The Rainbow* is a very close parallel to the dereliction, the despair, the sense of being pervious to death, in Paul Morel in this other book. The author is asserting that this cannot be the end, and wills his central characters into the effort to move towards the world, towards social human life. The rest of Lawrence's work engages first with marriage, and finds that that, at last, can be achieved. But the most characteristic final gesture of his central characters from now on is not to walk towards the town, but away from it, and away from twentieth-century social life.

7   Short Stories II

The two great masterpieces among the stories begun in the period 1909–11 are 'Daughters of the Vicar' and 'Odour of Chrysanthemums'. Neither reached its present version easily; it was in drastic revision in the period from 1911 until 1913 and 1914 that they reached the form in which we have them, and the changes that Lawrence made in revising them were crucial.[1] Their completion takes us into the first period of his maturity, so that they represent a substantial advance on *Sons and Lovers*, in his own grasp of what he wanted to say, and his ability to express it. Yet they are related to the material of that novel, as well as to the stories already considered.

They do a final justice to the mining community of Eastwood, to the men and women of that life; and they provide a comment also on the relationship of Walter and Gertrude Morel. The dead miner in 'Odour of Chrysanthemums' is called Walter; like Morel he is a drunkard, or in danger of becoming one; his wife Elizabeth is becoming estranged from him. They are imagined living not in one of the Lawrence homes, but in a cottage very close to and very like that in which the Durants live in 'Daughters of the Vicar'. In that story too there is a strong-minded capable wife, but the coarser husband has lived on into a moral eclipse. His beard and his manner remind us of Lawrence's father. Mrs Durant, like Lawrence's mother, has kept a little shop and dies of cancer, and her favourite son Alfred, 'centralised, polarised in his mother', finds it hard not to disintegrate when she is not there behind him. Like Paul Morel and the Wookeys, his mother's power over him has made it hard for him to approach a woman '. . . when the ready woman presented herself, the very fact that she was a palpable woman, made it impossible for him to touch her'.

His two daughters are brought up by the vicar, Mr Lindley, to feel separate because socially superior. One, Miss Mary, marries a 'good' but physically insignificant – indeed repulsive – priest, Mr

Massey, who revealingly prays to God as 'the higher Will'. Mr Massey represents one kind of will, associated with mind, with an abstract spirituality, and the power of money which is an instrument of the social will. The other daughter, Miss Louisa, loves Alfred Durant, who, being a miner, is beneath her socially. He is inarticulate and inhibited compared with Mr Massey's awful rationalising power; but appeals to her because of something she senses in him – life and warmth: he is 'a fine jet of life'. Since he is his mother's favourite, in that archetypal situation where the father is inadequate and is slighted by the mother who lives in and for the child, he is in danger of remaining isolated. It is his good fortune that he is loved by Louisa, since she is genuinely superior: not in the social sense, which would cut her off, but because she has eyes to see, heart to feel, and courage to step forward and claim what she sees is good. She is a true aristocrat, and can assert herself as George Saxton (for instance) could not.

At the outset she, like Alfred, is cut off, uncertain, and longing with the characteristic yearning of Lawrence's young people in all his early works. The emergency which finally crystallises their being by moving them together is the sickness and death of Mrs Durant. Louisa goes to the house to help, and finds that she has to cook for Alfred and wait on him at table. He comes in in his pit-dirt: this entrance is familiar from earlier stories but now has the significance that Lawrence has found in it – not just the miner's social difference, but essential strangeness, otherness:

> Her soul watched him, trying to see what he was. His black face and arms were uncouth, he was foreign. His face was masked black with coal-dust. She could not see him, she could not know him. The brown eyebrows, the steady eyes, the coarse, small moustache above the closed mouth – these were the only familiar indications. What was he, as he sat there in his pit-dirt? She could not see him, and it hurt her. (*PO*(C) 71)

She finds that she has to help further by washing his back. Her first reaction is a natural holding-back and not merely snobbish, but too nearly what her father would feel:

> Curious how it hurt her to take part in their fixed routine of life! Louisa felt the almost repulsive intimacy being forced upon her. It was all so common, so like herding. She lost her own distinctness. (*PO*(C) 72)

That loss is a condition of further life, as the grain of seed must fall into the earth and die. As she goes on, she removes the black mask, the foreignness, and she gets an answer, though not an easy or unequivocal one, to her question, 'what was he?':

> Mechanically, under the influence of habit, he groped in the black water, fished out the soap and flannel, and handed them backwards to Louisa. Then he remained rigid and submissive, his two arms thrust straight in the panchion, supporting the weight of his shoulders. His skin was beautifully white and unblemished, of an opaque, solid whiteness. Gradually Louisa saw it: this also was what he was. It fascinated her. Her feeling of separateness passed away: she ceased to draw back from contact with him and his mother. There was this living centre. Her heart ran hot. She had reached some goal in this beautiful, clear, male body. She loved him in a white, impersonal heat. But the sunburnt, reddish neck and ears: they were more personal, more curious. A tenderness rose in her, she loved even his queer ears. A person – an intimate being he was to her. She put down the towel and went upstairs again, troubled in her heart. (*PO*(C) 72–3)

The last phrase is Biblical, from the Gospels. Miss Louisa has had a kind of Annunciation.[2] We are by these words put in touch with the world where ritual washing (for instance, of Christ's feet by Mary Magdalene, or of the disciples' feet by Christ himself) expresses love and the desire to minister. And this is a world away from the other notion, of 'serving', which Miss Mary represents, for she finds herself serving another will, and so is locked into a reverse of spontaneity. Louisa's Annunciation is confirmed in these words:

> Now her soul was going to open, she was going to see another. She felt strange and pregnant. (*PO*(C) 73)

Alfred has an equivalent vision of Louisa, as this which is before him, strange and for a moment transfigured; causing him both to forget himself and to realise her too as miraculously other:

> As she sat writing, he placed another candle near her. The rather dense light fell in two places on the overfoldings of her

hair till it glistened heavy and bright, like a dense golden plumage folded up. Then the nape of her neck was very white, with fine down and pointed wisps of gold. He watched it as it were a vision, losing himself. She was all that was beyond him, of revelation and exquisiteness. All that was ideal and beyond him, she was that – and he was lost to himself in looking at her. She had no connection with him. He did not approach her. She was there like a wonderful distance. . . . And, when he got out of the house, he was afraid. He saw the stars above ringing with fine brightness, the snow beneath just visible, and a new night was gathering round him. He was afraid almost with obliteration. What was this new night ringing about him, and what was he? (*PO*(C) 75)

The language is very assured, without overt metaphorical display other than the remarkable figure about the hair; yet it is not the language of reflection or ratiocination. It conveys a situation very clearly grasped by the writer. What Alfred receives is something present to him as a vision, not something which he is putting, or could put, into words. The language is now coming close to that of *The Rainbow*, and especially its early part, which seems to me to be a summit of Lawrence's achievement. Alfred Durant's awe in the presence of Louisa is a religious feeling, not unlike Tom Brangwen's in the presence of Lydia; and his moving out into the night under the sky, and feeling the mystery of being there, in process in a world which is also in process, is characteristic of this point in Lawrence's writing. It links him with Hardy, but also shows him to be unique.

Having had this vision of the strangeness, the otherness and the magical attraction of the other, Louisa and Alfred have to cross the gap. This too is something which they do not grasp and could not propose as a considered course of action, though it is something they are moved to do. Part of the difficulty of grasping it consciously is that being able to recognise the other *as* other is related to the process of reaching a new phase of their own being, going beyond the old selves they thought they knew and were fixed in. This can hardly be a conscious thing, and must be rendered as an internal process which is not thinking, scarcely even feeling:

It had nothing to do with his thoughts. Almost it had nothing to do with him. Only it gripped him and he must submit. The whole tide of his soul, gathering in its unknown towards this expansion into death, carried him with it helplessly, all the fritter of his thought and consciousness caught up as nothing, the heave passing on towards its breaking, taking him further than he had ever been. (*PO*(C) 76)

Lawrence has a peculiar calm authority over his people, just saying as from himself what is passing through them. Much in the fiction takes this form. It is a narrative of strange internal events. The characters are not allowed to speak for themselves, or not able to; so that one gets a version of the stream of consciousness which is not that of an 'I'. This is a sign of his clarity about what he is doing. What takes place inside his characters is not consciousness in the strict sense, or not self-consciousness. In people like Alfred Durant or Tom Brangwen, the succession of perceptions or tides of feeling is more like something which simply grips them, moves them, changes them. It is in them, but might almost be outside them: it is the spontaneity of crisis (including prolonged crisis), which is unlike the introspectable and predictable movement of the ego.

So here the tide- or wave-image is no cliché. We meet it in other places, where it conveys the notion of an inexorable, not ulteriorly motivated internal movement. The falling back of the wave equally aptly conveys the idea of something deposited on the beach, beyond its own power of movement or mental range. The paradoxical association with death reminds us again of the death of the Biblical seed; and the two ideas come together in *The Rainbow* in the image of the tide or wave of spring being like a casting of seed, which leaves the newborn on the beach of the earth. Some way below these parable-metaphors is an appropriation of the Christian ideas of spiritual rebirth, symbolised by the Resurrection itself, as well as that rite in which John the Baptist took the new initiates down into the river and immersed them in a washing of the whole body. Louisa's washing of Alfred's body is an Annunciation to her and makes her 'pregnant'; but what she gives birth to is the next stage of herself. Lawrence also releases into the story by way of the Biblical language many of the elements of the old beliefs, but not as the hitherto revealed doctrines. It is as if he has the boldness to take back from Christianity something even older, which had been battened down to serve a puritanical use. He also takes it back into the realm of sexual love from which it had been deflected by Pauline theology; and he reverses the archetypal analogy. For Christians, human love had been dignified by being seen as a mirror, an exemplum, of divine love, so that it was acceptable to use the language of human love in order to speak of the love of God. Hence, perhaps, the Song of Songs, which is allegorised as Christ's love of the Church. But the unbiased reader knows that the Song of Songs is no allegory: it is not erotically divine, it is divinely erotic. It reveals an original substratum which first the Jews and then the Christians made subservient to a religion which in one of its aspects points out of humanity and slights it.[3]

There is in Lawrence, from this early point all the way to 'The Escaped Cock' and *Apocalypse*, a consistent though not always overt reference to Christianity. He is not so much trying to subvert it as to get back to a stage behind it. He is perfectly at home in the original world of the Bible, which is not the world of modern rationalism or positivism, but one filled with power and glory. But if he is against the modern thought-movements which have opposed Christianity, he is also against essential features of the nineteenth-century puritan Anglicanism and Dissent that he grew up with, and which he absorbed daily at chapel, in school, and at home with a pious mother. What he got from that was twofold: a grasp of the Bible, and through its language some ways of perceiving which are not 'thought'; and years in which to ponder human phenomena such as Mr Lindley, Mr Massey and Miss Mary, presented in this story as an ascending order of limited Christian beings.

Mr Lindley is scarcely Christian at all, for all that he is the vicar. His failure as a man is linked to the failure of his vocation, which is deftly conveyed in the first pages of the story with Lawrence's light but lethal touch. A ministry based on the assumption that the shepherd is superior to his flock is annihilated when the flock refuse to be treated as inferior. The Lindleys go on in genteel poverty masked by mad social pride, and this cripples the parents morally: Mrs Lindley becomes a hysterical invalid. But the social pride is not crippled, and when Mr Massey comes into view, and it is seen that he has money and wants Miss Mary, the parents easily persuade themselves that the solution of a money-problem is a match made in Heaven. This is a blasphemy.

The story sets in play various kinds of will and various kinds of faith. Mr Lindley's will is to be the conventional Anglican vicar who, as gentleman, is social as well as moral leader: he will sacrifice his daughter to that social faith. Miss Mary's will is to serve. Louisa's will is not to sacrifice herself that way; she is an intelligent girl, able to judge and form conscious aims, and she says of her family:

> "They are wrong – they are all wrong. They have ground out their souls for what isn't worth anything, and there isn't a grain of love in them anywhere. And I *will* have love. They want us to deny it. They've never found it, so they want to say it doesn't exist. But I *will* have it. I *will* love – it is my birthright. I will love the man I marry – that is all I care about." (*PO*(C) 58–9)

It is a formidable will that she demonstrates, and she shows herself stronger, in mere willpower, than anyone else in the story. So the will is not all bad, for Lawrence: it depends what kind of will it is, and what it does for you and others.

Before Louisa and Alfred manage to reach across to each other we have the very different account of the marriage of Mary to Mr Massey. It is no accident that she is called Mary. The Mary of Luke's Gospel is greeted by the Angel of the Annunciation, at which she is 'troubled'; and she 'ponders in her heart' what she is later told at the Nativity. These questionings are transferred to Louisa in Lawrence's story; his Mary is essentially the willing servitor who says 'behold the handmaid of the Lord'. Her self-sacrifice is presented as the opposite of Louisa's 'will'. Yet in its own way it is an effort of will, and the resistance is provided by something deep in Mary herself.

Mr Massey is slight and sickly, and we have Lawrence's word for it that he is repulsive. He is so to Louisa:

> She was unable to regard him save with aversion. When she saw him from behind, thin and bentshouldered, looking like a sickly lad of thirteen, she disliked him exceedingly, and felt a desire to put him out of existence. (*PO*(C) 50)

Through Louisa Lawrence conveys his own repulsion for the dream-figure of the little man that he conjures up and wants us to shrink from. But, for all the assertions that are made, he never becomes as real as the other characters, and he is a rather abstract repository for a number of things that Lawrence hated and went on hating. It is a mistake of tactics and a sign of animus to make him weak, insignificant and repulsive as a body, in the same way that it is a mistake that Clifford Chatterley is physically shattered and impotent. It loads the scale against him. Lawrence also makes firm judgemental assertions about him:

He had not normal powers of perception. They soon saw that he lacked the full range of human feelings, had rather a strong philosophical mind, from which he lived. His body was almost unthinkable, in intellect he was something definite. The conversation at once took a balanced, abstract tone when he participated. There was no spontaneous exclamation, no violent assertion or expression of personal conviction, but all cold, reasonable assertion. (*PO*(C) 48)

There is a skilful immediate amplification:

This was very hard on Mrs Lindley. The little man would look at her, after one of her pronouncements, and then give, in his thin voice, his own calculated version, so that she felt as if she were tumbling into thin air through a hole in the flimsy floor on which their conversation stood. It was she who felt a fool. Soon she was reduced to a hardy silence. (*PO*(C) 48–9)

But even that is stated, not shown. For dramatisation of what we have been told, we are reduced to the scene in which Mr Lindley visits the dying Mr Durant and with awful aptness 'prayed with a pure lucidity that they all might conform to the higher Will'. We see also that his own will is neatly exemplified in his proposal to Mary. Alfred and Louisa have the greatest difficulty in coming together in marriage, or even saying anything to each other: but Mr Lindley can, as will-driven entity, propose the course of marriage to himself, and then to Mr and Mrs Lindley, and then to Mary. Proposal is the right word: it is conceived, formulated, discussed, put forward, accepted – all a matter of the conscious personality negotiating social procedures and using accepted verbal forms.

It is too plain what Mr Massey stands for: the rational intellect, the life of the top layer of the mind, the social being, religion as a system of observances – all associated with a safe income and a puny body. The animus is shown in Lawrence's unwillingness to do much more than assert. If he had wanted to 'do' Mr Massey as more than a playing-card figure in one of the black suits he would have had to reckon with him as a human being, and he might not have made things easier for himself by making the man repulsive. In principle, it may not matter too much: the main concern is Mary's choice and what it does to *her*. But in practice there is this odd vibration of hatred, and Mary's choice seems more strange and disgusting because of the physical incompatibility: it seems overdone.

Mary and Louisa have a crucial conversation just after the invocation of the higher Will. In her first visit to the Durant's house Louisa has become aware of Alfred as 'a fine jet of life'. Her thoughts are warmed by a quiet undercurrent of Lawrence's favourite positive imagery:

> . . . she wanted to see his face more distinctly in her mind, ruddy with the sun, and his golden-brown eyes, kind and careless, strained now with a natural fear, the fine nose tanned hard by the sun, the mouth that could not help smiling at her. (*PO*(C) 53)

She contrasts him with Massey, feeling he had no right to be there. Mary demurs, saying:

> "He is *really* a Christian."
> "He seems to me nearly an imbecile," said Miss Louisa.
> Miss Mary, quiet and beautiful, was silent for a moment.
> "Oh, no," she said. "Not *imbecile* –"
> "Well, then – he reminds me of a six months child – or a five months child – as if he didn't have time to get developed enough before he was born."
> "Yes," said Miss Mary slowly. "There is something lacking. But there is something wonderful in him: and he is really *good* –"
> "Yes," said Miss Louisa, "it doesn't seem right that he should be. What right has *that* to be called goodness!"
> "But it *is* goodness," persisted Mary. Then she added, with a laugh: "And come, you wouldn't deny that as well."

There was a doggedness in her voice. She went about very quietly. In her soul, she knew what was going to happen. She knew that Mr Massey was stronger than she, and that she must submit to what he was. Her physical self was prouder, stronger than he, her physical self disliked and despised him. But she was in the grip of his moral, mental being. And she felt the days allotted out to her. And her family watched. (*PO*(C) 53)

That last phrase but one is like the Biblical 'the days were accomplished that she should be . . .'. Behold the hand-maid of Mr Massey, one thinks.

It is the effect of the marriage on Mary that mostly interests Lawrence, so that Mr Massey is primarily a mechanism to bring it about. Mary tries to become a 'pure reason' like her husband, a 'pure will'. In this she is like one aspect of Alfred Durant: the part of him that had made him go into the Navy and serve. He has that instinct even with Louisa:

. . . he was stiff before her now, treating her not like a person, but as if she were some sort of will in command, and he a separate, distinct will waiting in front of her. . . . And she hated the military discipline – she was antagonistic to it. Now he was not himself. (*PO*(C) 54)

It is a universal phenomenon, a fatal tendency in which people are 'not themselves'. Mary's choice is a variant of this:

She was a pure will acquiescing to him. She elected a certain kind of fate. She would be good and purely just, . . . she was a pure will towards right. She had sold herself, but had a new freedom. She had got rid of her body. She had sold a lower thing, her body, for a higher thing, her freedom from material things. . . . She had paid with her body: that was henceforward out of consideration. (*PO*(C) 56)

This too is strange in its equivocations. The notion of 'selling' introduces the idea of prostitution – but that does not free one from material things, but is worse than ordinary wage-slavery. Not that Mary is being equated with Mary Magdalene: the underlying parallel is with the Mother of Christ, and the ulterior vibration is that Mr Massey is an awful parody of the Holy Ghost as ordinarily received by 'social' Christians.

Mary recognises quite soon that 'after all, her body was not quite so easy to get rid of'. Mr Massey requires his marital rights: and the Biblical note returns:

> Then she found herself with child, and felt for the first time horror, afraid before God and man. This also she had to go through – it was the right. When the child arrived, it was a bonny, healthy lad. Her heart hurt in her body, as she took the baby between her hands. The flesh that was trampled and silent in her must speak again in the boy. After all, she had to live – it was not so simple after all. Nothing was finished completely. She looked and looked at the baby, and almost hated it, and suffered an anguish of love for it. She hated it because it made her live again in the flesh, when she *could* not live in the flesh, she could not. She wanted to trample her flesh down, down, extinct, to live in the mind. And now there was this child. (*PO*(C) 57)

The word 'flesh' became very important to Lawrence in the years 1911–14. The Biblical source is Jesus's words 'For this cause shall a man leave father and mother, and shall cleave to his wife: and they twain shall be one flesh. Wherefore they are no more twain, but one flesh. What therefore God hath joined together let no man put asunder.'[4] Both Mary and Louisa reflect the position of the woman in the Bible who becomes an instrument of revelation. Mary thinks she is entering a sacred, because spiritual marriage, as if mating a Holy Ghost. But Christ's words apply in the first place to the act of love: it is that which produces the union, and it is a union in the flesh. So Mary's union, in which she thought to deny the flesh, is no true marriage – yet it produces this child.

The complex of ideas here had been very briefly touched on in *The White Peacock* where Lettie, a precursor of Mary Lindley, had had some presentiment of her own unfitness for a real marriage, and had put it in similar terms, however halting:

> "Love – Love – I don't know anything about it. But I can't – we can't be – don't you see – oh what do they say – flesh of one flesh."

This might have been her perception that Lesley Tempest was a precursor of Mr Massey: but Lettie was also frightened of the body.

Louisa's rejection of false spirituality, misdirection of the will and denial of the flesh, is first felt as a fixing of the will:

> The two sisters stood apart. They still loved each other, they would love each other as long as they lived. But they had parted ways. A new solitariness came over the obstinate Louisa, and her heavy jaw set stubbornly. She was going on her own way. But which way? She was quite alone, with a blank world before her. How could she be said to have any way? Yet she had her fixed will to love, to have the man she loved. (*PO*(C) 59)

It happens that one afternoon she goes out in irritation, realises she is walking towards the Durant's cottage, led by the unconscious direction of a deeper will, and so finds the old woman desperately ill and in need of help. There is a link between the subsequent washing-scene, and this strange half-spiritual half-literal perception of the 'flesh'. The body she washes clean of its pit-dirt, and which is then clear and white before her, is the flesh of, the tangible life of, the being who was hitherto disguised under his clothes and his tendency to treat her as 'superior'. In ministering to him as a miner's wife naturally would, she receives her Annunciation, which is true where Mary's was false.

But between the first scene and their becoming one flesh, Alfred Durant has to answer for himself Lawrence's question 'what was he?' He has to allow the wave in him to deposit him on the further shore, to be reborn as himself, and able to claim Louisa, or to respond to her claim on him. And since he is, Lawrence-like, undergoing the trauma of the death of the mother who stabilised his earlier self, this is very difficult for him, and for Louisa. This is put in various ways: 'he was not very actual'; or 'He was so deferential, quick to take the slightest suggestion of an order from her, implicitly, that she could not get at the man in him'; 'How was she to approach him? For he would take not one step towards her'.

Near the end of the story, in a parallel to the washing-scene, the two do manage to come together. The words, the actions are very simple. She calls on him; he is once more in his pit-dirt, since he is in too purposeless a state to wash. He is very likely to go off to the mindless sociableness, the meaningless warmth of the pub, and forget his troubles. Ultimately he may emigrate. At this moment he is merely unfixed, disorientated. At the end of an unsatisfactory exchange of talk, the ritual of ordinary social behaviour requires her to go, and she gets ready to do that; but then she has the courage to ask him if he *wants* her to go. Even now he can scarcely answer, hardly has the courage to assert himself; but he can make the essential gesture – he puts his hand out to detain her. They embrace; she tells him she loves him. Still he can say nothing, but he has made himself clear. At the very end of the scene he makes his claim on her – that they should become 'flesh of one flesh'. Again he does it by the simple gesture of putting out his hand.

This most beautiful, most heartening, most subtle and touching scene ought to be as familiar as the washing-scene. I will comment on some of the language, to show the essential terms Lawrence is developing for what might be called a psychology – though it also borders on theology.

When she comes into the room, Louisa becomes aware of his 'reserve, and the simple neutrality towards her, which she dreaded in him. It made it impossible for her to approach him'. She will have to surmount this, and so puts a series of personal questions to him. His perception of her, initially, is that 'Her repose was exquisite and her dark grey eyes rich with understanding'. Though that is admiration, it is admiration of a superior being, so 'He felt afraid of her as she sat there, as he began to grow conscious of her.' At the end of her sequence of questions she has aroused him to consciousness of her, but it is painful for him, and he is still in awe of her. Lawrence puts it like this:

> He was leaning forward on the arms of his chair. He turned to her. Her face was pale and set. It looked heavy and impassive, her hair shone richer as she grew white. She was to him something steady and immovable and eternal presented to him. His heart was hot in an anguish of suspense. Sharp twitches of fear and pain were in his limbs. He turned his whole body away from her. The silence was unendurable. He could not bear her to sit there any more. It made his heart go hot and stifled in his breast.

She is at the end of her social resources: she has asked all the questions which someone playing the social game would recognise as displaying friendly, indeed warm interest, hoping for a response. But of course he *can't* manage that, so she is losing, and losing him:

. . . Yet she continued to pin on her hat; in a moment she would have to go. Something was carrying her.

Then suddenly a sharp pang, like lightning, seared her from head to foot, and she was beyond herself.

"Do you want me to go?" she asked, controlled, yet speaking out of a fiery anguish, as if the words were spoken from her without her intervention.

'She was beyond herself': it is a very economical formulation, and pregnant. He can still hardly answer; can only ask 'why?', which turns the initiative back to her again:

"Because I wanted to stay with you," she said, suffocated, with her lungs full of fire.

His face worked, he hung forward a little, suspended, staring straight into her eyes, in torment, in an agony of chaos, unable to collect himself.

The unbearable attempt to achieve a crossing goes on, and the crucial moment is this:

"Don't you want me?" she said helplessly.

A spasm of torture crossed his eyes, which held her fixed.

"I – I –" he began, but he could not speak. Something drew him from his chair to her. She stood motionless, spellbound, like a creature given up as prey. He put his hand tentatively, uncertainly, on her arm.

In the embrace which follows there are no words, but Lawrence unfurls his essential terms:

. . . he felt himself falling, falling from himself, and whilst she, yielded up, swooned to a kind of death of herself, a moment of utter darkness came over him, and they began to wake up again as if from a long sleep. He was himself.

That is, a new phase of himself, into which he has 'lapsed out'. And the corollary of 'being himself' is that in that further state

He was with her. She saw his face all sombre and inscrutable, and he seemed eternal to her.

'With her' is a very simple phrase, but has a deep meaning. They have been born again, and he has been born of her, because of her courage. They also have what might be called an inkling of immortality. What follows is the necessary rite, preceded by a washing. Even here, his hands speak for him:

> "What shall you do?" he asked.
> "How?" she said.
> He was awkward at a reply.
> "About me," he said.
> "What do you want me to do?" she laughed.
> He put his hand out slowly to her. What did it matter!
> "But make yourself clean," she said. (*PO*(C) 81–3)

By the old social morality, Louisa has been 'forward' and 'made herself cheap'. By Lawrence's standard, she has had the courage to move them both beyond an insecure or inchoate self to a new one, or to a state which is their true self, 'eternal'. The words 'falling, falling' are a premonition of Lawrence's later favourite parable-figure, of the nut falling from the tree, coming to earth, splitting and releasing the new life in it. It renders the paradox of a death which is also a birth, a natural continuous process of life. The relationship with religious ideas of being reborn or resurrected into a new life is also clear.

The postlude moves us out of these intensities and eases us back into ordinary life; it supplies a symmetrical pendant to the mordant opening pages about Mr Lindley. Alfred has to go through the humiliating process of presenting himself to the Lindley family as suitor. They are shocked at his social presumptuousness, but he steels himself to ride out their arrogance. This is ironically conveyed as his feeling 'not responsible'. That is, he is acting now at the prompting of something that supersedes mere social being: 'He must put himself aside: the matter was bigger than just his personal self. He must not feel. This was his highest duty.' By an inevitable paradox Mr Lindley puts forward his mere snobbery in similar terms: 'I cannot understand why Louisa should not behave in the normal way. I cannot see why she should only think of herself, and leave her family out of count.' A deeper normality has been vindicated; Louisa and Alfred in their great moment were not thinking of themselves: they were beyond egoism, which is why their encounter was a transcendence, and something they could not calculate. One might use an old phrase and say they had been in the hands of God: but not the God of Mr Lindley, Mr Massey and Miss Mary.

Like 'Daughters of the Vicar', 'Odour of Chrysanthemums' is widely accepted as among Lawrence's masterpieces. We are back in another cottage by the railway-side; the story is shorter, very concentrated, and 'dramatic' in that the events take place in a few hours and have the weight and inevitability of those climactic moments in which a fate is worked out. There is a sense of years being summed up and given a meaning; but no eventful 'plot', and only one central character – the miner's wife. All others are mere attendants. The mature embittered woman is shown awaiting her husband's return at the end of the day, at first in anger, then in dread. The anger is because she thinks he is getting drunk at the pub. But he is brought in dead, smothered by a fall of rock at the coal face. The wife and his mother lay out and wash the body in the greatest of all Lawrence's ritual lavings: and in the course of this Elizabeth, like Louisa in 'Daughters of the Vicar', seeing the body before her, comes, too late, upon an essential truth, a revelation about the otherness of the man – what he was.

In the page or two in which the laying-out is described – like a Deposition or a Pietá by a great artist – the simple language is again both Biblical and peculiarly Lawrentian. These paragraphs are one of the great set-pieces in the language. The passage begins:

> When they arose, saw him lying in the naive dignity of death, the women stood arrested in fear and respect. For a few moments they remained still, looking down, the old mother whimpering. Elizabeth felt countermanded. She saw him, how utterly inviolable he lay in himself. She had nothing to do with him. She could not accept it. Stooping, she laid her hands on him, in claim . . . (*PO*(C) 196)

It is a movement of the ego, in response to a feared loss. That gesture of the woman 'claiming' the man, as if she owned him, became peculiarly hateful to Lawrence, as we grasp from the poem 'She said as well to me' in *Look! We have come through*. So this is an initial hubris, provoked by the implicit denial which the body seems to offer. But Elizabeth is embarked on the process which will lead her to 'see', in the same way as Louisa comes to 'see' Alfred, though the two situations are polar opposites, since in the one case Alfred is alive, and coming more alive, while Walter is dead, and even his life with Elizabeth is being denied its previous significance.

She continues her anxious exploration; pursuing her claim, but still refused:

> . . . Elizabeth embraced the body of her husband, with cheek and lips. She seemed to be listening, inquiring, trying to get some connection. But she could not. She was driven away. He was impregnable.

Partly because she must do it anyway, and partly because it induces a different attitude to laying her hand on the body 'in claim', she prepares to wash him. The Biblical element in the syntax and language ('When they arose. . . .', 'She had nothing to do with him') begins to stir:

> She rose, went into the kitchen, where she poured warm water into a bowl, brought soap and flannel and a soft towel. "I must wash him," she said. Then the old mother rose stiffly, and watched Elizabeth as she carefully washed his face, carefully brushing the big blonde moustache from his mouth with the flannel. She was afraid with a bottomless fear, so she ministered to him.

There is the word. The act is now one of service, performed in awe.

> At last it was finished. He was a man of handsome body, and his face showed no traces of drink. He was blonde, full-fleshed, with fine limbs. But he was dead.

The word 'fleshed' generates, a few lines later, sentences in which both the Biblical doctrine and the physical reality lie side by side: again her attempt to reach him is repulsed:

> Elizabeth sank down again to the floor, and put her face against his neck, and trembled and shuddered. But she had to draw away again. He was dead, and her living flesh had no place against his.

The old mother breaks out into a lament, and her words remind us of Alfred Durant's living body, and of Miss Mary's baby son. Underneath the words (and she calls the man a lamb, twice) there may be a reference also to the other Mary's baby; immaculate:

> "White as milk he is, clear as a twelve-month baby, bless him, the darling!" the old mother murmured to herself. "Not a mark on him, clear and clean and white, as beautiful as ever a child was made."

Elizabeth then has her tragic recognition, accepting the dead man as unreachably other, as unknown:

> Life with its smoky burning gone from him, had left him apart and utterly alien to her. And she knew what a stranger he was to her. In her womb was ice of fear, because of this separate stranger with whom she had been living as one flesh. Was this what it all meant – utter, intact separateness, obscured by heat of living? In dread she turned her face away. The fact was too deadly. There had been nothing between them, and yet they had come together, exchanging their nakedness repeatedly. Each time he had taken her, they had been two isolated beings, far apart as now. He was no more responsible than she. The child was like ice in her womb. For as she looked at the dead man, her mind, cold and detached, said clearly: "Who am I? What have I been doing? I have been fighting a husband who did not exist. *He* existed all the time. What wrong have I done? What was that I have been living with? There lies the reality, this man." – And her soul died in her for fear: she knew she had never seen him, he had never seen her, they had met in the dark and had fought in the dark, not knowing whom they had met nor whom they fought. And now she saw, and turned silent in seeing. For she had been wrong. She had said he was something he was not; she had felt familiar with him. Whereas he was apart all the while, living as she never lived, feeling as she never felt.

The 'smoky burning' we have met before. The word 'womb', used several times, both of the mother and of Elizabeth, is distinctly Biblical. Here the striking phrase 'in her womb was ice of fear' reminds us that Elizabeth is pregnant; so that her

Annunciation, unlike Louisa's, is a negation of joyful prophecy. It is an annihilating negation that she faces; but her grief is not egoistic: she feels pity as well as awe and shame:

> She looked at his naked body and was ashamed, as if she had denied it. After all, it was itself. It seemed awful to her. She looked at his face, and she turned her own face to the wall. For his look was other than hers, his way was not her way. She had denied him what he was – she saw it now. She had refused him as himself. – And this had been her life and his life. – She was grateful to death, which restored the truth. And she knew she was not dead.
>
> And all the while her heart was bursting with grief and pity for him. What had he suffered? What stretch of horror for this helpless man! She was rigid with agony. She had not been able to help him. He had been cruelly injured, this naked man, this other being, and she could make no reparation. There were the children – but the children belonged to life. This dead man had nothing to do with them. He and she were only channels through which life had flowed to issue in the children. She was a mother – but how awful she knew it now to have been a wife. And he, dead now, how awful he must have felt it to be a husband. She felt that in the next world he would be a stranger to her. If they met there, in the beyond, they would only be ashamed of what had been before. The children had come, for some mysterious reason, out of both of them. But the children did not unite them. Now he was dead, she knew how eternally he was apart from her, how eternally he had nothing more to do with her. She saw this episode of her life closed. They had denied each other in life. Now he had withdrawn. An anguish came over her. It was finished then . . .

The Biblical phrase hints a kinship with the dead Christ. And the phrase about this episode of her life being closed is a comment on Cyril Mersham's cheerful wish to be done with this part of his life in 'A Modern Lover'. Her earlier gesture is now corrected:

> She was almost ashamed to handle him; what right had she or anyone to lay hands on him; but her touch was humble on his body.

The final sentences are again both Biblical (the repetition of 'it was finished' is deliberate) and characteristically Lawrentian:

> At last it was finished. They covered him with a sheet and left him lying, with his face bound. And she fastened the door of the little parlour, lest the children should see what was lying there. Then, with peace sunk heavy on her heart, she went about making tidy the kitchen. She knew she submitted to life, which was her immediate master. But from death, her ultimate master, she winced with fear and shame. (*PO*(C) 197–9)

That last cryptic judgement yields its meaning slowly. It had been made more immediately comprehensible in the cancelled reading in the page-proofs: 'For in death she would have no life, for she had never loved. She had life on earth with her children, that was all.' But it is a niggling explanation, and Lawrence did well to take it out.

The story, first drafted in 1909, has its origins in the period of *The White Peacock*. But it was rewritten more than once, and there are two published versions – one in the 'English Review' of June 1911 and one in the collection *The Prussian Officer* of 1914. These differ greatly from each other, and from the first manuscript versions. The most important changes come at the end, in the long sequence describing the washing of the body. Some decisive change took place in Lawrence between 1909 and 1914. His attitudes had changed, so that the story quite alters its point. In the very first version, when the two women strip the body, they feel an access of love, and it is comforting, almost euphoric. There is nothing of the later significance, the withering self-recognition which falls upon Elizabeth. It is hard to tell how much Lawrence himself in 1909 was feeling the warm gush that passes through the women. It is a maternal emotion: motherly pride and dominating complacency; and it leads the wife to handle the body in a spirit which later seemed sacrilegious to Lawrence:

> When they rose and looked at him lying naked in the grandeur of death, the women experienced suddenly the same feeling: the sense of motherhood. Elizabeth knelt and put her cheek against him and put her arms around him; the mother took his hand . . . and held it, sobbing, whispering "My son! – Oh my son!" . . . Elizabeth kissed him again and again, and touched him with her hands and her face.

There is more to this effect, reinforcing the idea of the two women acting as if they shared a sleeping child. Elizabeth handles the body very freely, smoothing his yellow hair from his forehead, and kissing him 'on the smooth clear ripples just below the breasts. She loved him very much now – and she was content. Her tears were all for the pity of it – and for the pity of him. Ah, the pity of it! . . . Ah, she loved him, how she loved him now!' The story ends 'Poor dear, he was more helpless than a baby – and so beautiful.'[5]

All this easy emotion, and the easy manipulation of the body, might have been noted with savage irony: a satire on an assumed tendency of women to turn their loss into an indulgence of maternal self-satisfaction. It is hard to be sure; it seems possible that Lawrence is divided here: part of him is reacting against what in another part of him flows very freely. But his intelligence would not let him rest there, nor would his developing experience. Between 1909 and 1914 he rejected that reaching-out of the mother to claim her child, and the wife reaching out to claim her husband as if he too were a child. If we turn to the story as we now have it, certain key words have a new resonance. The corpse lies 'inviolable'. It is not open to claims for emotional satisfaction, still less dominance or possession. The wife still, at first, lays her hand on the body 'in claim', but already she is 'listening, inquiring. But she could not. She was driven away. He was impregnable'. She is 'unavailing' and 'countermanded'.

The sense that he is 'apart and utterly alien' then leads to her bitter discovery about the meaninglessness of their life together: the futility, the error of their struggle. What she now feels is a just emotion, since it does retrospective justice to the man and is a judgement on herself. J. C. F. Littlewood has pointed out that it is very like a comment on the struggle between Gertrude and Walter Morel in *Sons and Lovers*, and therefore like a step towards a just account of Lawrence's father. That is true, but is not all: Lawrence is not only shifting his emotional balance away from his mother, but from all women who 'claim' men – the betraying gesture is her laying her hand on his body in the wrong spirit.

'Daughters of the Vicar' and 'Odour of Chrysanthemums' are like a great diptych, the wings of an altarpiece. They both portray the same central figure being ministered to, being washed, by a woman: the body of the miner in his physical beauty, mature, powerful and unblemished. The firm flesh and the white skin are revealed as the soiling mask of labour is washed away and he is uncovered as this other, strange and wonderful. In the first story the wonder is released and is potent; in the other it has been lost, negated. In both cases it is a revelation, and if revelations have meaning it is as a mystery conveyed alive into the soul of the beholder. The two stories capture different facets of one truth, and reflect a moral on each other. Since at the end of 'Daughters of the Vicar' life is left open into the future, the moral is usable. If people like Louisa are to deal justly with people like Alfred, they must never assume that the other is entirely known: he must remain a mystery. If Louisa were to come to think that she knows him, then in that sense she claims to possess him, to shut off the possibility of growth, to be like a dominant mother, and to find that to the egoist the great advantage of death is that the other can be finally possessed as complete. It is striking that Lawrence first wrote and then rejected this end to the story:

> She found she had a love that would wear. He did not always understand. But he was always hers, always there, always reliable. And they had some very happy times, at evening, talking and reading, for he was intelligent and straight forward in his mind, if not very profound. Moreover, when she thought she knew him altogether, she would find she had been too ready. Queer little things he said, or a few half articulate words he spoke in his sleep, showed her his feeling went much deeper than it seemed, and she was ashamed, for she had been tempted to draw a line under her estimate of him, and say, that was all.
>
> He was very happy, working all his life for her. She liked the house and garden, and therefore he spent most of his leisure planning out improvements, little conveniences. He was always busy, and she felt as if he were building his own little world round her. (*PO*(C) 281–2)

There is the temptation ('she thought she knew him') and it is recognised and avoided. Even so, there is a complacency about the ending, the lapse into the humdrum and the evident patronising of Alfred, which doesn't fit the rest of the story, and Lawrence was right to change it. The tragic end of the one story implies that there is no necessarily happy ending to the other: we have seen a moment of revelation which is likely to be succeeded by the light of common day. Not much of life is lived on that plane.

The reader has another after-thought, not merely mean-minded, about 'Odour of Chrysanthemums'. Suppose that the wife's assumption at the beginning of the story – he's out getting drunk again – had been right? That is improper, literary critics will say: the story is as we have it, and it records the wife being shocked out of her commonplace situation and her merely natural exasperation. But Elizabeth's husband has given enough evidence, to others in the story as well as to her, of being on the way to becoming a lost man, a drunkard. She is jolted out of that judgement, and we are jolted with her; and her second, exalted judgement must either produce a sense of hopelessness – neither of them could do anything about it; the condition of life is futile struggle and fatal incomprehension – or a sense that they share any blame that can fairly be laid. It would not be just to infer as a moral that hardworking women of puritan instincts trying to cope with tipsy and improvident husbands in that harsh world should just let go and enjoy their tipsy husbands. It is one aspect of the tragedy that they can't. Or, more philosophically, if the doctrine is to be 'take me as I am and enjoy me for what I am', serious-minded women have as much right to say that as their tipsy husbands, and as much hope of being heard.

In 'Women are so Cocksure', written years later, Lawrence admitted that he had not been fair to his father in *Sons and Lovers*; and that his mother realised, too late, that she had been wrong to struggle against her husband:

> And then what would she not have given to have her life again, her young children, her tipsy husband, and a proper natural insouciance, to get the best out of it all? (*PI* 168)

One says such things, with hindsight, and a 'proper natural insouciance' is a winning characteristic and a kind of wisdom. But if you don't have it, you don't, and to those people it just seems like not caring, and letting others do the caring. Lydia Lawrence didn't have it, like all her kind, and it is an admirable kind. 'Odour of Chrysanthemums' tells one deep truth: you are what you are: you may make others pay for it and will certainly pay for it yourself. You may be given a moment of vision: usually too late. 'Daughters of the Vicar' tells another deep truth: you may by an act of grace be able to evolve into another phase of your being.

8 Short Stories III

The Prussian Officer as a collection forms a bridge. The stories dealt with in previous chapters, though revised by the mature Lawrence, make use of his early experience of childhood in Eastwood and the teaching years in Croydon. But two of the twelve stories are of a very different kind. 'The Thorn in the Flesh' and 'The Prussian Officer' come from a new range of experience. So does 'New Eve and Old Adam', which was written at the same time, though it was not included in the volume. The first two are set in Germany and deal with the life of the Bavarian and Imperial armies, which Lawrence observed in 1912–13 in Metz, Frieda's parents' home, in Trier and near Munich. The third introduces a new woman into the world of Lawrence's fiction. So we are in the different world that he began to inhabit after his elopement with Frieda in May 1912. She took him where he had meant to go anyway, to Germany; and she offered him the absorbing new human spectacle, herself.[1]

The title-story, now called 'The Prussian Officer' though Lawrence wanted it to be called 'Honour and Arms', is remarkably powerful, though readers are unwilling to admit its success, because it forces us to face things which are not just unpalatable but frightening, and the drama is presented with an economical and unremitting clarity, like a nightmare. It goes through the wall of ordered social life and conventional social feeling, and offers no accommodation or comfort. It is therefore ducked, as 'too intense', or just an unpleasant excursion down a psychological side-alley. Yet it is one of the works which should be put forward whenever it is said – as it reasonably can be – that Lawrence was not only obsessed by his own experience but limited by it. So far as we know, 'The Prussian Officer' is a pure exercise of the imagination. Lawrence may have heard the gist of the story from Frieda or her family or friends, many of them officers in the Imperial Army, but it was not something he knew at first hand. He had to imagine the strange relationship of the unnamed Prussian captain and his batman or orderly, Schöner. Once again the important action takes place at the level below or before words: very little is said in the story, and then in simple terms of everyday meaning, mostly the laconic words of military relationship. Everything else has to be in Lawrence's evocation of the situation, and his presentation of the action.

Much of the story is concerned with capturing a deep level of feeling, often fleeting or unstable. This may issue as action, as violence, but it is not entertained at the conscious level – cannot be. So, for instance, the story opens with what seems like an external landscape, described as if it were just a setting. Lawrence may seem to be neutrally describing the country through which the orderly marches with his fellows, but the vividness of the description is the outward-turning anguish of a consciousness which is not just constrained but in physical pain, and baffled by a situation which it dare not comprehend. The mountain-and-plain scenery is vivid to the point of hallucination, yet real, and the mind which is keeping a grip on the world by seeing it so intensely is also unconsciously keeping a grip on itself. It is using the world to keep out any other consciousness. Correspondingly, at the end of the story, the equally vivid forest-scenery is flashed meaninglessly on a consciousness which has lost that grip, and is unable to realise what it sees. The type of person involved is itself a factor: Lawrence is seized by the idea of a very simple nature in the orderly, who does not reflect, even in a calm state:

> He had firmly marked eyebrows over dark, expressionless eyes, that seemed never to have thought, only to have received life direct through his senses, and acted straight from instinct. (*PO*(C) 2–3)

The orderly is caught in a human relationship which he could not afford to comprehend even if he were more conscious. Partly it is a matter of his being a naive and direct creature, peasant-like or even animal-like (the words are not meant pejoratively) and therefore not self-conscious. Partly it is a matter of his being in an extreme situation where even self-conscious people might need time to reach some vantage-point sufficiently outside themselves in order to grasp the situation and diagnose it. Partly the orderly cannot afford to let the situation crystallise in that way, because that would be to face his intolerable subjection and to have either to accept it, or to burst out in a focused hatred. That finally happens, though not by a process of thought.

So at the outset, the orderly marching in his hot uniform, and beginning to recover from the pain of a severe kicking given to him by the captain the previous evening, is in this kind of suspended consciousness. The strange conflict between the two men is such that neither can afford to be objectively aware of it; but the captain, as the more conscious of the two, is shown as having to fight down his consciousness, as well as other things, as part of his nature:

> Perhaps the man was the more handsome for the deep lines in his face, the irritable tension of his brow, which gave him the look of a man who fights with life. (*PO*(C) 2)

An essential contrast between the two is established in the two sentences quoted. It is an attraction in the orderly that he has the direct, instinctive life that the other man fights against. The reaction is a strange perverted love, the desire to negate what is contemplated with jealousy, as other. The other is either desirable because strange, or a criticism and a threat for the same reason: often both. The captain fends off full daylight knowledge; but has a dawning awareness that something is happening to him:

> Gradually the officer had become aware of his servant's young, vigorous, unconscious presence about him. He could not get away from the sense of the youth's person, while he was in attendance. It was like a warm flame upon the older man's tense, rigid body, that had become almost unliving, fixed. There was something so free and self-contained about him, and something in the young fellow's movement, that made the officer aware of him. And this irritated the Prussian. He did not choose to be touched into life by his servant. . . . And yet as the young soldier moved unthinking about the apartment, the elder watched him, and would notice the movement of his strong young shoulders under the blue cloth, the bend of his neck. And it irritated him. To see the soldier's young, brown, shapely peasant's hands grasp the loaf or the wine-bottle sent a flash of hate or of anger through the elder man's blood. It was not that the youth was clumsy: it was rather the blind, instinctive sureness of movement of an unhampered young animal that irritated the officer to such a degree. (*PO*(C) 3)

Signals are being given here of a kind the reader has learnt to recognise. The 'warm flame' is, as always, a powerfully positive note; so is the sunburnt skin; the characteristic concentration on the bend of the neck. The comparison with 'an unhampered young animal' might even seem a Lawrence-cliché, but the reader who is saturated in Lawrence will detect beneath it a stirring of what he has come to think of as the 'gamekeeper motif'. More obvious is the Biblical reminiscence in 'did not choose to be touched into life by his servant'. In the Gospels, miracles are worked by Jesus's touch, or by people touching him;[2] and he even brought the dead back to life. The resonance plays back over the previous lines about the 'older man's tense rigid body, that had become almost unliving, fixed.' That is presented baldly as Lawrence's firmly held idea about the difference between the two men, considered as types, and as an idea it was always in danger of becoming fixed. It is given a fresh metaphoric life by 'touched into life'. 'By his servant' is also a tonal modification: it seems a mere class-superiority at first, but the idea of the suffering servant is a metaphoric enrichment, an activating force from Lawrence's own thought-world.

There is a further element of Lawrence's instinctive, even obsessive preoccupations. In other stories such as 'Love Among the Haystacks', or 'A Modern Lover' or 'The Shades of Spring', he presents two men who become aware that they are rivals for a woman, and entertain odd feelings for each other nevertheless – or for that reason. In the first story they are brothers, yet they fight, and one for a moment hopes he has killed the other. In the second and third the relationship is scarcely entertained, just sketched as a possibility: but the Lawrence-figure feels an affinity for the other more robust man, who is in one case a gamekeeper, and is in both cases desirable to the woman and also felt as desirable by the man. In 'The Old Adam' the Lawrence-figure fights with the husband, an older man, and after the shock of finding their hostility has broken out, they become tender to each other. In *Sons and Lovers* Paul Morel and Baxter Dawes are rivals, have a murderous fight with each other, and end in a strange friendship.

In 'The Prussian Officer' these beginnings, sketches, hints, are fully developed and transformed into a lethal love-hate, with the woman removed from the scene. We are aware that the orderly has a girl, and their relationship is briefly described in simple but important terms which recur elsewhere.[3] The captain cannot afford to keep up a society marriage on his pay, and has no private means. He has brief predatory relationships with various mistresses. This failure or lack is a pressure on his equilibrium, leading him to act violently towards the orderly, who is in his power, and who is apparently happy in love. But to present the case as merely one of jealousy, or even to 'psychologize' the situation and present it as suppressed homosexuality, is to simplify. The effect of the language is always to deflect the reader away from such obviousness, and this is especially so with the animal-references, which take us away from the world of social humanity. The phrase about 'the blind, instinctive sureness of movement of an unhampered young animal that irritated the officer to such a degree' points to something intrinsic and other which escapes social categorisation. It is reinforced by this repetition of the motif:

> [The captain] knew himself to be always on the point of breaking out. But he kept himself hard to the idea of the Service. Whereas the young soldier seemed to live out his warm full nature, to give it off in his very movements, which had a certain zest, such as wild animals have in free movement. And this irritated the officer more and more. (*PO*(C) 4)

This is Lawrence commenting from his own perception: the captain could not present that constatation without exposing himself to self-criticism, as being envious. The envy comes out as what the officer is conscious of – irritation, merely. An aristocrat might well reject a peasant as an 'animal'. But the 'animal' reference is more widely suggestive, and we are reminded of the powerful ambiguity of the gamekeeper-figure in the other fictions. He is associated not with conservation but mainly with the destruction of what is free, unbroken-in, and natural. Annable is an emblem of ruin and waste and especially the ruin within himself; and even the more sympathetically-considered figures have a lack; the later Mellors in *Lady Chatterley's Lover* still has this bitterness and frustration. This undertone makes the two central figures of 'The Prussian Officer' less schematic and more mysterious. The captain is repressed by a savage discipline imposed on his inner chaos by a fierce will which is not thought but social reaction; the orderly is naturally free and vital, therefore enviable, desirable, complete, and a reproach: also a natural prey, given the situation the men are in. The military code places together in an impossible situation these two opposite natures – one whole but innocent, the other warped but potent, and unholily tempted to violate the other. In different situations (a school for instance) the bully might savour the situation by first indulging, even petting, the prey initially, but in the army only the bullying is permitted, indeed encouraged, so the captain has a disciplinary pretext for following his secret passion. The two men are bound into a conflict which only one of them can win. The servant cannot avoid it: military discipline fixes him there. The officer will not avoid it, for something compels him. The repulsion is a fascination, the hatred is the negative inversion, intensified, of an attraction.

So they are in a life-and-death struggle, if neither will swerve aside or give in. Lawrence has taken a situation he always hated – the military life, in which men have to give way or be broken: it is of the essence that they serve the machine. He has pursued the situation to a fatality. The orderly kills the captain, and then goes off in a delirious state, partly from the effects of his beating, compounded by sunstroke and thirst, partly from his own feeling of having gone beyond some natural frontier, and partly because he has been broken in upon and violated earlier. He goes on wandering until he dies. The reader is swept along, riveted and appalled by the entirely natural and vivid narrative, intensely perceiving with the wide unblinking eye of fascinated horror what Lawrence renders very concretely – scene, sun, atmosphere and the wordless conflict of the protagonists. Nothing is presented except the facts. There is no reflection, no debate. At the end, this strange opposition, like a lust, has worked itself out, and two people are dead. But one cannot dismiss the story as a mere quirk – like Maupassant's taste for the oddities of human behaviour served up by a knowing raconteur with repellent irony (here's a strange little tale: feel only a remote kinship with these primitives). No more than *The Trespasser* is this what the French call a *fait divers*: the sort of event given a newspaper paragraph as 'soldier kills officer in motiveless crime'.

The graded sequence of events is very carefully established. First there is just the officer's nameless or undefinable irritation. Then there is a little incident which crystallises something:

Once, when a bottle of wine had gone over, and the red gushed out onto the table-cloth, the officer had started up with an oath, and his eyes, bluey like fire, had held those of the confused youth for a moment. It was a shock for the young soldier. He felt something sink deeper, deeper into his soul, where nothing had ever gone before. It left him rather blank and wondering. Some of his natural completeness in himself was gone, a little uneasiness took its place. And from that time an undiscovered feeling had held between the two men. (*PO*(C) 3)

That is so well and simply put that we forget the gift that has captured it. 'Some of his natural completeness in himself was gone' realises the sudden loss of invulnerability in someone who was before entirely unconscious and was going to get through his military service successfully by dint of *being* unconscious, and so able to serve the machine mechanically. If he is forced to interact with his masters, and especially if they turn vicious, he is under threat. But he can't see that or say it, because he is free, unbroken, instinctive and not given to thinking or verbalising. So Lawrence has to find the words which will convey this dawning of something, this inkling.

The cruel process goes on: the officer allowing himself to bully the man without asking himself what he is doing or why; the man trapped in the situation and not allowing himself to discover conscious resentment or justified hatred. Finding finally that the orderly is writing a poem to his girl, the captain kicks him repeatedly: ostensibly because the man does not satisfactorily answer his questions. He would justify himself, if called upon to do so, by invoking 'dumb insolence', the ultimate Service arbitrariness of authority.

So a long and well-constructed flash-back returns us to the opening scene, where the orderly is marching in the heat. Something happens to him during this day on manoeuvres. He has during his persecution simply had the instinct to save himself – which means that if he can get to the end of his service he can afford to admit on returning to civilian life what he had not admitted before: that he had been abominably treated by the captain and hated him. But during this day crucial things take place within him. First there is this sense of being dominated, or annulled, as he sees the captain, proud on horseback in the sunlight, self-possessed, and watching him:

The orderly must move under the presence of the figure of the horseman. It was not that he was afraid, or cowed. It was as if he was disembowelled, made empty, like an empty shell. He felt himself as nothing, a shadow creeping under the sunshine. And, thirsty as he was, he could scarcely drink, feeling the captain near him. He would not take off his helmet to wipe his wet hair. He wanted to stay in shadow, not to be forced into consciousness. Starting, he saw the light heel of the officer prick the belly of the horse; the captain cantered away, and he himelf could relapse into vacancy.

Nothing, however, could give him back his living place in the hot, bright morning. He felt like a gap among it all. Whereas the captain was prouder, overriding. A hot flash went through the young servant's body. The captain was firmer and prouder with life, he himself was empty as a shadow. Again the flash went through him, dazing him out. But his heart ran a little firmer. (*PO*(C) 11)

It is as if the words 'domination', 'resentment' and 'rancour' had been taken back to the mint and reforged: the concepts recovered as original feeling. In such situations, people do not say to themselves 'I feel resentment'; still less the more analytical 'I feel as if that man dominated me in a way which prevents me from acting naturally and having a drink. Yet I am desperately thirsty.' What takes place is like what Lawrence has conveyed. The moment of feeling inferior or beaten, or incapable of asserting oneself in reply is then replaced, as the internal balance swings the other way. Two pages later we read this (the orderly is being sent off to bring the captain something to eat and drink):

But it was only the outside of the orderly's body that was obeying so humbly and mechanically. Inside had gradually accumulated a core into which all the energy of that young life was compact and concentrated. He executed his commission, and plodded quickly back uphill. There was a pain in his head, as he walked, that made him twist his features unknowingly. But hard there in the centre of his chest was himself, himself, firm, and not to be plucked to pieces.

The captain had gone up into the wood. The orderly . . . had a curious mass of energy inside him now. The captain was less real than himself. (*PO*(C) 13)

These are Lawrence's representations of 'confidence', 'self-assertion'. Again, one doesn't say 'Suddenly, mysteriously, I feel much more confident.' It is not a thought, but a feeling, and it is felt where Lawrence says it is felt, down below the place which does any thinking which may be going on. 'Hard there in the centre of his chest was himself, himself, firm' is one of the massive central Lawrentian perceptions: one core or central node of the system – though one must also note how brief is this moment of self-possession in the orderly's case. Within minutes he has disintegrated. But for this brief space he has evolved into a state in which he can act. The self in the centre of the chest is not like the inchoate, rudimentary or dominated social self which was prepared as a half-sketched calculation to do nothing, to suffer and last out until he was free. The newly formed power is not going to be cheated. It too says nothing; it does not think; it just waits its moment. In this respect it is like an animal, but it has ceased to be a prey; it has been harried into becoming a predator. The climactic moment comes when it sees its enemy well placed as victim, and acts. The key words below, after the succession of tiny sounds intensely noted, are 'And then he saw . . .'. What he sees is not what Miss Louisa sees in her moment of vision, but its polar opposite.

And he heard the sound of the captain's drinking, and he clenched his fists, such a strong torment came into his wrists. Then came the faint clang of the closing of the pot-lid. He looked up. The captain was watching him. He glanced swiftly away. Then he saw the officer stoop and take a piece of bread from the tree-base. Again the flash of flame went through the young soldier, seeing the stiff body stoop beneath him, and his hands jerked. He looked away. He could feel the officer was nervous. The bread fell as it was being broken. The officer ate the other piece. The two men stood tense and still, the master laboriously chewing his bread, the servant staring with averted face, his fist clenched.

Then the young soldier started. The officer had pressed open the lid of the mug again. The orderly watched the lid of the mug, and the white hand that clutched the handle, as if he were fascinated. It was raised. The youth followed it with his eyes. And then he saw the thin, strong throat of the elder man moving up and down as he drank, the strong jaw working. And the

instinct which had been jerking at the young man's wrists
suddenly jerked free. He jumped, feeling as if he were rent in
two by a strong flame. (*PO*(C) 14)

He presses the captain's head back, and breaks his neck.

It is not just that the watchful animal has caught its prey in an
unguarded moment. The processes going on here are human,
though 'mental' would obviously be the wrong word. The activity,
like an electric current, is felt in the wrists, the hands. The eyes
which watch so intently and the ears which catch the tiny sounds
are not at the service of a calculation but of an instant reaction.
The closing of the pot-lid has associations of defence, of denial,
and is a 'no'. But its reopening is a 'yes' because it means the
officer will raise the mug, turn up his unguarded throat and be
momentarily unable to see. What is caught here is the extremity of
human awareness at a level of danger, subtlety and speed, and
with a weight of consequence that is rarely experienced, and
where the conscious person is even at a disadvantage because
thought is slow and inhibiting. Here it pays to be as much like an
animal as possible. One can do what George Saxton was only able
to do to animals ('If you can run . . . you should be able to run to
death. When your blood's up you don't hang half-way. . . . If you
feel like doing a thing – you'd better do it'.) Cyril Beardsall
couldn't even catch a rabbit, being an intellectual; but Frances in
'Second-Best' had found herself able deliberately to kill a mole, as
necessary offering; and now the orderly finds himself very well
able to kill the captain, to make a good job of it, and to enjoy it:

> . . . the orderly, with serious, earnest young face, and underlip
> between his teeth, had got his knee in the officer's chest and was
> pressing the chin backwards over the farther edge of the
> tree-stump, pressing, with all his heart behind in a passion of
> relief, the tension of his wrists exquisite with relief. And with the
> base of his palms he shoved at the chin, with all his might. And
> it was pleasant too to have that chin, that hard jaw already
> slightly rough with beard, in his hands. He did not relax one
> hair's-breadth but all the force of all his blood exulting in his
> thrust, he shoved back the head of the other man, till there was a
> little "cluck" and a crunching sensation. Then he felt as if his
> heart went to vapour. Heavy convulsions shook the body of the
> officer, frightening and horrifying the young soldier. Yet it

pleased him too to repress them. It pleased him to keep his hands pressing back the chin, to feel the chest of the other man yield in expiration to the weight of his strong young knee, to feel the hard twitchings of the prostrate body jerking his own whole frame, which was pressed down on it. (*PO*(C) 15)

How it is imagined! The little 'cluck' is the last of the tiny sounds in the wordless scene, and what the other sounds had been leading up to. And how it is enjoyed! But the enjoyment is broken by the sight of the blood:

> But it went still. He could look into the nostrils of the other man; the eyes he could scarcely see. . . . Then, with a start, he noticed the nostrils gradually filled with blood. The red brimmed, hesitated, ran over, and went in a thin trickle down the face to the eyes. It shocked and distressed him. (*PO*(C) 15)

He wanders off, the shock now added to the pain of his bruises, his thirst and increasing sunstroke. He is found dying, later, on his own in the forest. Indeed Lawrence says, as the orderly leaves the body of the captain 'Here his own life also ended', though there are several pages which follow, about his last hours of hallucinated semi-consciousness, wandering among the trees. One of the things he is dimly aware of is that he no longer belongs to the world:

> And he no longer belonged to it – he sat there, beyond, like a man outside in the dark. He had gone out from everyday life into the unknown and he could not, he even did not want to go back. (*PO*(C) 16)

And again:

> It was all right, somehow. It was peace. But now he had got beyond himself. He had never been here before. Was it life, or not-life? He was by himself. They were in a big, bright place, those others, and he was outside. The town, all the country, a big bright place of light: and he was outside, here, in the darkened open beyond, where each thing existed alone. But they would all have to come out there sometime, those others. Little, and left behind him, they all were. There had been father and mother and sweetheart. What did they all matter. This was the open land. (*PO*(C) 18)

Here is an extreme transmutation of one of Lawrence's most instinctive perceptions: the circle of light surrounded by darkness. The orderly, like a trespasser, has passed beyond the known, and is alone outside in a place without known features or boundaries. Now that he is there, he is in no state to justify his over-stepping, but the story itself conveys an inevitability, if not a justification. The words guilt, crime, sin, are not used, and the concepts are not entertained at all; it seems scarcely possible that they are to be found back in the world he has left.

At the end of the story Lawrence presents the tableau of the two bodies, recovered and laid side by side, as if they were the only moral:

> The bodies of the two men lay together, side by side, in the mortuary, the one white and slender, but laid rigidly at rest, the other looking as if every moment it must rouse into life again, so young and unused, from a slumber. (*PO*(C) 20–1)

We must make what we can of that. It seems clear that the orderly has Lawrence's heart: the words 'rouse into life again' are an endorsement. He has the reader's sympathy too, no doubt. The captain is a tyrant, and not less hateful for being understood. But there are not many great writers, and fewer still before Nietzsche, who would present a homicide with that intensity and not feel some strong compulsion to indicate guilt or retribution. The death that the orderly departs into seems a natural sequel to what has gone before; is prepared for in the story, seems appropriate, and forestalls a human trial and punishment. But it is also a way of avoiding the moral issues. I assume that there are some, and do so not only out of habit; but Lawrence does not obviously make that assumption. Something related, but not identical, is offered in the passages about having passed 'beyond', or being 'outside'. Beyond good and evil, we wonder? Is that 'the open land'?

Lawrence did offer a moral, of a reductive sort, in a letter to Edward Garnett of 11? November 1912:

> Cruelty is a form of perverted sex. I want to dogmatise. Priests in their celibacy get their sex lustful, then perverted, then insane, hence Inquisitions – all sexual in origin. And soldiers,

being herded together, men without women, never being *satisfied* by a woman, as a man never is from a street affair, get their surplus sex and their frustration and dissatisfaction into the blood, and love cruelty. It is sex lust fermented makes atrocity.[4] (*Letters* I 469)

As simple rationalising, that goes some way to account for the captain's behaviour – but not all the way. The story goes far beyond that perception. The captain's cruelty to the orderly may have a sexual origin and an element of sexual jealousy; but that could only be one strand. 'Satisfied' people are perfectly capable of being tyrannical bullies; and any argument which runs 'he did A because he was B' tends to discount the intrinsic joy of doing A. And (for instance) the orderly, who has a reason for killing the captain, has better reasons for not killing him; and nothing compels him to kill the captain with enjoyment. But he does. In the story there are no reasons; only the events from which reasons might be inferred, no more or less plausibly than usual. The force of the story is to make the reasons look like what they are: after-the-event rationalisations which are a reduction of the situation.

What exists between the two men, however unwilled or perverse, is a bond. That, I think, is the point of the final tableau: the two naked bodies lying side by side in a parody of marriage. It is an unequal marriage in that one partner is 'rigidly at rest', while the other looks – even in death – as if the lost life in him might still cause him to rise and escape. Many marriages yoke incompatible partners, as if people sought an opposite; nonetheless the hint about the orderly's life after death seems to me opportunistic and sentimental, as if Lawrence wanted to soften the offence of the story.

One is also led to think further about the murder. Are we faced here with something Lawrence posited elsewhere: that there is no chance killing, but that every murder unites a murderer and a murderee, who has a profound but hidden desire to be killed? Could the captain be said to have willed both deaths? When Birkin comes out with his maxim in *Women in Love*, most of us respond like Gerald Crich, and refuse to accept it. But Lawrence means it there, and I think he is implying it here. At any rate, it needs to be thought about, and Lawrence will force us to return to the idea.

'The Thorn in the Flesh' is a pendant or companion-piece to 'The Prussian Officer'. It is part of a diptych, and related in the same way as 'Daughters of the Vicar' is to 'Odour of Chrysanthemums': the same way of life is being seen from a different viewpoint, and while one story ends with an opening into the future, in the other death closes off that possibility. Again, a young man, unconscious, instinctive or 'animal' is the centre of interest. Again he is in the grip of blind authority, and likely to be broken by it. Again there is an instinctive movement of rebellion, a gesture of reaction. But this time the man is saved, by the love of a woman who is 'there' for him. Schöner's girl was never brought into view in 'The Prussian Officer' and her absence, or her negation, are part of the catastrophe. Bachmann's Emilie, in 'The Thorn in the Flesh', keeps the man whole and safe, even though he is at the end of the story arrested and taken off to trial and punishment. He is saved because he is brought into a new life, as if in a religious conversion.

Again, near the beginning of the story the central character is being marched towards a crucial ordeal. Bachmann is one degree more conscious than Schöner, so that his attitude towards authority is more complex. He half gives himself to the life:

> . . . he had something of military consciousness, as if he believed in the discipline for himself, and found satisfaction in delivering himself to his duty. There was also a trace of youthful swagger and dare-devilry about his mouth and his limber body, but this was in suppression now. (*PO*(C) 22–3)

He is also half-aware, as he marches along, that some danger is impending:

> . . . But he was bound in a very dark enclosure of anxiety within himself.
> He marched with his usual ease, being healthy and well adjusted. But his body went on by itself. His spirit was clenched apart. And ever the few soldiers drew nearer and nearer to the town, ever the consciousness of the youth became more gripped and separate, his body worked by a kind of mechanical intelligence, a mere presence of mind. (*PO*(C) 23)

Here are words which were not applied in the earlier story to the central character: consciousness, intelligence, mind. Bachmann is distinguished from Schöner in important ways: nonetheless, the thing which happens to him impinges on consciousness but is not directed by it.

He finds he has to climb the wall of the fortifications on a siege-ladder. He has a horror of heights – a thing which possesses him and which he cannot control. He is paralysed with fear halfway up the ladder, and has the added humiliation of wetting himself. Pulled up to the top and bullied by the sergeant, he pushes the officer away in an automatic reflex action, and the man goes over the edge into the moat. Horrified, Bachmann runs away, goes into the town, and takes refuge at the house where his girl works (Frieda's parents' house in Metz). He is found, arrested, and taken away the following morning; but before this happens he and Emilie find each other, if I can use that term. The knowledge of their love for each other is the other central event: it balances the experience of the siege-ladder where in another way Bachmann learnt something about himself – learnt what he could not do or be because his body would not let him.

The words about the marching body with its 'mere presence of mind' paradoxically convey how the mixture of the socially adjusted and the mechanical will could get Bachmann to the foot of the ladder. His dread is powerfully present, but not recognised or in control, and the social will urges the body on. But this mechanism fails half-way up the ladder, where he hangs paralysed. In a passage of brilliant intuition Lawrence conveys this wild unconscious terror, represented by the man's lack of control over the sphincter – a natural representation of the body's own spontaneous activity:

> There came into his consciousness a small, foreign sensation. He woke up a little. What was it? Then slowly it penetrated him. His water had run down his leg. He lay there, clinging, still with shame. . . . He waited, in depths of shame beginning to recover himself. He had been shamed so deeply. Then he could go on, for his fear for himself was conquered. His shame was known and published. He must go on. (*PO*(C) 25)

The psychological notation is acute. The physiological event, purely instinctive, brings him back to a social consciousness, a shame, which is greater than the blind terror, and brings it under control. So the body wakes the mind, which then works the body.

He has to get away, and this is put in terms which look forward to the chapter 'The Nightmare' in *Kangaroo*, where Lawrence recounted his own experience of having to face the hateful military discipline; though the word 'flesh' with its manifold associations also links back and forward to the other fictions discussed in this book:

> He could not bear his shamed flesh to be put again between the hands of authority. Already the hands had been laid upon him, brutally upon his nakedness, ripping open his shame and making him maimed, crippled in his own control. (*PO*(C) 27)

Once again the Biblical resonances enrich and complicate the utterance. Among the many uses of 'flesh' in the Bible, a whole group brings the meaning very close to the sexual organs themselves; 'nakedness' has the same meaning.[5] Also, the flesh is weak where the spirit is willing: so the word has a range of potent meanings which Lawrence can call upon. This brings us to the significance of the title, and the Biblical text it refers to, but that is best deferred until the second half of the story has given 'the flesh' its whole meaning. Meanwhile one might put forward the suggestion that the 'shamed flesh' which has hung upon the ladder, having been put 'between the hands of authority', having 'hands laid upon him, brutally upon his nakedness' is a very discreet reference to Christ, who did indeed come 'in the flesh', had hands laid upon him brutally, and 'suffered in the flesh'.[6] The first episode in the story has analogies with the Crucifixion, and suggests that many people daily face such an annihilating experience at the hands of authority. It is like a death, and requires a resurrection if we are to recover. And from this vantage point, if we look back on 'The Prussian Officer' and think of its last cryptic sentence, we see that the idea of some kind of resurrection is fleetingly entertained. But there can be no literal resurrection for physically dead men: the resurrection of the body as Lawrence conceives it takes place at the hands of the right woman.

The second section of the story takes Bachmann to Emilie, who is a servant. That status is carefully explained. In the first place she is described as having 'the proud, timid eyes of some wild animal, some proud animal.' That is the badge of approval. But she can serve quite willingly where she thinks she serves superior beings:

And her contempt of the common men in general was ineffable. But she loved the Baroness, and she revered the Baron, and she was at her ease when she was doing something for the service of a gentleman. Her whole nature was at peace in the service of real masters or mistresses. For her, a gentleman had some mystic quality that left her free and proud in service. The common soldiers were brutes, merely nothing. Her desire was to serve. (*PO*(C) 31)

So her service is not mechanical and compelled, like that of conscripts. It is voluntary service of the higher: something reverential, as in 'behold the handmaid of the lord', (and lady, in this case). It gives her a demand on life: if she is to leave that service it must be for another that she accepts as equivalent: and the course of the story shows her transferring her allegiance to Bachmann. For that to happen, she has to have something like a revelation of him, in the flesh.

She takes him into her room, to hide him:

The curious simplicity and severity of the little Roman Catholic bedroom was foreign but restoring to him. He looked at the crucifix. It was a long, lean, peasant Christ carved by a peasant in the Black Forest. For the first time in his life, Bachmann saw the figure as a human thing. It represented a man hanging there in helpless torture. He stared at it, closely, as if for new knowledge.

Within his own flesh burned and smouldered the restless shame. He could not gather himself together. There was a gap in his soul. The shame within him seemed to displace his strength and his manhood. (*PO*(C) 30)

The passage makes the connection. Bachmann sees the Christ intensely,[7] and then moves to his own sense of humiliation (notated as Schöner's resentment and defeat were notated just before he swung back into his desperately brief moment of self-assertion and victory). Being humble and unreflecting, Bachmann makes no blasphemous comparison, but it is made for him.

Emilie then comes in and sees him sleeping; and what she sees is, in a way now characteristic of Lawrence, troubling to her soul; and she goes away asking what manner of thing this is:

Emilie came in a little while, and looked at him. But he was sunk in sleep. She saw him lying there inert, and terribly still, and she was afraid. His shirt was unfastened at the throat. She saw his pure white flesh, very clean and beautiful. And he slept inert. His legs, in the blue uniform trousers, his feet in the coarse stockings, lay foreign on her bed. She went away.

III

She was uneasy, perturbed, to her last fibre. She wanted to remain clear, with no touch on her. A wild instinct made her shrink away from any hands that might be laid on her. (*PO*(C) 30–1)

A symmetry is being set up. Emilie, like Bachmann, has a virgin instinct. As with him, this is expressed as rejection of the 'hands' that may be 'laid on her'. She will only give herself in a proper spirit. Meanwhile she is troubled, for she has had, like Louisa, a revelation of 'his pure white flesh, very clean and beautiful', through that characteristically Lawrentian glimpse of the point at the throat where open face joins hidden body: the place where enemies and predators attack. For the moment, however, the uniform makes him 'foreign', because (presumably) it associates him with the 'common men', who are 'brutes'. So she has a partial vision, of the flesh masked by the uniform.

His presence in her room brings two things into conflict. The order, the trust, of the household is disturbed; yet her impulse to transfer her service to Bachmann is powerfully in play. So for the moment

> . . . she was no longer the faithful in service serving with religious surety . . . she had the insupportable feeling of being out of the order, self-responsible, bewildered. The control of her life should come from those above her, and she should move within that control. But now she was out of it, uncontrolled and troubled. More than that, the man, the lover, Bachmann, who was he, what was he? He alone of all men contained for her the unknown quality which terrified her beyond her service. (*PO*(C) 33)

Her question 'who was he, what was he?' echoes Louisa's (and contrasts with the awful answer given to Elizabeth in 'Odour of

Chrysanthemums'). The question has to be answered and the tension resolved; and this happens in one of Lawrence's by now characteristic love scenes where all that is said is 'Do you want anything to eat?' and the answer, 'yes'.

As if in a spell she waited, standing motionless and looming there, he sat rather crouching on the side of the bed. A second will in him was powerful and dominating. She drew gradually nearer to him, coming up slowly, as if unconscious. His heart beat up swiftly. He was going to move.

The tension is not totally unlike that in which the orderly watches the Captain eating, waiting for his own moment to move. But the result is this, instead (and again it is the hands which communicate):

As she came quite close, almost invisibly he lifted his arms and put them round her waist, drawing her with his will and desire. He buried his face into her apron, into the terrible softness of her belly. And he was a flame of passion intense about her. He had forgotten. Shame and memory were gone in a whole, furious flame of passion.

She was quite helpless. Her hands leapt, fluttered, and closed over his head, pressing it deeper into her belly, vibrating as she did so. And his arms tightened on her, his hands spread over her loins, warm as flame on her loveliness. It was intense anguish of bliss for her, and she lost consciousness.

When she recovered, she lay translated in the peace of satisfaction.

It was what she had had no inkling of, never known could be. She was strong with eternal gratitude. And he was there with her. Instinctively with an instinct of reverence and gratitude, her arms tightened in a little embrace upon him who held her thoroughly embraced.

And he was restored and completed, close to her. That little, twitching, momentary clasp of acknowledgement that she gave him in her satisfaction, roused his pride unconquerable. They loved each other, and all was whole. She loved him, he had taken her, she was given to him. It was right. He was given to her, and they were one, complete.

> Warm, with a glow in their hearts and faces, they rose again, modest, but transfigured with happiness.
> "I will get you something to eat," she said, and in a joy and security of service again, she left him, making a curious little homage of departure. He sat on the side of the bed, escaped, liberated, wondering, and happy. (*PO*(C) 34)

The words 'they rose again' have their ordinary meaning, but 'transfigured' brings in a further significance as well. There is a delicate reference to the Resurrection, because this rite is meant to counterbalance Bachmann's earlier experience, with its delicate hint of Crucifixion. And Emilie's own attitudes 'eternal gratitude', 'reverence', 'homage' are those of the Virgin, in a new 'security of service'. These things are not crudely rendered: if we had not come upon the deeper more insistent note in 'Daughters of the Vicar' and 'Odour of Chrysanthemums' we might scarcely hear these.

But a serious Biblical parallel is being made throughout these stories. What the two characters achieve is that they are 'there' with each other; that they have moved beyond an earlier state, so that Bachmann can say 'He had won to his own being, in himself and Emilie, he had drawn the stigma from his shame, he was beginning to be himself.' This achievement, for ordinary people, is the way in which a crucifixion which is of every day and in this world can be succeeded by a resurrection of the same kind. The process and the achievement allow Bachmann a firm ground on which he can stand and consciously reflect on the earlier experience. Things now come into clear focus and are actually thought about:

> Again he went over the events of the afternoon, remembering his own anguish of apprehension because he had known he could not climb the wall without fainting with fear. Still, a flush of shame came alight in him at the memory. But he said to himself: "What does it matter? – I can't help it, well then I can't. If I go up a height, I get absolutely weak, and can't help myself." Again memory came over him, and a gush of shame, like fire. But he sat and endured it. It had to be endured, admitted, and accepted – " 'I'm not a coward, for all that," he continued. "I'm not afraid of danger. If I'm made that way, that heights melt me and make me let go my water" – it was

torture for him to pluck at this truth – "if I'm made like that, I shall have to abide by it, that's all. It isn't all of me." He thought of Emilie, and was satisfied. "What I am, I am; and let it be enough," he thought. (*PO*(C) 35–6)

This is the 'thorn in the flesh' of the title. The reference is to 2 Corinthians 12, where Paul writes how he had known a man in Christ, 'how that he was caught up into paradise, and heard unspeakable words, which it is not lawful for a man to utter'. He goes on:

> Of such an one will I glory: yet of myself I will not glory, but in mine infirmities.
>
> For though I would desire to glory, I shall not be a fool . . .
>
> And lest I should be exalted above measure through the abundance of the revelations, there was given to me a thorn in the flesh, the messenger of Satan to buffet me, lest I should be exalted above measure.
>
> For this thing I besought the Lord thrice, that it might depart from me.
>
> And he said unto me, My grace is sufficient for thee: for my strength is made perfect in weakness. Most gladly therefore will I rather glory in my infirmities.

To press the Biblical parallels, one might say that what has taken place is first like a crucifixion, then like an annunciation (when Emilie sees Bachmann asleep), then a joint resurrection which might also be thought of as a nativity, since the new Bachmann is born of Emilie. The central notions are the flesh, and the hands that are laid on it – whether the blind hand of authority or the reverent hand of love. The one conceals what a man is, as the uniform conceals it; the other reveals. So there is a subtle relationship between the two parts of the story. Bachmann's instinctive reaction on the ladder, the thorn in his flesh, is a genital weakness. But that shame is redeemed in Emilie's bedroom, where the man is established as glorious and desirable in the same flesh, where hands are laid on it in reverence. Yeats was pointing to the same mystery when he said that love has pitched his mansion in the place of excrement.

Both Bachmann and Emilie thought they needed some kind of external authority to which they could submit. He had thought it was the army; but that was wrong: the army had no reciprocal respect for him. She had thought it was her employers. Instead they both find that the thing they want is to be 'there' for each other. For Emilie the upshot is that she is 'in joy and security of service again'. Her allegiance is safely transferred. When Bachmann is arrested and taken away, he does not need to look at Emilie: 'They knew each other. They were themselves'.

To come into oneself is therefore a necessary achievement, but may be an ordeal like a rite of passage, and also a religious experience. It involves being revealed in the flesh, perhaps literally, perhaps figuratively. When Christ became flesh he could be seen as a man: he could also suffer as men suffer. Some kind of crucifixion is the lot of most people; but they may rise again in the flesh and be more truly known because more truly themselves. The women who minister to the sons of men may find them sons of God. They may see, or even wash, the living body; and so came upon the reality of 'the flesh'; they may find themselves washing the dead body. How hands are laid upon the flesh conveys the essential truth about the relationship.

9   Short Stories IV

This chapter deals mainly with 'New Eve and Old Adam', a story hitherto neglected, but of great interest and importance, both in itself and because it points towards the next phase of Lawrence's fiction, and especially the conflict of Will and Anna Brangwen in *The Rainbow*. It is unlike anything else in the early stories: yet it is linked with them, and with *The White Peacock*, because, for instance, it requires us to think once more what Lawrence means by 'flesh of one flesh'. Certain other motifs are familiar: the central character bathes himself; the man and woman make well-known gestures of the hands. There are even small Lawrentian peculiarities of observation: the heroine takes off her wedding-ring and spins it round, as Clara Dawes does in *Sons and Lovers*; she puts flowers in her hair (a mysteriously powerful gesture, associated with witchcraft); like Miriam she sucks a finger when thinking. There is even a rival male, and he is a *Doppelgänger*. These and other symbolic filaments tie the story into the world of the early fiction.

The story is about being married, and so having embarked on a different struggle, a different search, and feeling different yearnings from those of the other early fictions. It is true that in *The White Peacock* George and Lettie both marry and their marriages go badly. In the relatively mature third part of the novel Lawrence attempts to imagine how that might have gone. But it is a shrewd guess by an observer, who is sympathetic and troubled but inspecting from a distant perspective the experience of imagined others. 'New Eve and Old Adam' is the report of a participant, for all that it is a third-person narrative. Lawrence brings back from the front line of the marital war something that only he could report, because only he could feel it in the terms he uses, and they are so original as to redefine the struggle.

The only story from the period which can be compared is 'The White Stocking', because it too is about young married people in conflict. It is a deft and touching story, finely imagined; but it is observed from the outside, and it is, for lack of a better word, 'closed off' in a satisfactory conclusion which makes it a neat little anecdote with a happy ending, as if a danger had been circumvented, resolution reached. There is no such ending in 'New Eve and Old Adam', which is the more disturbing for that.

'The White Stocking' is among the stories with a long genesis. It was one of the first Lawrence ever started, being based on an anecdote that his mother had told him. She had gone to a dance, and was embarrassed to find that in that company she had pulled out a white stocking when she thought she was pulling out a silk handkerchief. As the story was finally revised, the little incident drops into a long perspective, becoming part of a very carefully constructed flashback, and projected back to a dance which took place two years before the story opens. It is now the second Valentine's Day since that dance, and the very charming and kitten-like Elsie Whiston has on each 14 February received a white silk stocking and a little gift of jewellery from her coarse ex-employer Sam Adams, whom she aroused at that original dance, and who picked up the stocking as a substitute-triumph. So the stocking is turned into an emblem of desire, and Adams's gifts are like a renewal of courtship. Her husband, during the course of the narrative, comes to know of the gifts, the whole sequence of events being skilfully recounted through reminiscence attached to the events of the day which is the 'now' of the story. A central perception of the story is Elsie's power to attract, which is a natural force. Her husband, very solid and a little dull compared with the flashy Sam Adams, knows of this power; but he has it in him to stabilise her. He watches over her carefully; and fundamentally she relies on him. This is wittily caught early in the story. Secretly Elsie puts on her illicit jewels:

> She wore her ear-rings all morning, in the house. She was self-conscious, and quite brilliantly winsome, when the baker came, wondering if he would notice. All the tradesmen left her door with a glow in them, feeling elated, and unconsciously favouring the delightful little creature, though there had been nothing to notice in her behaviour.
>
> She was stimulated all the day. She did not think about her husband. He was the permanent basis from which she took these giddy little flights into nowhere. At night, like chickens and curses, she would come home to him, to roost. (*PO*(C) 148–9)

So she feels certain of him: a certainty he does not yet have.

The second part of the story is the eventual climax and resolution; the first is the recollected narrative of the Christmas party and dance two years before. This is brilliantly done. Lawrence conveys the mute movements towards each other of Sam Adams and Elsie Whiston, who have the same physical magnetism and self-assuredness: who are able to expand into a situation and relax where Whiston naturally contracts and goes stiff, and who achieve an elation, an intoxication, where he becomes steadily more sober. This is naturally expressed in the dance, and we are reminded of the strange night scene in *The White Peacock* where George Saxton and Lettie dance together, achieving a spiritual consummation that they can't manage sexually or socially. So with Elsie and Sam:

> He was an excellent dancer. He seemed to draw her close in to him by some male warmth of attraction, so that she became all soft and pliant to him, flowing to his form, whilst he united her with him and they lapsed along in one movement. She was just carried in a kind of strong, warm flood, her feet moved of themselves, and only the music threw her away from him, threw her back to him, to his clasp, in his strong form moving against her rhythmically, deliciously. (*PO*(C) 151)

The sexual analogy is clear but not crude, for this is something not limited to sexuality, but including it. The whole course of the evening is presented as a sequence in which Sam Adams exerts his power over Elsie, and she responds to it. But there is an element of predatory calculation in him, and she is aware of it as a lack:

> When it was over, he was pleased and his eyes had a curious gleam which thrilled her and yet had nothing to do with her. Yet it held her. He did not speak to her. He only looked straight into her eyes with a curious, gleaming look that disturbed her fearfully and deliciously. But also there was in his look some of the automatic irony of the *roué*. It left her partly cold. She was not carried away. (*PO*(C) 151)

So she is, as Whiston perceives, roused to the other man, but doesn't find a complete answer in him. In her roused state she goes to watch Whiston, quietly playing cribbage, and he is disturbed by his consciousness of her being so roused. This is a matter of the antennae, of receptivity to what is purely sensed, and Lawrence conveys it very vividly. She returns to the dance with Adams, and the tension rises further:

> That dance was an intoxication to her. After the first few steps, she felt herself slipping away from herself. She almost knew she was going, she did not even want to go. Yet she must have chosen to go. She lay in the arm of the steady, close man with whom she was dancing, and she seemed to swim away out of contact with the room, into him. She had passed into another, denser element of him, an essential privacy. The room was all vague around her, like an atmosphere, like under sea, with a flow of ghostly, dumb movements. . . . Every moment, and every moment, she felt she would give way utterly, and sink molten: the fusion point was coming when she would fuse down into perfect unconsciousness at his feet and knees. (*PO*(C) 153)

The language is familiar. Yet in this near-fusion she retains a small centre of resistance because of the persisting awareness of the man's predatoriness:

> . . . There was a strange impersonality about his low exultant call that appealed to her irresistibly. Yet why was she aware of some part shut off in her . . .?
> She was not aware of what she was doing, only a little grain of resistant trouble was in her. The man, possessed, yet with a superficial presence of mind, made way to the dining-room, as if to give her refreshment, cunningly working to his own escape with her. He was molten hot, filmed over with presence of mind, and bottomed with cold disbelief. (*PO*(C) 153)

That brilliant formula is Lawrence's swift summary, as ever-present and fully analytical consciousness, yet dealing in entirely new terms. It goes on with the same self-possessed clarity, neatness, and complete originality:

> In the dining-room was Whiston, carrying coffee to the plain, neglected ladies. Elsie saw him, but felt as if he could not see her. She was beyond his reach and ken. A sort of fusion existed between her and the large man at her side. She ate her custard,

but an incomplete fusion all the while sustained and contained within the being of her employer.

But she was growing cooler. Whiston came up. She looked at him, and saw him with different eyes. She saw his slim, young man's figure real and enduring before her. That was he. But she was in the spell with the other man, fused with him, and she could not be taken away. (*PO*(C) 153–4)

'That was he': it could not be more economical, and indicates that Whiston is 'there' for her. Once she has become aware of him as 'real and enduring', Whiston can try to make her conscious of the situation, and of him. But it is a struggle, since she resists: 'He was only a heavy place in her consciousness.'

The tension is broken rather than resolved by the incident with the stocking which has been so well prepared for. Adams picks it up as she stands there in an agony of embarrassment, and it is plain that his taking it is like a claim on her, a substitute for possession. Whiston is furious, and insists on leaving. When they are alone together she finally releases all her tension in a storm of tears, and commits herself to Whiston's ultimate tenderness. The whole sequence of her internal states, so intelligently and sympathetically divined, is conducted to a restabilisation.

It is this which is tested by the final turn of the story. When Whiston discovers that she has received the gifts of jewellery, has not told him about them, has also seen Adams again, he is jealous and angry. The formula in which Lawrence sums up their marriage is that

She was quite happy at first, carried away by her adoration of her husband. Then gradually she got used to him. He always was the ground of her happiness, but she got used to him, as to the air she breathed. He never got used to her in the same way.

Inside of marriage she found her liberty. She was rid of the responsibility of herself. Her husband must look after that. She was free to get what she could out of her time. (*PO*(C) 158)

Lawrence as dramatist shows her, within a page of this comment, testing Whiston by putting on the white stockings she has received from Adams.

"Don't they look nice?" she said. "One from last year and one from this, they just do. Save you buying a pair."

And she looked over her shoulders at her pretty calves, and at the dangling frills of her knickers.

"Put your skirts down and don't make a fool of yourself," he said.

"Why a fool of myself?" she asked.

And she began to dance slowly round the room, kicking up her feet half reckless, half jeering, in a ballet-dancer's fashion. Almost fearfully, yet in defiance, she kicked up her legs at him, singing as she did so. She resented him. (*PO*(C) 159–60)

This other dance, the solo dance of the defiant woman, is the prototype of the one that Anna Brangwen dances before Will, as *Anna Victrix*. She dances her independence, her defiance, her will to be separate, her scorn for him. But Whiston is not Will Brangwen. When as her final challenge Elsie tells him about the earrings and the brooch, in the spirit of 'and what are you going to do about that?', he answers with sheer violence. He has twice told her in their angry exchange that he will break her neck: an idea frequently entertained in Lawrence's world, and once actually carried out; and he now makes a start:

He seemed to thrust his face and his eyes forward at her, as he rose slowly and came to her. She watched transfixed in terror. Her throat made a small sound, as she tried to scream.

Then, quick as lightning, the back of his hand struck her with a crash across the mouth, and she was flung back blinded against the wall. The shock shook a queer sound out of her. And then she saw him still coming on, his eyes holding her, his fist drawn back, advancing slowly. At any instant the blow might crash into her.

Mad with terror, she raised her hands with a queer clawing movement to cover her eyes and her temples, opening her mouth in a dumb shriek. There was no sound. But the sight of her slowly arrested him. He hung before her, looking at her fixedly, as she stood crouched against the wall with open, bleeding mouth, and wide-staring eyes, and two hands clawing over her temples. And his lust to see her bleed, to break her and destroy her, rose from an old source against her. It carried him. he wanted satisfaction. (*PO*(C) 162)

As in 'The Prussian Officer' the violence is intensely seen, its strange sounds heard. Lawrence enters fully into it, as something which he wants to realise. There is no deprecation: this is what the man feels, what he wants, what he has it in him to do. But there is something else in him equally real, and more powerful: his sense of pity springing from his sense of responsibility for her:

> But he had seen her standing there, a piteous, horrified thing, and he turned his face aside in shame and nausea. He went and sat heavily in his chair, and a curious ease, almost like sleep, came over his brain. (*PO*(C) 162)

When he has returned the jewels to Adams, there is a poignant reconciliation, made more sweet by the tears and the blood:

> "I'm sleeping down here," he said. "Go you to bed."
> In a few moments she lifted her tear-stained, swollen face and looked at him with eyes all forlorn and pathetic. A great flash of anguish went over his body. He went over, slowly, and very gently took her in his hands. She let herself be taken. Then as she lay against his shoulders, she sobbed aloud:
> "I never meant –"
> "My love – my little love –" he cried, in anguish of spirit, holding her in his arms. (*PO*(C) 164)

The psychological penetration in the story is very remarkable; especially the challenges offered by Elsie, Adams's greedy opportunism, Whiston's slow wrath. The whole recollected sequence of the party, and the climactic present day of reckoning, where the morning prompts the long flashback and the evening follows and clinches it – it is all brilliantly constructed and, as a succession of actions and states of consciousness, imagined as only genius can imagine. Yet it has a limitation. I would not want to offer the conventional criticism that it is a day-dream of masculine dominance, since the story seems to me to be truthful, and faithful to the nature of the imagined people. It also renders with grace and assurance a stream of notations well beyond the reach of other writers. And in any case, Elsie's dance more than half-hints that neither violence nor tenderness can finally quell the spirit in her: something is invoked and released which might be more powerful than Lawrence's ostensible moral, the position where he wants to

end, that 'within his grasp, she could dart about excitingly', or
that 'he was the permanent basis from which she took these giddy
little flights into nowhere'. Whiston puts this something more
coarsely when in his anger he calls her a 'stray-running little
bitch': there he betrays a fear which may be natural, well-founded
and not merely angry. Bitches run astray as part of nature: so the
ending of the story may not be entirely an easy 'happy ever after';
rather a moment of reconciliation in a process which may recur.

Yet though one can point to such implications, one must admit
that the whole drive of the story is meant to confirm the moral:
that Whiston's masculine strength can from now on cradle Elsie's
feminine waywardness and charm, even if it has to offer a salutary
violence at the right moments. A more important criticism might
be that the sheer achievement of the story tells against it: its very
brilliance is created by Lawrence's complete knowledge of these
people, whom he has created and who pose no challenge to that
domination since they are not a mystery to him. He sees right
through them and all round them; and while we are startled,
touched, and impressed by all that he can see (more than we could
see ourselves) it threatens to leave his characters finished, closed
off, and known. 'New Eve and Old Adam' challenges the
comfortable male security, making it seem old-fashioned –
something from Lawrence's mother's young days. It also shows
him struggling with a major challenge that he can't see all round,
so that he will have to embark on his major fictions in order to
comprehend it.

One of the odd little filaments which I have mentioned links 'New
Eve and Old Adam' to 'The White Stocking' itself:

> And her quilted dressing-gown – it was a little bit torn, like
> most of her things – and her pearl-backed mirror, with one of
> the pieces of pearl missing – all her untidy, flimsy, lovable
> things hurt him as he went about the bedroom . . .
> (P/H SSI 80)

That reminds us of Elsie Whiston:

> Her slovenliness and untidiness did not trouble him. When she
> picked up the edge of her petticoat, ripped off a torn string of
> white lace, and flung it on the dressing-table, her careless

abandon made his spirit glow. . . . She wore an old, sack-like
dressing-jacket of black silk pinned across her breast. But one of
the sleeves, coming unfastened, showed some delightful pink
upper arm. (*PO*(C) 144–5)

Perhaps something of Lawrence's later experience is projected
back into the anecdote that his mother told him, and perhaps
something of his own marriage makes the observation of the
Whistons' so penetrating. But the little toy or pet Elsie is entirely
different from the New Eve, who is

a beautiful woman of about thirty, fair, luxuriant, with proud
shoulders and a face borne up by a fierce, native vitality. Her
green eyes had a curious puzzled contraction just now. (*P/H
SS* I 71)

This fair woman of 'about thirty' (Frieda was now thirty-three),
with her green or (in later fictions) 'tawny' eyes is a new person
altogether: not Jessie Chambers or Helen Corke or Louie
Burrows.[1] Lawrence has passed his twenty-sixth year and met
Frieda. If much of the early fiction was about not finding the right
woman, or not being able to reach across to any woman, the
problem is now, having found the woman, how to live with her:
how to be married. It remains the problem for a long time,
perhaps for the rest of his writing career.

'The Prussian Officer' and 'The Thorn in the Flesh' also took us
away from Nottinghamshire and London, away from England
altogether, and to the Germany that Lawrence knew in 1912–13.
The stories are new experience in another world, but it is
important to remember how much they are concerned with the
hardy peasant men and the peasant unconsciousness which
Lawrence divined in Bavaria and in Italy. His letters during the
period drop the essential hints,[2] and the experiences which found
their way into the difficult speculations of *Twilight in Italy* amplify
those hints. It is as if in this remote region he came upon what
George Saxton might have been if he had not had the bad luck to
be born in Protestant and industrial England. Something had
happened here which started working people or country people
into a damaging beginning of self-consciousness. Bachmann in
'The Thorn in the Flesh' is dangerously near it, but not yet lost; so
he and Emilie can find each other and be 'there' for each other in a

way which is easier than it is for Louisa Lindley and Alfred Durant.

'New Eve and Old Adam' introduces, with the Frieda-figure Paula and the Lawrence-figure Peter Moest, a new world of highly conscious and self-conscious people, inhabitants of England in Lawrence's present day, not his or his mother's youth. Moest is a businessman moving freely between London and Milan; and his cosmopolitan name suggests a sophisticated background. The Moests live in ease and tasteful luxury at a good London address. Nothing is said about Paula's background, but she is beautiful and obviously has a past; we infer that like Frieda she feels free, as a consciously liberated woman, to take lovers. She has her own income, which makes her independent of her husband. Another of the filaments I mention is this curious action, which mirrors a gesture by Clara Dawes in *Sons and Lovers*:

> With a quick movement she glanced down at her hands. She took off her wedding ring, reached to the bowl for a long flower-stalk, and shook the ring glittering round and round upon it, regarding the spinning gold, and spinning it as if she would spurn it. Yet there was something about her of a fretful naughty child as she did so.[3] (*P/H SS*I 72)

The action is unconscious, but the significance is obvious. The Moests have been married just over a year, and as Lawrence quickly points out, 'during the last three months there had gone on almost continuously that battle between them which so many married people fight, without knowing why'.

Though the story is tense with that conflict, almost nothing happens, in the crude sense. The passages between the two main characters are more verbal or analytical than the scenes in which the Whistons quarrel and are reconciled; yet despite this lively exchange at the conversational level, Lawrence is also uncannily receptive, as ever, to bodily posture, gesture and the quasi-electrical discharges which pass between people who may be silent ('His wife was all the time, in spite of herself, conscious of him, as if the cheek that was turned towards him had a sense which perceived him'). The silence may be eloquent ('He was sitting still motionless, and detached from her, hard; held absolutely away from her by his will'). This would *look* like a tender love-scene, but is more complex:

She crouched between his knees and put her arms round him. She was smiling into his face, her green eyes looking into his, were bright and wide. But somewhere in them, as he looked back, was a little twist that could not come loose to him, a little cast, that was like an aversion from him, a strain of hate for him.[4] The hot waves of blood flushed over his body, and his heart seemed to dissolve under her caresses. But at last, after many months, he knew her well enough. He knew that curious little strain in her eyes, which was waiting for him to submit to her, and then would spurn him again. He resisted her while ever it was there. (*P/H SS*I 75–6)

At this crucial moment in their relationship, when it may decline into an ordinary unsatisfactory marriage, a more or less mute battle of wills, there is an odd misunderstanding which precipitates the events of the story (they are mostly internal events). A telegram arrives for 'Moest', who happens to be someone of the same name staying in the same apartment building. Discounting this almost impossible coincidence, and seeing that the telegram suggests a rendez-vous, Moest thinks it must be a message to his wife from a lover: his insecurity betrays itself in this instant (yet reasonable) conviction. She, at odds with him anyway, pays him out by going out to see this unknown person, while Moest goes off in sadness to a nearby hotel, in preparation for his next business trip. In effect they are agreeing to part for a while, estranged, and this is a confession of failure. She discovers the misunderstanding about the telegram, summons him back next day, and introduces the other Moest, another hyperconscious intellectual. By an odd trick of habit, Lawrence produces another of the 'filaments': his fictional representative Moest responds, like the Lawrence-figure in other stories, to the attraction of the feared rival ('really lovable, evidently a gentleman'). This time the alter ego even has the same name; you can hardly go further without becoming a mirror-image. When he has gone, the Moests have another prolonged scene of conflict, verbal and non-verbal, leading to a love-making which is almost a reconciliation, but is really only another patching up. The battle will go on. The story ends with a sudden jump to a month later, and ends with counter-accusations from both of them, in letters written between her in London and him in Milan.

The story takes us deep into the other country of Lawrence's heart: not Eastwood, nor even Italy or New Mexico, but the interior landscape of people painfully involved with each other, making demands on and resisting the demands of each other. It can be thought of as like a landscape, of the kind Hopkins knew: with abrupt features, mountains and abysses. For some of its movements there has also been a traditional language, that of the introspective self. During these chapters of commentary I have pointed to the elements of a new language, necessary for things not notated before, and so new to consciousness. Lawrence's lovers are often articulate enough, and we are now entering the period where mature and conscious people become his central characters and offer their own attempt at an analysis of what they seek and what is happening to them. Peter Moest is the precursor of Rupert Birkin, in that respect. But like Birkin, and also like George Saxton, Siegmund Macnair, and Paul Morel, he is struggling for something, and obsessed with a desire, a lack. He must get this into words if he can, and in the attempt he faces the same difficulty as Cyril Mersham in 'A Modern Lover' who was looking for an 'algebra', or Bernard Coutts in 'The Witch à la Mode' who complained of the 'foggy weather of symbolism'. So another filament which ties 'New Eve and Old Adam' to the early stories is the search for a language, represented by this familiar phrase, which Peter Moest blurts out obsessively, though not managing to convey his need:

> Later, when he lay holding her with a passion intense like pain, the words blurted from him:
> "Flesh of my flesh – Paula! – Will you –?"
> "Yes my love," she answered, consolingly.
> He bit his mouth with pain. For him it was almost an agony of appeal.
> "But Paula – I mean it – flesh of my flesh – a wife –?"
> She tightened her arms round him without answering. And he knew, and she knew, that she put him off like that. (*P/H SS*I 93)

That is, she offers him the automatic comforting noise that a mother makes to a child.[5] Does she really know what he means? Probably not, though she offers to soothe him. Does *he* quite know what he means? Probably not, though these are the only words he has for it, and they press themselves on him like a half-remembered tune. She is ultimately aware of it, and wary of it, as a demand on her.

But she too makes demands, and her words are familiar:

> "I can't put it into words – but there it is. You – you don't love. I pour myself out to you, and then – there's nothing there – you simply aren't there."
>
> He was silent for some time. His jaw had set hard with fury and hate.
>
> "We have come to the incomprehensible," he said. (*P/H SS*I 77)

It might seem that they want something similar: he wants 'a wife', she wants him to be 'there'. But if they are so tragically at odds, the words must cover some essential gulf which their experience daily reveals to them. They have come to the edge of what is verbally communicable.

But Lawrence has been developing his own verbal resources, so that by the end of the story we have a better sense than the characters of what unites and divides them. Moest in his alienation goes off to a hotel. He does nothing there but have a bath and go to bed; and he says nothing, since he is alone. Lawrence however can deploy a set of language-equivalents for his blank wordless internal movements of depression, loss, bafflement and obsessive struggle.

His experience that night has two phases: one in the light, one in the dark. The first is familiar from the stories of George Saxton, Siegmund and Maurice Wookey: Moest ministers to his own body by washing it. But his feelings are the direct opposite of Maurice Wookey's, since he is in a state of feared defeat, not anticipated triumph, and is not being revealed to another person as a life that is 'there':

> He was trying, with the voluptuous warm water, and the exciting thrill of the shower-bath, to bring back the life into his dazed body. Since she had begun to hate him, he had gradually lost that physical pride and pleasure in his own physique which the first months of married life had given him. His body had gone meaningless to him again, almost as if it were not there. It had wakened up, there had been the physical glow and satisfaction about his movements of a creature which rejoices in

itself; a glow which comes on a man who loves and is loved passionately and successfully. Now this was going again. All the life was accumulating in his mental consciousness, and his body felt like a piece of waste. He was not aware of this. It was instinct that made him want to bath. But that, too, was a failure. He went under the shower-spray with his mind occupied by business, or some care of affairs, taking the tingling water almost without knowing it, stepping out mechanically, as a man going through a barren routine. He was dry again, and looking out of the window, without having experienced anything during the last hour. (*P/H SS*I 81)

The second movement is the more important:

As soon as he had turned out the light, and there was nothing left for his mental consciousness to flourish amongst, it dropped, and it was dark inside him as without. It was his blood, and the elemental male in it, that now rose from him; unknown instincts and unperceived movements out of the depths of his physical being rose and heaved blindly. The darkness almost suffocated him, and he could not bear it, that he was shut in this great, warm building. He wanted to be outside, with space springing from him. (*P/H SS*I 82)

The 'blood' is something whose meaning we have to feel for, and also his 'life'. The two are related but not identical. 'Space springing from him' is familiar as one of Lawrence's basic instinctive perceptions. The passage continues:

But again, the reasonable being in him knew it was ridiculous, and he remained staring at the dark, having the horrible sensation of a roof low down over him; whilst that dark, unknown being, which lived below all his consciousness in the eternal gloom of his blood, heaved and raged blindly against him. (*P/H SS*I 82)

Here, the 'life' and the 'blood' are moving nearer to consciousness – something they are naturally unwilling to do, since they are unconscious forces: not in the equivocal sense that we are unconscious of them, but in the strict sense that they are apart from and not under the control of the consciousness which can often glimpse them, and may even be set against them. The root-image here is of a stream or tide, naturally suggested by the idea of 'blood'. In that stream there lives an unidentified creature. Lawrence goes on:

> It was not his thoughts that represented him. They spun like straws or the iridescence of oil on a dark stream.

This is a deeper perception of thought than Cyril Mersham's. For him 'thought' had been distinct from 'life' in the sense that it was a residue or precipitate: a sum of experience, deposited by the events. Here, on the other hand, the thoughts are going on; but they are the film on a flowing surface, something swept along or carried away by a deeper and more powerful current than the stream of consciousness itself.

Now Lawrence begins to focus on Moest's aggrieved thoughts, having established that they are riding on the back of something else, which agitates them:

> . . . He had the dark, powerful sense of her, how she wanted to get away from him and from the deep, underneath intimacy which had gradually come between them, back to the easy, everyday life, where one knows nothing of the underneath, so that it takes its way apart from the consciousness.

That is a sharp perception: that the special relationship of two people in love sets the stream flowing more forcibly, as if the normal subterranean course, invisible, silent and calm, is forced up nearer to the surface, and one is bound to be uncomfortably aware of it. So thought is no fool, since it has given him this flash of conscious insight. But thought, riding on the stream, is also subject to one's grievances or obsessions, and so goes on to add, with the normal mixture of truth and parti pris:

> She did not want to have the deeper part of herself in direct contact with or under the influence of any other intrinsic being. She wanted, in the deepest sense, to be free of him. She could not bear the close, basic intimacy into which she had been drawn. She wanted her life for herself.

We begin to see what 'flesh of my flesh – a wife' might mean for Peter Moest. Lawrence is defining it by putting these obsessive or aggrieved feelings into words. We glimpse also how this obsession on the man's part could come across to the woman as a demand, an ivy-grip upon her. The conflict focuses on the ambiguous word 'life', which she wants 'for herself'. Actually, she *must* want that. But he sees it as fending him off, in a self-defensive unwillingness to commit herself as fully as he has done. The passage goes on:

> It was true, her strongest desire had been previously to know the contact through the whole of her being, down to the very bottom. Now it troubled her . . .

The idea of the contact between two beings has two aspects. We are aware of the importance for Lawrence of touch. Throughout the early fictions we have watched for the moment at which the hands, almost like climbing plants reaching out for a purchase-point, move out towards the other person. The hand, the instrument of touch, of contact, may be laid on the 'flesh', the body, of the other, either in a good love, or in an impertinent one, or in repudiation, hatred or violence. Where bodies touch, two streams of blood converge: most obviously in the act of love itself. But the notion of a constant contact throughout the whole of one's being evidently leaves no space between the two, and it is an idea that Lawrence himself moved away from (in Birkin's maxims or dicta about love, for instance[6]). But Moest is desperately trying to maintain this total contact, as if he feared to be totally cast off. He pursues:

> She wanted to disengage her roots. Above, in the open, she would give. But she must live perfectly free of herself, and not, at her source, be connected with anybody – –. She was using this symbolical Richard [the other Moest, the alter ego and rival] as a spade to dig him away from her. And he felt like a thing whose roots are all straining on their hold, . . .

The metaphor has strikingly changed. The plant-figure was dear to Lawrence, and we are familiar with its uses (faces as flowers, hands as tendrils). Its special aptness here (apart from the subdued ironic reflection on Moest's clinging, so that he may seem like an ivy or other plant-parasite) is that the 'out in the air' aspect – stem, leaves and flower – conveys the public, active, conscious nature of a life, and the touch of flamboyant display in Paula's nature. The 'down in the ground' aspect – the burrowing, clinging roots – gives an equivalent for the idea of the 'blood' and the 'life', or their original source below the surface. There is this important difference – often overlooked in some of Lawrence's key analogies – that the plant does indeed receive its life from the earth below, in the interaction of root and soil. But humans have no literal roots, so where does the life flow in? Where is the 'source', at which people are literally connected, and where the life flows between them? Only, and momentarily, in the sex-act. But Moest is not thinking of that, so there is an incoherence in his thought, concealed by the associative aptness of his changing metaphors. Nonetheless, the idea of the intertwining roots of two neighbouring plants conveys a quality of marriage which can be good or bad. The interconnection can be tranquil and natural; or it can be parasitic and predatory, and may cause one partner to want a separation of roots which seems painful or life-threatening to the other.

Moest's thought is still shaped, at the deeper level, by the image of the underneath-motion, the heaving, of his stream of life, so that the earth round his roots trembles from that seismic force as much as the feared spade that Paula threatens him with. One metaphor shifts into the other, and the poetic process renders as no other verbal process could both the subconscious or elemental drive of the mental stream and its inescapable partiality, indeed its near-panic. The node linking the two images, the pivot, is found in the completion of the sentence broken off above:

> straining on their hold, and whose elemental life, that blind source, surges backwards and forwards darkly, in a chaos, like something which is threatened with spilling out of its own vessel.

So he is both his own stream of life, and a pot-plant; the word 'vessel' neatly provides the idea of a container which may hold a plant, or a liquid; and the alternative meaning (a ship) takes him from an underground stream to the open sea:

This tremendous swaying of the most elemental part of him continued through the hours, accomplishing his being, whilst superficially he thought at random of the journey, of the Italian he would speak, how he had left his coat in the train . . .

'Accomplishing his being' is a strong phrase; but it is the essential Lawrentian process, which goes on whether one knows it or wants it. After the associative train of superficial thoughts:

. . . Underneath it all, like the sea under a pleasure-pier, his elemental, physical soul was heaving in great waves through his blood and his tissue, the sob, the silent lift, the slightly-washing fall away again. So his blood, out of whose darkness everything rose, being moved to its depth by her revulsion, heaved and swung towards its own rest, surging blindly to its own re-settling.

Without knowing it, he suffered that night almost more than he had ever suffered during his life. But it was all below his consciousness. It was his life itself at storm, not his mind and will engaged at all.

In the morning he got up, thin and quiet, without much movement anywhere, only with some of the clearness of after-storm. His body felt like a clean, empty shell. (*P/H SS*I 82–3)

Lawrence is surely one of the great introspectives: especially great because he did not see exactly the same mechanism as his predecessors in the European tradition of self-analysis. He saw more than others, or rather he was looking for different things. Only a superb power of self-awareness could render these processes. The paradox is that self-awareness must mean self-consciousness, and 'self' and 'conscious' are bad words or limiting definitions for Lawrence. What we see here is a new breadth or depth of consciousness, which does not attend merely to what the so-called self is normally thought to be urging on us. We are not here questioning obvious motives, and especially we are not in the presence of someone who is only doing the normal thing in self-examination; that is, trying to reach a balance between the self's representation of its own actions, its own view of itself and the world, and the suspected judgement of others. So there is nothing here which is ordinarily self-defensive or ordinarily self-critical or self-analytical. The total aim is not dissimilar (Lawrence was a man like other men) but it is more inclusive and deeper (Lawrence had a more powerful mind, to use that word, than we do). Alongside thought or underneath thought, he is representing something more fundamental, which most people do not recognise at all, and which the best people (defined as the best hitherto) would distrust precisely *because* it comes from that deep level and might be identified as a baser self which simply urges the demands of an instinctive need for self-satisfaction. But the puritan conscience which shuts them out as – to appropriate Lawrence's word – the 'flesh', or even the devil, may in that movement be shutting out something vital to which we absolutely must attend. We are flesh and blood, Lawrence is reminding us, and the representation of the world which we habitually manufacture up in the head, and which comes out in words, typically under-represents or even thwarts that other sense of the world which we take in, so to speak, at the breast where 'space starts', or which we touch with the hands. Especially it distrusts what comes welling up from within. The astonishing metaphor of the pleasure-pier is peculiarly apt. It is a rickety structure which goes out into the element, the sea. But we are also that element: it is only the pier, the consciousness, that thinks it is different. Our pier-legs go down into it, and when there are waves we feel them. When there is a storm, the pier may collapse.

Again Lawrence had had an inkling of that relationship in a rapid notation in 'A Modern Lover': 'His disappointment rose as water suddenly heaves up the side of a ship.' But the ship is external to the water: the pier is rooted in it, as plants are rooted in their soil. So what looks in this long passage like a mixed metaphor reveals itself as a poetic analogical process. All the best poetry mixes its metaphors: or rather, poetry offers a way of progressing which is unlike other thoughts in that the logic leaps apparent gaps, is inductive in the way that electricity is, and can be intuitive and personal: but with the right person doing it, the process rapidly brings together things we had not thought related. For Lawrence it is the instrument through which he can apprehend and convey the width and depth of the internal personal goings-on which he wishes to substitute for the narrower traditional notation of the stream of consciousness. It is no accident that that phrase is a metaphor; no accident either that Lawrence's capacity to

entertain both the conscious and the unconscious elements of the
stream has moral consequences. He is bringing up to the bar, and
allowing to plead, the element which others had dismissed as
'lower', as anti-social, as the consequence of 'original sin'. If the
prophet could call it 'the heart', he could immediately denounce it
as 'desperately wicked'.[7] If it is what Freud called the 'id', he
expressed by the very name the alienation of the social self from
what it feels to be other, and merely anonymous and universal.
Freud's categorisation is traditional, and entails traditional
paradoxes: if the 'id' is 'that', how can it also be me? Or am I split
into warring, separate elements? Traditional Christian belief,
shrewd as it was, allowed the prompting of an external devil. But
that, like Freud, enables one to disown something which one
ought to own. Lawrence is saying it is not 'that'; or the 'devil'. It *is*
human nature and universal; it is also essentially me. Indeed it is
'my life', needing to be heard, and I ignore it to my ultimate great
cost.

But traditional psychological schemata and the great European
tradition of moral judgement based on introspection are not
foolish either. Lawrence is here pressing on us as 'life' what would
by others, earlier, have been dismissed or suspected as the
promptings of the 'self'. And this is supported by the obvious fact
that Moest, pressing the demands of his 'blood' or his 'life' is
resisted by his wife, who senses a predatory demand on her by a
will which wants her to submit, and to which she might both
acutely and credibly reply that *her* 'life', *her* 'blood', required that
she should in at least a corner of her being remain free of him. The
image of roots intertwining can easily turn into that of ivy sucking
the life out of a tree. Finally they are left saying to each other 'You
are not me. You cannot see yourself as I see you. I fear and resent
your demand on me, your resistance to me'. If implicitly Moest is
saying (as I think Lawrence often did, with some reason) 'My
insight is deeper than yours. Trust me.', Paula's reply can be 'It's
not your insight I fear, but your motives. You want me to submit
to you. You have a basic fear, of being alone, which you translate
into a wish for dominance.'

So the battleground is essentially set out, and the terms, or the
weapons, of the conflict displayed. This brief story at last fully
announces one of Lawrence's main themes, encapsulates some of
his insights, and for the first time brings into focus many of the
shadowy inklings which had haunted the earlier fictions like

things wanting to be recognised, but not yet seen nor heard clearly enough. The other thing to be noted about the story is its scrupulous fairness to both characters struggling with each other. There isn't much doubt that Moest represents what Lawrence himself had at one stage felt. What strikes the reader is how firmly Moest is dramatically 'placed': there is a desperation in him, and an incoherence, which a self-possessed woman like his wife could both look down on from her greater security, laugh at a little, be irritated by, and finally be exhausted by. So her feeling that after months of struggle she needs 'rest' is perfectly understandable. But one senses also a kind of moral indolence in her, and her own form of domination, which is essentially her power to charm when she decides to charm, her power to give when she feels like giving, and a slightly childish hurt when the recipient of her favours is not either pliantly delighted to be charmed for the moment or content when she withdraws for another moment. She wants him always 'there', in that sense. He, for his part, anxious and tense, sees himself being manipulated by a mistress, when what he wants, he says, is a 'wife', 'flesh of my flesh'. It is here that his incoherence lies: the meaning of those words is obsessively clear to him, but not to her, or to us. It sounds like a demand in part-consequence. This almost comes through to him:

> Was there something in it? Did he only want the attributes which went along with her, the peace of heart which a man has in living to one woman, even if the love between them be not complete; the singleness and unity in his life that made it easy; the fixed establishment of himself as a married man with a home; the feeling that he belonged to somewhere, that one woman existed – not was paid but *existed* – really to take care of him; was it these things he wanted, and not her? But he wanted her for these purposes – her, and nobody else. But was that not enough for her? Perhaps he wronged her – it was possible. What she said against him was in earnest. And what she said in earnest he had to believe, in the long run, since it was the utterance of her being. He felt miserable and tired. (*P/H SS*I 89)

These are, we see, thoughts – daylight thoughts: they are shrewd ones, too. He is representing to himself one ordinary but good kind of marriage. He also accepts his needs and sees that they come out

as demands, at least to her. And in the last phrase about 'the
utterance of her being' he is recognising that the 'life', the 'blood'
in her can be set against his 'life' and his 'blood' as firmly as any
conflict of self: indeed the two things here merge.

This moment of thought and self-knowledge becomes a
moment of pure grace. Not shut off in his suffering, he can
recognise hers:

> When he looked at her, across the gathering twilight of the
> room, she was staring into the fire, and biting her finger-nail,
> restlessly, restlessly, without knowing. And all his limbs went
> suddenly weak, as he realised that she suffered too, that
> something was gnawing at her. Something in the look of her, the
> crouching, dogged, wondering look, made him faint with
> tenderness for her.
> "Don't bite your fingernails", he said quietly, and
> obediently, she took her hand from her mouth.[8] His heart was
> beating quickly. He could feel the atmosphere of the room
> changing. It had stood aloof, the room, like something placed
> round him, like a great box. Now everything got softer, as if it
> partook of the atmosphere, of which he partook himself, and
> they were all one. (*P/H SS*I 89)

These are *not* thoughts, but feelings caught as only Lawrence
can catch these fugitive, largely physiological inner movements.
The relaxation, the softening, is a real tenderness, and it is odd but
truthful that he sees it as projected onto the room around him, so
that he creates the atmosphere he feels (we remember the similar
projection in 'Second-Best'). It is odd, but truthful also, that his
tenderness betrays itself as an instruction, and that she obeys.

By another flash of insight, Lawrence shows that such moments
pass; Moest reverts at once into his anguished and obsessional
questioning of himself, and of her. And in so doing he proves the
point he is resisting – her charge that 'he cannot come out of
himself'. For here, now, he does not:

> His mind reverted to her accusations, and his heart beat like
> a caged thing against what he could not understand. She said he
> did not love her. But he knew that in his way he did. In his way
> – but was his way wrong? His way was himself, he thought,
> struggling. Was there something wrong, something missing in

his nature, that he could not love? He struggled madly, as if he were in a mesh, and could not get out. . . . She said he could not come out of himself, that he was no good to her, because he could not get outside himself. What did she mean? Get outside himself! It seemed like some acrobatic feat, some slippery contortionist trick. . . . His heart flashed hot with resentment. (*P/H SS*I 89–90)

But we know what she means, and we see him proving her point. He now feels he must get away from all this complication, and 'casually' says he must go. She then proves that *she* can get outside herself, but simultaneously proves his point about her, that she manipulates him:

> She did not answer. Then she turned and looked at him with a queer, half bewildered, half perverse smile that seemed conscious of pain. Her eyes, shining rather dilated and triumphant, and yet with something heavily yearning behind them, looked into his. He could not understand, and, between her appeal and her defiant triumph, he felt as if his chest were crushed so that he could not breathe.
>
> "My love" she said, in a little singing, abstract fashion, her lips somehow sipping towards him, her eyes shining dilated; and yet he felt as if he were not in it, himself. (*P/H SS*I 90)

It is his consciousness we see through, but I think that, transfixed, it is a truthful consciousness here – candid in the old sense. We do see in her 'triumph' her ability both to move towards him, which is a grace denied him, and her ability to manage him. The essential gestures follow: a hand is put out to touch him; he touches her hand. They embrace.

It is a moving moment, but the deeper truth in it, which Lawrence grasps and conveys, is that even here the struggle and the resistance goes on. The gesture of lifting the arms, familiar from the earlier fiction, and the word 'fusing' that we have met before and will face again, make their not unexpected appearance:

> His wife, when she came back, as soon as she had closed the door, lifted her arms to him in a little ecstasy, coming to him. They clasped each other close, body to body. And the intensity of his feeling was so fierce, he felt himself going dim, fusing into

something soft and plastic between her hands. And this connection with her was bigger than life or death. And at the bottom of his heart was a sob. (*P/H SS*I 91)

And later, he reaches another kind of summary:

He loved her, and it would never be peace between them, she would never belong to him, as a wife. She would take and reject him, like a mistress. And perhaps for that reason he would love her all the more; it might be so. (*P/H SS*I 92)

What he means by 'like a mistress' we have seen. What he means by 'like a wife' cannot be given the same definition, since she is not like that. So when at last he stammers out his longing, his demand ('flesh of my flesh – a wife'), and she says 'Yes, my love' consolingly ('and he knew, and she knew, that she put him off like that'), she has acted like a mother, soothing a child but not looking beyond the soothing noise to the real need. Nor can she, really, since it would seem that he is fundamentally asking her to be someone else, just as her demand that 'he come out of himself' is an evident demand for him to do the same.

So they are locked in a conflict of a common enough kind. The triumph of the story is how sharply, how deeply it is realised on both sides, and how important it is shown to be for those who must undergo it.

The two rather despairing statements which close the story are extracts from letters stating once more the irreconcilable positions. Paula's is shrewd, starting 'Your idea of your woman is that she is an expansion, no a *rib* of yourself, without any existence of her own.' This gives us the title, and something to think about. The New Eve is determined not to be Adam's rib; in consequence she *cannot* be what Adam called 'bone of my bones and flesh of my flesh'.[9] The Old Adam, it seems, is something about human nature that will not change. Moest's last words are either a total expression of their failure and his despair, or a merely obstinate repetition of his point of view, and an injustice to her:

'For my side, without you, I am done – But you lie to yourself. You *wouldn't* love *me*, and you won't be able to love anybody else – except generally'. (*P/H SS*I 94)

Notes

CHAPTER 1   THE CRITICISM OF LAWRENCE

1. 'I think the real tragedy is in the inner war which is waged between people who love each other, a war out of which comes knowledge and –' (Letter to Edward Garnett of 29 June 1912 in *Letters I* 419). One might complete the sentence by saying 'stories like 'New Eve and Old Adam' ' – discussed below. The better-known statements come in a letter to Sallie Hopkin of 25 December 1912 (*Letters I* 492): 'I'll do my life-work, sticking up for the love between man and woman', and the letter to Arthur McLeod of 23 April 1913 (*Letters I* 543–4): 'And I am so sure that only through a readjustment between men and women, and a making free and healthy of the sex, will she [England] get out of her present atrophy . . . I do write because I want folk – English folk – to alter, and have more sense.' These three letters were printed in Huxley's collection of 1932, and were much quoted by Lawrence's supporters. The last must have seemed progressive; since 'free' implies a liberation, and 'healthy' a hygienic enterprise.
2. Published in 1955. Leavis's first publication on Lawrence was the 'Minority Pamphlet' Number 6 published in 1930 by Gordon Fraser. He there took the position that Lawrence's greatest work was *Lady Chatterley's Lover*. He reviewed the Huxley *Letters* in *The Listener* in 1932, and in a longer review in the first volume of *Scrutiny* in the same year.
3. '. . . Love was once a Little Boy' is reprinted in *Phoenix II*. It is part of *Reflections on the Death of a Porcupine*, first published in Philadelphia in 1925.
4. F. R. Leavis: *Thoughts, Words and Creativity: Art and Thought in Lawrence* (London, 1976) pp. 122, 124.
5. Ibid., p. 54.
6. J. C. F. Littlewood: *D. H. Lawrence, 1885–1914* (British Council 'Writers and their Work' Series), (London, 1976) p. 20.
7. Ed. Carl Baron: *A Memoir of D. H. Lawrence (The Betrayal)*, by G. H. Neville (Cambridge, 1981) p. 2.

CHAPTER 2   METHOD

1. I know how hard it is. One needs something to make one's mood deep and sincere. There are so many little frets that prevent our coming at the real naked essence of our vision. It sounds boshy, doesn't it. I often think one ought to be able to pray, before one works – and then leave it to the Lord.

Isn't it hard, hard work to come to real grips with one's imagination –
throw everything overboard. I always feel as if I stood naked for the fire of
Almighty God to go through me – and it's rather an awful feeling. (*Letters
I* 519)

2. *Letters I* 109. The poem is 'Cherry Robbers', later published in *Love Poems and
   Others* in 1913.
3. *Letters I* 113–14. '. . . and the new-fangled madness of 'Hedda Gabler'. . . .
   'Hedda Gabler' is subtlest, profoundest – and, I think, truest; least
   imaginary.'
4. 'Miss Whale is quite right when she says I am good – I *am* good. Give her my
   love. Only the women have eyes for goodness – and they wear green moral
   spectacles, most of 'em.' Letter to Edward Garnett, in *Letters I* 410. Lawrence
   is joking, but means it nonetheless.

CHAPTER 3   *THE WHITE PEACOCK*

1. Lawrence was struck by something spontaneous and uninhibited in her
   cheeky courage, and she reappears as Beatrice Wyld in *Sons and Lovers*. But in
   The White Peacock she is simply a tiring voice.
2. George also has in him some elements of George Neville. This is an early
   example of the danger of saying that George 'was' Alan Chambers, since he
   is a composite figure. It is also an example of the reverse danger of saying
   that George Neville 'became' George Saxton, since some of Neville's
   characteristics are given in the early pages to Leslie Tempest. Leslie's
   characterisation wavers: this is not a matter yet, of Lawrence's deep
   perception of the instability of the ego – more a matter of not making up his
   mind what he wanted Leslie to be, or simply not seeing him clearly. He starts
   as a complacent bounder, and is at first crudely drawn. He turns into a
   dependent nature, and becomes interesting; he ends as a merely social
   personality.
3. He is careful to tell us that he was born, like Lawrence, in September, and
   that he is twenty-three – as Lawrence was in 1908. This is the first example of
   a habit. Annable concludes his own story by saying that his life effectively
   came to an end at 26, Lawrence's age when the novel was published, and the
   age at which he thought his own first life had ended, with the death of his
   mother, and the end of the relationships with Jessie Chambers, Louie
   Burrows and Helen Corke. See the comment by Murry, in *Son of Woman*,
   39–46.
4. In Part II, Chapter V, 'An Arrow from the Impatient God'. The scene is like
   the breakdown of Skrebensky when he is rejected by Ursula Brangwen in *The
   Rainbow*.
5. The reader is struck by this as an imaginative stroke, without knowing what
   to make of it. Later fictions enable us to see it as a characteristic female
   hubris. In 'St Mawr', Mrs Witt decides to cut the hair of her groom Lewis.
   He submits (like Samson, but awake). He is made aware that a woman who
   can lay a hand on his body in this way, both proprietory and frivolous,

cannot have a deep respect for him; and that is his reason for rejecting Mrs Witt's later offer of marriage. See also the other instances of irreverent handling below, in 'Odour of Chrysanthemums', 'Daughters of the Vicar', *Sons and Lovers*. A personal experience is recorded in the poem 'She said as well to me' in *Look! We Have Come Through!* Touching the hair recurs in 'New Eve and Old Adam'.

6. See *Letters I* 97, 99, to May Holbrook and Blanche Jennings, in December 1908; especially the second:

> I have kissed dozens of girls – on the cheek – never on the mouth – I could not. Such a touch is the connection between the vigorous flow of two lives. Like a positive electricity, a current of creative life runs through two persons, and they are instinct with the same life force – the same vitality – the same I know not what – when they kiss on the mouth – when they kiss as lovers do. Come to think of it and it is exceedingly rare that two people participate in entirely the same sensation and emotion; but they do when they kiss as lovers, I am sure. Then a certain life-current passes through them which changes them forever; another such effect is produced in a mother by the continual soft touchings of her baby. Somehow, I think we come into knowledge (unconscious) of the most vital parts of the cosmos through touching things. You do not know how I feel my soul enlarged through contact with the soft arms and face and body of my Hilda Mary – who is nine months old today. I know my phraseology is vague and impossible.

7. Lawrence felt that Orion was 'his' constellation, though he also had a strong affinity with the evening and morning star.

8. We may see in the 'hoary imp' the prototype of the 'wizard rat' which swims ahead of the others in *Women in Love*, and whose human representative is Loerke the sculptor. In Lawrence's own life Gertler and Maurice Magnus seemed to him mysteriously rat-like.

9. See below, p. 170, for an expansion of the potential in 'stately barbaric hordes'.

10. Cf in *Women in Love* the passage in the chapter 'Breadalby' where Birkin, having been assaulted by Hermione, leaves the house and 'saturates himself with the touch' of the bushes and flowers. They are the alternative to people, as inhabitants of the universe and things one can relate to; and at moments of crisis, much preferred alternatives.

11. Isa 40.6; Job 14.2. The first text in its complete form reads:

> The Voice said, Cry. And he said, What shall I cry?
> All flesh is grass and all the goodliness thereof is as the flower of the field: The grass withereth, the flower fadeth: because the spirit of the LORD bloweth upon it: surely the people is grass.

12. Cf *Letters I* 202 '. . . we have to struggle like water-beetles stranded and toiling in mud'.

13. The reader familiar with the biographical record will know that in implying that Lettie and Meg are representative Lawrence was speaking from his own dilemma. He felt at this time that there were two sorts of women, the 'spiritual' and the 'physical', and that a man could not expect to have both sorts of satisfaction from one woman. He saw Jessie Chambers as only spiritual, and Louie Burrows as only 'natural' or desirable. He feared a fate

in which, married to a Louie or a Meg, the husband, like George, finds he cannot give himself entirely to the wife, because she answers to his physical need only. She would be naturally offended and jealous, because (like all women?) she would also want 'the soul of him'. Refused it, she would turn away to the children. He shows this happening in *The White Peacock*, and presents it as inevitable, and, since there is no example of anything happier, as a universal consequence of all women wanting the man's 'soul', whether they are 'spiritual' or not.

Jessie Chambers thought Lawrence was fundamentally muddled about this. He projected on to her *his* inability to desire *her*, and type-cast her as spiritual, 'a holy nun'. He felt desire for Louie, but only that; and he did them both an injury by splitting his own needs between them and implying that neither wanted both parts of *him*.

The White Peacock is somewhat diminished in its power because of this premature generalising, and its universality is to that degree specious.

See Jessie Chambers: *A Personal Record*, especially pp. 138–40, and in *Letters I* 30 July 1908 to Blanche Jennings, 66–7, where Lawrence puts his own position more subtly.

CHAPTER 4   *THE TRESPASSER*

1. This letter has another interest. At the end of it, Lawrence rather mysteriously says:

> I can never decide whether my dreams are the result of my thoughts, or my thoughts the result of my dreams. It is very queer. But my dreams make conclusions for me. They decide things finally. I dream a decision. Sleep seems to hammer out for me the logical conclusions of my vague days, and offer me them as dreams. It is a horrid feeling, not to be able to escape from one's own – what? – self – daemon, fate, or something. I hate to have my own judgments clinched inside me involuntarily. But it is so.
>
> What tosh to write. I don't know what ails me.

There is the moment of self-deprecation, after the moment of insight. The reader wonders, what *was* the decision? He then sees a few pages later that on the 4 February Lawrence wrote to Louie Burrows, breaking off their engagement. The interest for us here is that throughout *The Trespasser* he shows his main character Siegmund evolving by the same process towards the same kind of decision. It crystallises at this point, without more words:

> At half past six in the morning he suddenly opened his eyes.
>
> "What is it?" he asked, and almost without interruption answered:
>
> "Well, I've got to go through it."
>
> His sleep had shaped him perfect premonition, which, like a dream, he forgot when he awoke. Only this naïve question and answer betrayed what had taken place in his sleep. Immediately he awoke, this subordinate knowledge vanished. (*T*(C) 175)

2. Especially the 'Freshwater Diary' now reprinted in the Cambridge Edition. This shows that Lawrence followed the incidents carefully, and worked actual fragments of conversation into his own narrative. To see how he

amplifies the Diary is to see how carefully he imagined how it might all have been, and especially the inner movements in the people which produce the words and the actions.

3. 'Siegmund' is only the Wagnerian nick-name given to him by Helena. His name is Bertram. Siegmund dies a fated death in Wagner's *Die Walküre*. Helena and Siegmund think of her as like Sieglinde, Siegmund's twin sister, for whom he has an incestuous love, leaving her carrying his child after a single night of enchanted passion. Helena's true part is more like that of Brünnhilde, sent to announce and to secure Siegmund's death. Certainly she is fatal to him.

4. As the letters record. See also 'The Witch à la Mode', discussed below. In the last stages of writing *The White Peacock* Lawrence knew Helen Corke well and was painfully involved with her.

5. At the very end, 'He sat up suddenly, threw away the bedclothes, from which came a puff of hot steam, and began to rub his pyjamas against his sides and legs.' (199). This is *too* neat a symmetry.

6. Cf Cyril's gesture to Annable: 'I held out my hand from the shadow. I was startled myself by the white sympathy it expressed extended towards him in the moonlight.' (*WP*(C) 151). Or Lettie's gesture: 'The soft outreaching of her hand was like the whispering of strange words into the blood' (*WP*(C) 255).

7. The word is one of Lawrence's favourites: or it was until 'loins' became the preoccupation. The source-document is the letter to Blanche Jennings (p. 64 above) but the word recurs very frequently. For instance:

> Then, tucking her head in his breast, hiding her face, she timidly slid her hands along his sides, pressing softly, to find the contours of his figure. (*T*(C) 63)

Or, in *Sons and Lovers*:

> He straightened himself. His back was towards her. She put her two hands on his sides, and ran them quickly down.
> 'You are so *fine!*' she said. (*S & L*(P) 242)

8. Cf a few pages later: 'She had given him this new, soft beauty. She was the earth in which his strange flowers grew' (69).

9. Annable thought of his Lady Chrystabel as 'souly', and associated her with Waterhouse's picture, *The Lady of Shalott*. Tennyson's poem gives 'the crystal mirror' in which the fated lady sees the world reflected. For a working out of the image, see 'The Witch à la Mode' below.

10. Lawrence was peculiarly conscious of the junction between head and body. In *The White Peacock* Cyril advised George, if he wanted to attract Lettie, to 'leave your neck showing' (162). That would draw her attention again to what she had earlier noticed with excitement: 'the sudden meeting of the sun-hot skin with the white flesh in his throat' (14). In *The Trespasser* Helena's 'cool thick throat' (55) is mentioned several times. Helena, characteristically, is a little shocked when Siegmund leaves his collar off 'so his throat was bare above the neck band of his flannel shirt. Altogether she disapproved of his slovenly appearance.' (75). His 'bare throat', and 'strong throat' are mentioned in the exchange with Hampson, and again on p. 114. See also 'The Thorn in the Flesh' below; and of course 'The Prussian Officer', where the temptation in a letter to Helen Corke is indulged: 'You

see, I know Siegmund is there all the time. I know you would go back to him, after me, and disclaim me. I know it very deeply. I know I could not bear it. I feel often inclined, when I think of you, to put my thumbs on your throat.' (*Letters I* 160, 11 May 1910).

11. In particular, the idea of a central patch of light, a circle, round which there is shadow, is transformed later into the idea of a circle of firelight outside which wild beasts may prowl. See below, on *Sons and Lovers*, p. 170ff.

A related idea may have been suggested by images such as Pater's 'burning with a hard gem-like flame,' but is extended into the thought that people burn with various kinds of flame, at varying rates. George Saxton is taken with the idea of burning up fiercely and brightly like a wood-fire, but does the opposite. Miriam Leivers and Mrs Morel burn like pressure-lamps, with a fierce white light. Walter Morel has the natural golden glow of the candle.

Lawrence used the idea of the 'hidden level' or 'real substratum' in talking about his dying mother: "She was when well, incredibly bright, with more smile-wrinkles than anything: you'd never know that this was the permanent structure on which the other floated'. (Letter to Arthur McLeod of 5 December 1910 in *Letters I*, 1912). The word 'floated', seemingly inappropriate to a 'structure', takes us back subliminally to the oil-level in the lamp, and the sea beneath the sand.

12. George Saxton has the same momentary ecstasy. He turns to Cyril, who has just given him, as wedding present, watercolour paintings of the scenes of their shared happy youth. ' "It's been wonderful, Cyril, all the time," he said, with surprised joy.'

13. In the old days of lead toy soldiers and open fires, children often put a broken soldier in the fire. They saw, first, the paint burn off in a rapid shrivelling: then amazed, they saw the figure collapse into a little caterpillar of brilliant silver lead which wriggled down through the burning coal to drop like a bright bead into the ash below. I think Lawrence has this in his memory; but also of course his experimental work in the laboratory at University College Nottingham.

14. Cf the letters to Blanche Jennings of 15 December 1908 (*Letters I* 98): 'You women, when you turn, you are like Lot's wife, pillars of salt, immutable; you can never turn again and look with calm generous eyes on a thing that has disappointed and disillusioned you.'

15. Cf *Sons and Lovers* below, for permutations on Madonna-lilies, golden light and white light. Further treatments of the woman as moon-creature are found in *The Rainbow* and *Women in Love* in particular.

CHAPTER 5   SHORT STORIES I

1. The reader will find the clearest and most up-to-date statement in the chronologies in Cambridge Edition of *The Prussian Officer* and *Love Among the Haystacks*, edited by John Worthen (Cambridge, 1983, 1986).
2. Emily in *The White Peacock*, Muriel in 'The Fly in the Ointment' and 'A Modern Lover'; Hilda in 'Shades of Spring', Miriam in *Sons and Lovers*.

3. Cf in 'The Fly in the Ointment':

> I rejoiced exceedingly when night came, with the evening star, and the sky flushed dark blue, purple, over the golden pomegranates of the lamps.

4. The rival, Tom Vickers, is not a gamekeeper, but an electrical engineer, reminding one of the younger Tom Brangwen in *The Rainbow*. But the image establishes a link with Annable, with Arthur Pilbeam in 'Shades of Spring' (see below) and with Mellors. The attribution of these murdered-vermin hands to the Lawrence-figure implies something striking about the relationship with the rival, or the alter ego, or the father-figure – all shapes which the gamekeeper takes. A further complication is the insistence by Mersham that the rival is 'strictly lovable'; has a 'beautiful lustihood that is unconscious like a blossom', is 'like summer, brown and full of warmth', 'very desirable', and so on.

5. Mrs Thomas is thirty-four; eight years older than Severn, who is therefore twenty-six, rising twenty-seven.

6. Severn cannot box, and makes straight for the other man's throat: like Paul Morel with Baxter Dawes and the orderly in 'The Prussian Officer'.

7. Worthen points out that the passage quoted above is from a redrafting of 1914. The story has three layers; of 1911, 1912, 1914. The relevant passage of 'Odour of Chrysanthemums' was also written in 1914.

8. The reference is to the Persephone legend, which was touched on more than once in *The White Peacock*. Annable called his wife 'Persephone'.

9. The perception links Annable, who knew his Lady Chrystabel was also a Lady of Shalott and a Belle dame sans merci, and Siegmund Macnair and Lawrence himself. The witchcraft motif is also found in *Sons and Lovers*, where 'Gipsy' Lily Denys ensnares William Morel, while the young Paul watches, himself entranced. *Sons and Lovers* also gives a sub-theme of the witch motif, where Paul puts flowers in the hair of the enchantress:

> Paul went gathering the big daisies. She had taken off her hat; her hair was black as a horse's mane. Paul came back and threaded daisies in her jet-black hair – big spangles of white and yellow, and just a pink touch of ragged robin.
>
> 'Now you look like a young witch-woman' the boy said to her. (*S & L*(P) 173)

In 'New Eve and Old Adam' the wife put flowers in her hair, with an unexplained intention. The husband's resistance to her is the resistance to an enchantment. (See below, pp. 240ff.)

In 'Once' the short story currently printed in *Phoenix II*, the heroine makes her soldier-lover 'have roses in his hair'.

10. The picture is reproduced in Baron (ed): G. H. Neville *A Memoir of D. H. Lawrence* (Cambridge, 1981) facing page 73; and see Appendix B: 'Lawrence, Neville and Geiffenhagen's "Idyll" '.

11. 'A Modern Lover' gives the first of the miners' washing-scenes:

> The boys had stripped to their waists, and had knelt on the hearth-rug and washed themselves in a large tin bowl, the mother sponging and drying their backs. Now they stood wiping themselves, the firelight bright and rosy on their fine torses, their heavy arms swelling and sinking with a life. They seemed to cherish the firelight on their bodies. Benjamin, the younger, leaned his breast to the warmth, and threw back his head,

showing his teeth in a voluptuous little smile. Mersham watched them, as he had watched the peewits and the sunset. (*P/H SS*I 4–5)

Bernard and Hubert Chambers probably worked in the pit; and Lawrence has casually imported this note without as yet making much of it or tying it into the story. It becomes significant in 'Odour of Chrysanthemums' and 'Daughters of the Vicar', as revealing what the man 'is' (see the comment on those stories). But we are also reminded of George Saxton and Siegmund Macnair stripping to swim, and other loci.

12. The work of historians, art historians and literary scholars on Renaissance topics was made more widely available in England and distilled into literary theory by writers like Symonds, following Pater. At another level still, it became popular in (for instance) the historical novels of Maurice Hewlett, which made the condottiere or the troubadour glamorous, like the English knight. The trend becomes more literary in the early poems of Yeats and Pound. One story in the collection *The Prussian Officer* which Lawrence's literary friends praised to him was the worst one – 'A Fragment of Stained Glass'. It is 'historical' and uses a strong variant of Hewlett's mannered narrative style, which mingles reminiscences of Cellini's autobiography, Malory, and the Arthurian poems of Tennyson and the Pre-Raphaelites. The attraction for Lawrence's contemporaries of that old world was that it went behind naturalism and prose into a world of passion, violent action, striking costume, and magic. But Lawrence's everyday world is magical, and he had no need to put on a Wardour-Street costume. Helen Corke read Maurice Hewlett, and Lawrence, having felt Hewlett's spurious charm, first turned it to effect in his own story, and then made the discovery that the real woman he knew was a Belle Dame Sans Merci.

CHAPTER 6 *SONS AND LOVERS*

1. See, for instance, the discussion of 'The Prussian Officer' and 'The Thorn in the Flesh' in Chapter 8; and note 6 below.

2. Wisely, and not immodestly, Jessie wrote to Emile Delavenay on 21 June 1935: '. . . no critic, so far as I have seen, has been at the trouble to remark upon the really astonishing fact that so unpropitious an environment should produce Lawrence and me in such close proximity. (I know you'll pardon anything that sounds like conceit; I am not speaking of myself in the *personal* sense). When I look back upon the early surroundings of both of us I feel both amazement and reverence at the sheer pertinacity of all the spiritual powers of life'.

3. J. C. F. Littlewood points out that retrospective justice is done to Jessie in the character and experience of the young Ursula Brangwen in *The Rainbow* (in his article already cited). The Miriam-figure in the short stories 'The Shades of Spring' and 'A Modern Lover' is also given more strength and independence than the Miriam of *Sons and Lovers*; and in 'A Modern Lover', which predates *Paul Morel*, Cyril Mersham has the grace to admit that "I used to shrink from the thought of having to kiss you, didn't I?" (p. 119 above). So Lawrence was capable of admitting that at one time he could not

approach Jessie sexually; so that it was unjust to present only her as bound in by her virginity. And in 'New Eve and Old Adam' Paula Moest says to the Lawrence-figure Peter Moest some of the bitter things that Miriam once says to Paul Morel.

4. By this time Mrs Morel was trembling violently. Struggles of this kind often took place between her and her son, when she seemed to fight for his very life against his own will to die. (*S & L*(P) 316)

[After her death] The lesser things he began to let go from him, for fear of this big thing, the lapse towards death, following in the wake of his beloved. (*S & L*(P) 478)

He would not admit that he wanted to die, to have done. He would not own that life had beaten him, or that death had beaten him. (*S & L*(P) 484–4)

5. In the sense that like many mothers, she puts up with an unsatisfactory marriage for the sake of the children ('Wouldn't I have gone long ago, but for these children?' *S & L*(P) 58). But she also requires the children to make up for it: makes them her justification and consolation, lives through them, and so sacrifices them.

6. 'No: he never got there', Clara says of her husband. Paul asks 'Got where?' and she replies 'At me. He never really mattered to me' (*S & L*(P) 334). Clara finally rejects Paul on the same ground: ' "I feel", she continued slowly, "as if I hadn't got you, as if all of you weren't there, and as if it weren't *me* you were taking" ' (431).

7. And an ambiguity resolved (are they grains of sand, or of corn?). In the later passage they are corn.

8. He knew that Dawes often thought about him, and that the man was drawn to him by some bond or other. (*S & L*(P) 408)

Paul had a curious sensation of pity, almost of affection, mingled with violent hate, for the man. (*S & L*(P) 411)

And being in such a state of soul himself, he felt an almost painful nearness to Dawes, who was suffering and despairing, too. Besides, they had met in a naked extremity of hate, and it was a bond. (*S & L*(P) 449)

9. Compare the attitudes of Miriam and Paul to the flowers that they pick. Miriam is given the reverence that Emily showed in *The White Peacock* (p. 60 above):

"I think," said Miriam, "if you treat them with reverence you don't do them any harm. It is the spirit you pluck them in that matters."

"Yes" he said. "But no, you get 'em because you want 'em, and that's all." (*S & L*(P) 295)

10. But it concludes the references to Paul as Christ, and to his women as Marys. We remember Miriam's 'annunciation', when she sees him in the sun's glow. Cf also: 'And she, with her little finger in her mouth, would ponder these sayings' (202); 'Mrs Leivers and her children were almost his disciples' (198); 'She [Miriam] might have been one of the women who went with Mary when Jesus was dead' (203); ' "Your face is bright," he said "like a transfiguration" ' (350), and the passage about the rose-bush at night, mentioned below. The reader has some difficulty in deciding whether this is

just a habit, or whether it conveys a serious intention. Lawrence fell instinctively into Biblical or Christian turns of phrase in contexts which are not evidently highly charged, and he sometimes produced anomalies or illogicalities (e.g. 'This act of masculine clumsiness was the spear through the side of her love for Morel' (*S & L*(P) 51). Mrs Morel is not Christ; but she can perhaps be seen as the *Mater Dolorosa*). I suggest below that in the great short stories the references to the Gospel story make a serious parallel, suggesting that many ordinary men have something of Christ in them, and women something of Mary. In *Sons and Lovers* the implication is that Paul Morel is more special. Mrs Morel hopes, before holding the baby up to the sun that perhaps her son 'would be a Joseph'. It is not extravagant to suppose that Lawrence thought he had a unique mission, and it is striking how friends like Murry became disciples, Judases or apostles. George Neville suggests that Lawrence's childhood friends called themselves the Pagans; but in *Sons and Lovers* the friendly term used is ''postle': appropriately, given Paul's name.

11. Revelation 6.12: 'And I beheld when he had opened the sixth seal, and, lo, there was a great earthquake; and the sun became black as sack cloth of hair, and the moon became as blood'. The moon as messenger has been met in *The White Peacock* and *The Trespasser*.

12. This was a constant in Lawrence's imagination, but particularly active at this time. In the Letters, for instance, in December 1913:

> We were the week-end at Aulla with Waterfield, who has quite a wonderful castle, in a sort of arena, like the victim, with the Appennines all round. It is a wonderful place, but it gives me the creeps down my back, just as if one sat in a chair down in the middle of the amphitheatre at Verona, and the great banks of stone took no notice, but gathered round. (17 December 1913, *Letters II* 120)

Lina Waterfield gives her memory of a letter he wrote to her:

> He described his first impression when he walked in the roof-garden one evening and looked at the mountains. It seemed to him as though wild beasts were circling round a fire, and he was filled with a feeling of apprehension. (*Letters II* 122)

A few days later, he wrote to Garnett:

> It is a wonderful place: a squat, square castle on a bluff of rock, with all the jagged Appennines prowling round (21 December 1913, *Letters II* 127)

and to Cynthia Asquith, the same day:

> There it [the castle] sits keeping an eye on two rivers that come crawling insidiously out of the jaggy Appennines, as if expecting them to pounce. (*Letters II* 128)

13. Is it coincidence that when Paul finally decides, as an act of will, to possess Miriam, an instinct leads him out of the light and into a circle of darkness?

> They went down the fields and into the thick plantation of fir-trees and pines.
> "Shall we go in among the trees?" he asked.
> "Do you want to?"
> "Yes."
> It was very dark among the firs, and the sharp spines pricked her face. She was afraid. Paul was silent and strange.

"I like the darkness," he said. "I wish it were thicker – good, thick darkness"

He seemed to be almost unaware of her as a person: she was only to him then a woman. She was afraid. (*S & L*(P) 347–8)

If the mother is associated with the moonlight, to move out of the light is to escape her influence.

14. E.g. 'Naked tribal man breast to breast with the naked cosmos', in *Apocalypse*, Fragment 2 (ed. Kalnins, Cambridge edition, p. 180).

15. References to the hands and to touch in *Sons and Lovers* are too numerous to list and the point has been made in the comment on earlier fictions. The hands of another are watched as they perform tasks, as if they were independent, yet a representative of their owner. The watcher wonders if he will put his own hand on the hand of the other. Sometimes, as in *The Trespasser*, two people stand side by side with their hands on something in front of them, as here:

Their two hands lay on the rough stone parapet of the Castle wall. He had inherited from his mother a fineness of mould, so that his hands were small and vigorous. Hers were large, to match her large limbs, but white and powerful-looking. As Paul looked at them he knew her. "She is wanting somebody to take her hands – for all she is so contemptuous of us", he said to himself. And she saw nothing but his two hands, so warm and alive, which seemed to live for her. (*S & L*(P) 332)

In this sort of relationship, the crucial gesture is to touch the other. Miriam often wants, but only once dares, 'to run her hands down his sides'.

When Paul is about to start the affair with Clara, the critical moment is when he shows her how he might design a dress specially for her:

He stood in front of her, his eyes glittering as he expounded. He kept her eyes fixed with his. Then suddenly he took hold of her. She half-started back. He drew the stuff of her blouse tighter, smoothed it over her breast.

"More *so!*" he explained.

But they were both of them flaming with blushes, and immediately he ran away. He had touched her. His whole body was quivering with sensation. (*S & L*(P) 365)

Touch is not only what children call a dare: it is a declaration, a commitment, a claim: also a consolation, a support.

16. Cf the important conversation in which Mrs Morel urges Paul to be happy. He is realistic about the chances of being happy, and even its importance; and he has an insight into the value of her life-struggle. She says

". . . How could I bear to think your life wouldn't be a happy one!"

"Your own's been bad enough, mater, but it hasn't left you so much worse off than the folk who've been happier. I reckon you've done well. and I am the same. Aren't I well enough off?"

"You're not, my son. Battle – battle – and suffer. It's about all you do, as far as I can see."

"But why not, my dear? I tell you it's the best –" (*S & L*(P) 316)

She diagnoses this as his will to die, and is not far wrong. But he is not wrong about the dignity and value of her long battle.

17. The moon appears more often than the sun in *Sons and Lovers*, and this is no accident, given the way in which Mrs Morel and Miriam eclipse Walter

Morel. However, the moon has no fixed or algebraic significance. One can say it is always feminine, and it is always bearing a message, but the message varies. When the children fought round the lamp-post, and the 'big red moon' lifted itself up 'like a great bird', it was like one of Wordsworth's accusing presences, signifying guilt in the watcher. But when at the seaside Paul and Miriam see 'an enormous orange moon' staring at them, and Miriam asks 'What is it?' a possible answer is that it is announcing to them that sexless childhood is past, and they have to face their sexuality.

18. A gesture first seen in George Saxton, in *The White Peacock*:

"Is she at home?" he said.

"No, she's gone to Nottingham. She'll be home before dark."

"I'll see her then. Can you smell violets?"

I replied that I could not. He was sure that he could, and he seemed uneasy till he had justified the sensation. So he arose, very leisurely, and went along the bank, looking closely for the flowers.

"I knew I could – white ones!"

He sat down and picked three flowers, and held them to his nostrils, and inhaled their fragrance. Then he put them to his mouth, and I saw his strong white teeth crush them. He chewed them for a while without speaking; then he spat them out and gathered more.

"They remind me of her too," he said . . . (*WP*(C) 161)

CHAPTER 7   SHORT STORIES II

1. The history is set out in John Worthen's Introduction to the Cambridge Edition of *The Prussian Officer and other Stories*. He shows that the writing and revision of 'Odour of Chrysanthemums' extended over the whole period Autumn 1909 to October 1914. During that period it was written in a first draft (Autumn 1909) and sent to the *English Review* and accepted for publication. While in proof it was heavily revised and cut: this version was published in 1911. For the collected volume it was revised extensively in July 1914, and even in proof was further heavily corrected.

'Daughters of the Vicar' was written in 1911 as 'Two Marriages', and revised in the same year. In 1913 it was revised again, twice, and got its present title. It was revised again in 1914 for collection in the *Prussian Officer* volume, and, again, the proofs were heavily corrected.

In both stories the stages of revision carried them from the early Lawrence of 1909 and 1911 to the mature Lawrence of 1914. They are type-cases of the difficulty of treating the writings in chronological order. Between the first and last drafts of 'Odour of Chrysanthemums' the first three novels had been published.

2. And in the sixth month the angel Gabriel was sent from God unto a city of Galilee, named Nazareth, to a virgin espoused to a man whose name was Joseph, of the house of David; and the virgin's name was Mary. And the

angel came in unto her, and said, Hail, thou that art highly favoured, the Lord is with thee; blessed art thou among women. And when she saw him, she was troubled at this saying, and cast in her mind what manner of salutation this should be. And the angel said unto her, Fear not, Mary: for thou hast found favour with God. And behold, thou shalt conceive in thy womb, and bring forth a son, and shalt call his name Jesus . . .

Then said Mary unto the angel, How shall this be, seeing I know not a man? And the angel answered and said unto her, The Holy Ghost shall come upon thee, and the power of the Highest shall overshadow thee: therefore also that holy thing which shall be born of thee shall be called Son of God . . .

And Mary said, Behold the handmaid of the Lord; be it unto me according to thy word. And the angel departed from her. Luke I, 26–38.

3. A Christian would reply that this is not the whole of Christianity, is even a perversion; and that the Incarnation properly understood lends divinity to the body that Christ assumed, and hallows the ordinary course of life. That is true, but Lawrence was envisaging the provincial puritan Christianity he saw about him.

4. Matthew, 19, 5–6. Jesus is quoting Genesis 2, 23–4:

And Adam said, This is now bone of my bones, and flesh of my flesh: she shall be called Woman, because she was taken out of Man. Therefore shall a man leave his father and his mother, and shall cleave unto his wife: and they shall be one flesh.

Compare 'New Eve and Old Adam', below.

5. In Appendix I in the Cambridge edition.

CHAPTER 8 SHORT STORIES III

1. The story 'Once', now included in *Love Among the Haystacks and Other Stories* in the Cambridge edition unites the two interests, since the woman who recounts her experience in it is a Frieda-figure, (she is thirty-one), and she is telling a Lawrence-figure of her experiences (mingled with a sister's experiences), and especially an affair with a young German officer 'just bursting with life, a splendid creature: the German aristocrat at his best . . . simply firm with life'.

2. Mentioned above, in the chapter on *The Trespasser* (p. 87). The Biblical references are Matthew 9:20; Mark 5:27; Luke 8:44; Mark and Luke use the expression about 'virtue' going out of Jesus and into the woman.

3. 'The soldier had a sweetheart, a girl from the mountains, independent and primitive. The two walked together, rather silently. He went with her, not to talk, but to have his arm round her, and for the physical contact. This eased him, made it easier for him to ignore the captain; for he could rest with her held fast against his chest. And she, in some unspoken fashion, was there for him. They loved each other.

The captain perceived it, and was mad with irritation' (*PO*(C) 5). The girl is like Emilie in 'The Thorn in the Flesh'; where the idea of being 'there' for each other is developed.

4. Lawrence was commenting on Garnett's play about Joan of Arc.

5. For instance, Genesis 17, 11: 'And ye shall circumcise the flesh of your foreskin'; and of course Genesis 2.24 again: '. . . and shall cleave unto his wife: and they shall be one flesh'. In Leviticus 15, 'running issue out of his flesh' and 'if her issue in her flesh be blood' refer to sexual emissions and menstruation.

For 'nakedness' the classic text is the drunkenness of Noah in Genesis 9. In later life Lawrence painted a picture of the gardener in Boccaccio's tale, who falls asleep, exposes his nakedness, and is seen by nuns. It is a modern and bawdy variation on the same topos, and Lawrence sees it as a comic triumph over prudishness.

6. Cf. 1 Tim. 3:16; 1 Pet. 4:1, and other texts.

7. The reader will remember the attention given to similar crucifixes seen in the Tirol, especially in *Twilight in Italy*. There is no doubt that these images haunted Lawrence, and he looked for their significance in the daily life that produced them and gave them meaning. There was a special significance for him and Frieda: the figure on the cross reminded them of Ernest Weekley, whom they had injured. Cf Frieda's remarks in a letter to Edward Garnett of 13 August 1912: 'My husband is a perfect agony, the loads of crucifixes round here seem joyful round-about-horses [Lawrence interjects: She means merry-go-rounds] compared to him. I wanted love, now I have more than I can bear.' (*Letters I*, 438)

CHAPTER 9   SHORT STORIES IV

1. I must qualify this remark. Paula Moest is modelled mostly on Frieda, but some of the things she is given to say are like those that Clara Dawes says to Paul Morel in *Sons and Lovers*. For instance:

   ". . . you've never come near to me. You can't come out of yourself, you can't. . . ."

   "I feel," she continued slowly, "as if I hadn't got you, as if all of you weren't there . . ." (*S & L*(P) 430–1)

   There is a lot of Frieda in Clara Dawes, of course. But also among the things Paula Moest says to her husband are some that remind us of Miriam's bitter charges against Paul. This suggests that Lawrence, in his honesty, is collecting together in Paula Moest's grievances all that had been said against him by the two most important women in his life. It may strike the reader that Peter Moest shares Paul Morel's initials, but has progressed from being 'more' to being 'most'. Other links are noted below.

2. 'That is why I like to live in Italy. The people are so unconscious. They only feel and want: they don't know. We know too much.' (To Ernest Collings, 17 January 1913; *Letters I* 504)

   'They are a spunky lot, and no soul or intellect. It's an awful relief to live among them.' (To May Holbrook, 31 January 1913, *Letters I* 508).

3. Cf:

   After tea, she stared broodingly into her tea cup, twisting her wedding-ring all the time. In her abstraction she took the ring off her finger, stood it up, and spun it upon the table. The gold became a diaphanous, glittering globe. It fell, and the ring was quivering upon the table. She spun it again and again. Paul watched, fascinated. (*S & L*(P) 335)

4. Cf 'What cattle were you bred by, that you can't keep straight eyes? Look me in the eyes when I speak to you.'

And the soldier turned his dark eyes to the other's face, but there was no sight in them: he stared with the slightest possible cast, holding back his sight, perceiving the blue of his master's eyes, but receiving no look from them. (*PO*(C) 5)

5. Another of the filaments, and one of the most mysterious: one of her ways of manipulating him is to rearrange his hair:

"My love," she murmured consolingly. "My love."

And she put her fingers through his hair, arranging it in little, loose curves, playing with it and forgetting everything else. He loved that dearly, to feel the light lift and touch – touch of her finger-tips making his hair, as she said, like an apollo's. (*P/H SS*I 92)

We remember the occasion in *The White Peacock* when Lettie puts aside George's final challenge by combing his hair into two wings, with a central parting.

Is there a Delilah-reference here? There certainly is in the later incident when Mrs Witt cuts off the hair of Lewis the groom in *St Mawr*. There may be some connection with the fact that Paula Moest twice puts flowers into her own hair. She puts primroses in her hair in the opening scene, and daisies in the closing scene, as if to increase her power to charm, to bewitch.

6. Cf also, in a letter to Edward Garnett of 13 August 1912, this early formulation about the relationship with Frieda:

We want remarkably the same thing in life – sort of freedom, nakedness of intimacy, free breathing-space between us. (*Letters I* 439)

7. Jeremiah 17.9: The heart is deceitful above all things, and desperately wicked: who can know it?

Cruden defines the Biblical heart: 'The word heart is used in Scripture as the seat of life or strength; hence it means mind, soul, spirit, or one's entire emotional nature and understanding. It is also used as the centre or inner part of a thing'. This is an important instance of the consonance of Lawrence's way of using words like heart or blood, and the Biblical network of meanings.

8. Jessie Chambers seems to have put her fingers in her mouth as a habitual unconscious gesture. It is noted often in *Sons and Lovers*, also in 'A Modern Lover'. It was usually her little finger, and she withdrew it with 'a little pop'.

9. Genesis 2:23.

Index

Adam, 95, 164, 256
age of characters, 119, 122–3, 137, 185, 241, 258, 263, 269
algebra (of speech), 119–20, 131
altar, altar-stone, 86, 91, 138
amphitheatre, arena, 266
anger, DHL on, 38
animal, animals, 26, 212, 215, 219–20
  in the darkness, 31, 172, 262
  'her animal', 63
  animal imagery, 63, 65, 74
  a. that she feared, 101
  a. life like . . . a fountain, 124, 149
  unhampered young a., 213
  wild a. in free movement, 215
  proud timid eyes of, 226
  circling round a fire, 266
Annunciation, 182
  to Helena, 109
  to Miriam, 157, 183, 265
  to Mrs Morel, 181
  to Miss Louisa, 190, 192, 199
  to Miss Mary, 197, 199
  to Elizabeth, 205
  to Emilie, 227–8, 231
apple
  Eve's, 29–30
  forbidden, 60, 66
arm, arms, 24, 53, 115, 129, 134, 190, 241, 255
  see also hand, touch
Austen, Jane, 6

Bacchus, bacchanal, bacchante, 29, 30
back
  a woman at one's b., 30–3, 171, 173
  muscles of, 53
baptism, 165, 192
barbarians, barbaric horde, 31, 51, 60, 170, 259
Baron, Carl, 16, 18, 257
bathing, 65, 70, 85, 86, 115–16, 130, 147, 233, 245–6
  see also washing, ritual

bats wing, 90, 92, 93, 97
be, being, 45
  we cannot be, 35
  what to be, 43
  content to be, 69–70
  new phase of being, 105, 118, 127, 165, 191, 192, 201, 202, 210, 232
  won to his own b., 230
  dark unknown b., 246
  accomplishing his b., 249
  utterance of her b., 253
bee, bees, 73, 90, 93–4, 103, 129
  the world as heavy b., 92
  delights like a b., 97
  great burning b., 99
  thoughts like b., 104
  city as beehive, 99, 186

berries in the hair, 28–30
beyond, 221, 222
  b. herself, 201
  b. himself, 221
  open b., 221
Bible, the: quotations, allusions, parallels, 62–3, 72, 105, 184, 190, 192, 193, 197, 198, 203, 204, 205–7, 214, 226, 229–31, 266, 271
  Gen. 2, 269, 270, 271
  Gen. 9, 270
  Gen. 17, 270
  Lev. 15, 270
  Job, 20, 72, 259
  Isa. 40, 72, 259
  Matt. 5, 85
  Matt. 9, 214, 269
  Matt. 19, 198, 269
  Mark 5, 87, 214, 269
  Luke 8, 214, 269
  John 12, 175
  1 Tim. 3, 270
  1 Pet. 4, 270
  2 Cor. 12, 231
  Rev. 6, 172, 266

birds, 90
    wood-pigeon, 67
    larks, 69, 128
    white sea-b., 93, 97, 115
    wild geese, 104
    peewits, 163, 264
Blake, William, 8, 10, 14
blood, the blood, 13, 15, 92, 108, 148,
    221, 248, 249, 252, 254
    wiser than the intellect, 34
    answering to the b. direct, 34
    the scent of b., 50
    when your b.'s up, 51
    that is I, 85–6
    virtue passing out of the b., 87
    dreams were the flowers of his b., 88
    brightness of b., 88
    = sap, 90, 92
    in the bat's wing, 90, 92
    b. cool and sharp, 113–14, 148
    delicious sublimation of, 124, 148
    length of b. and bone, 134
    pulsing of, 135
    one ruby drop of, 144
    moon turned to b., 172
    a sense of b., 172
    flash of hate through, 213
    force of all his b., 220
    surplus sex into the b., 223
    lust to see her bleed, 238
    hot waves of b., 243
    b. and the elemental male, 246
    eternal gloom of his b., 246
    waves through her b., 250
    out of whose darkness everything rose,
        250
    strange words into the b., 261
    see also vein
'blue room', the, 95, 97
body, the; bodies
    as flame, 34–5
    George Saxton as healthy b., 45
    the baby's b., 49
    pride of the b., 53, 63, 86, 139–40
    life of the, 84
    as offering, 160
    almost unthinkable b., 195
    b. a lower thing, 197
    not easy to get rid of, 198
    touch humble on the b., 206
    b. side by side, 222
    b. went on by itself, 224
    b. wakes the mind, 225
    resurrection of, 226

bread, bitter, 107, 108
breast, the; breast-to-breast, 20, 170, 173,
    175, 263, 267
    lifting of the b., 137, 147
    space starting at the b., 170, 173, 251
    see also chest, space
Brontë, Emily, *Wuthering Heights*, 47, 75
bud, budding, 60
    of life, 55, 65
bulb, bulbs
    in summer, 65
    underground, 66, 70
'Burne-Jones damsels', 29–30, 63
burning as metaphor, 147, 262
    smoky b., 33, 205
    banked-up fire, 33, 118
    clear flame (candle), 33, 34, 35, 36, 98
    pressure-lamp, 35, 96
    burning bright, 99
    smouldering embers, 115
    white hot fire, 118
    see also fire, flame, life
Burrows, Louie, 6, 28–30, 122, 130, 241,
    258, 259–60

candle, candle-flame
    associations, 33–5, 36, 98, 178–9
    candles in a fog, 132
    candle-light, 190
Carswell, Catherine, 1–2, 5
Chambers, Jessie ('E.T.'), 1–2, 28–30, 43,
    55, 111, 112, 122, 179, 241, 258,
    259–60, 261
    as Muriel, 117–22, 130, 133
    as Hilda, 123–9, 142, 146
    as Miriam, 152ff, 262
Chambers family, 23, 43, 111, 137, 258,
    263–4
change, 119, 127, 132
chest
    hard there in the centre of his c., 218
    as if his c. were crushed, 255
    see also breast
Christ, 4–5, 169–70, 190, 198, 206, 214,
    226, 227, 232, 265–6
Christianity, DHL and, 192–3, 269
cold
    deep mass of, 94
    relentless mass of, 95
Collings, Ernest, letters to, 34–6, 270
communion, 108, 183, 186
Conrad, Joseph, 6, 9, 148

conscious, consciousness, 35, 40, 45, 46, 70, 75, 200, 212–13, 217–18, 224–6, 237, 250
  stream of, 104, 192, 235, 246–7, 251
  and the will, 161–2
  gripped and separate, 224
  self-c., 212, 241, 250
  mental c., 246
  apart from the c., 247
Corke, Helen, 17, 30, 38, 39, 79, 80, 82, 83, 112, 116, 122, 129, 130, 133, 146, 241, 258, 261, 264
corruption, 45, 46, 56, 62
  see also rats, rot
cross, crucifix, crucifixion, 132, 133, 226, 227, 230, 231–2, 270
crystal
  witch's ball, 89, 134
  c. cup, 108
cup (ritual), 107–8, 121

dance, dancing, 59, 177, 235–6, 238, 239
dark, darkness, 106, 176
  circle of, 31–3, 171–3, 175, 221, 262, 266
  see the d. through its petals, 97
  the same that fills in my soul, 97
  flame off the surface of, 97–8
  great width of the d., 121–2
  moment of utter d., 202
  fought in the d., 205
  outside in the d., 221
  d. enclosure of anxiety, 224
  d. inside him, 246
  d. unknown being, 246
  good thick d., 267
death
  of plants, 65–6
  of trees, 67
  of sunlight, 72
  = the mass of life, 95
  the fuel of d., 97
  thrill of pleasure in, 145
  necessary, 146
  the drift towards, 154–5
  expansion into, 192
  d. of herself, 201
  d. her ultimate master, 207
  lapse towards d., 265
Dickens, Charles, 6, 8, 9–10, 11
Dionysus, 30
Doppelgänger, 84, 95, 233, 243
dream, dreams, dreaming, 88, 133, 260

Dreaming Women, 88, 102, 129
dusky, 178, 180, 181

ear of wheat, 31, 175
electricity, 12, 55, 87, 90, 121, 220
  women as accumulators, 88
  conducted by kissing, 259
  see also hand, touch
Eliot, George, 6, 47
Eliot, T. S., 4, 7, 11, 15
enchantress, *see* witch
eternal, 201, 202
Eve, 29–30, 164, 256
evening star, 114–16, 130, 131, 149, 259, 263

falling from himself, 201, 202
  see also lapsing
farmer, farmers, 51, 71, 72, 141–6
fatal women, 43, 45, 55, 83, 88, 102, 108–9, 110, 129–36
father, father-figures, 41, 43, 44, 52, 64, 66, 189, 263
  hated by mother, 65
  sun as f., 52, 65–6, 114
fingers
  of trees, 66
  of ivy, 67
  over the thumbs, 83–5
  in the mouth, 254, 271
  see also hand, thumb
fircone image, 117
fire, 88, 99, 115, 118, 147, 205, 230, 258, 266
  see also burning, flame, life
flame
  candle-f., 33, 35, 178
  man's body as f., 34–5
  because it is itself, 35
  living my full f., 35
  feed with oxygen, 96
  off the surface of darkness, 97
  an invisible f., 97
  f. coming off of sadness, 178
  like a conflagration, 178
  like a warm f., 213–14
  flash of f., 219
  rent in two by a f., 220
  whole furious f., 229
  hands warm as f., 229
fleece (thought as), 118
flesh
  of the apple, 29

flesh – *continued*
  flesh of his/my/one f., 31, 55, 186, 198,
    200, 205, 233, 244, 248, 253, 256,
    269
  speck of f., 31, 175
  wiser than the intellect, 34
  hard f., 53
  f. of bulbs, 65
  all f. is grass, 72
  off his f. like the flame, 178
  the same f., 185
  f. that was trampled, 198
  live in the f., 198
  full-fleshed, 204
  her living f., 204
  shamed f., 226
  in the Bible, 226
  within his f. the shame, 227
  pure white f., 228
  hands laid on f., 231, 248
  revelation in the f., 232
  f. or the devil, 251
  f. in his throat, 261
flower, flowers, 12, 26, 90, 103, 104, 128,
    139, 259, 261, 265
  in the hair, 28–30, 233, 263, 221
  guelder roses, 29
  cowslips, 29, 182
  daisies, 29, 263, 271
  snowdrops, 60–1
  forget-me-nots, 127
  pinks, 127, 181–2
  orchids, 135
  face as flower, 135, 177
  bluebells, 170
  lilies, 180–1, 262
  iris, 181
  rosebush, 183, 265
  sunflowers, 184
  violets, 268
  f. in the grass, 71–2
  f. of the spirit, 88
  f. of his blood, 88
  the head as f., 89
  bees in f., 94, 97
  fresh bell f., 97
flowering, passion of, 65–6, 67, 71, 89, 98
'form' in DHL, 4, 37–8, 154
fountain-image, 124, 149
free, freedom, 158–9, 197, 213, 227, 271
  of birds, 67, 103
  f. and proud in service, 227
  found her liberty, 237
  free of him, 247

free of herself, 248
fuse, fused, fusing, fused down, 12, 88, 89,
    91–2, 101–3, 106, 236–7, 255, 262

gamekeeper motif, 42, 61–4, 70, 74, 112,
    117, 122, 124–9, 147, 214–15, 263
Garnett, Edward, 25, 33, 37, 39, 78, 154,
    257, 258, 269, 271
gesture as communication, 147, 194
  see also hands
God, the; unknown God, 15, 100, 107,
    126, 145
  the fire of God, 109
  God at home, 109
gold, golden, 12
  of light, 35, 98–9, 113, 262
  of honey, 35
  of waves, 93
  of moonlight, 107
  horn, 107
  cup, 107
  g. and black snake, 131
  city's g. phosphorescence, 176, 186
  dusky g. softness of flame, 178
  pointed wisps of g., 191
  golden-brown eyes, 196
  see also candle, dusky, honey
grain, grains, 31, 164, 175, 194, 236, 265
Greiffenhagen, Maurice, 'Idyll', 129, 136,
    147, 263

hair
  flowers, berries in the, 28–30, 233, 263,
    271
  vineleaves in, 29
  manipulated by the woman, 47, 271
  stroked, 141, 169
  like golden plumage, 191
  cut by the woman, 258
hand, hands, 24, 53, 54, 55, 64, 140–1,
    143, 147, 169, 175, 176, 185, 207,
    213, 219, 232, 233, 239, 248, 251,
    255, 258, 261, 267
  h. disclaim me, 54
  h. refuting me, 84
  h. are me, 84
  of thine h. offend thee, 85
  h. as flowers, 85, 87, 90
  conduct electricity, 55, 87, 88
  lifted, 113, 114, 117, 127, 157, 160, 183,
    238
  as ambassadors, 141, 146, 200, 201,
    202, 229
  like dead stoats, 117, 168

hand, hands – *continued*
  like orchids, 135
  burning-red h., 136
  h. of flowers, 181–2
  h. laid in claim, 186, 203–4
  lay h. on him, 206
  h. of authority, 226, 231
  h. laid on her, 228
  h. warm as flame, 229
  h. along his sides, 261
Haggs Farm, the, as setting, 23 43–4,
  111ff, 114, 148
Hardy, Thomas, 31, 75, 93, 114, 148, 170,
  174, 191
  The Return of the Native, 23
  Far from the Madding Crowd, 47
head as flower, 89
Hewlett, Maurice, 264
homosexuality, 65, 215
honey, 35, 36, 98, 99, 103, 114
Hopkin, Sallie, 257
Hopkins, Gerard Manley, 244
Hueffer (Ford), Ford Madox, 78
Huxley, Aldous, 1, 2, 257

I
  I am I, 85
  that is I, 86
  what I am, I am, 230
  that was he, 237
Ibsen, Henrik, *Hedda Gabler*, 28–9, 258
ice of fear, 205
  in her womb, 205
initiation, 160, 164, 165
intellect, only a bit and bridle, 34
  the light shed on things, 34–5
intelligence, 224
Italy, Italians, DHL on, 35, 36, 241, 270
ivy, 67, 248, 252

Jaffe, Else, 155
James, Henry, 6, 9, 25
Jennings, Blanche, 28, 39, 41, 64, 87, 140,
  259, 260, 261, 262
Jones family, 49, 123, 146, 259

killing, 50–1, 56, 126–7, 143–6, 165,
  219–23
kiss, kissing, 68, 101, 129
  desire accomplished in a, 88, 136
  vampire's k., 96, 135, 147
  k. on the mouth, 259
  k. as lovers, 259
Kobolds, the, 134

Lady Chrystabel, 53–4, 55, 62–3, 129,
  261, 263
Lady of Shalott, 30, 63, 96, 129, 133, 135,
  261, 263
  her crystal, 89, 133, 134, 147
lamp, lamp-flame, pressure-lamp, 35, 96,
  98, 135–6, 178–9
  see also light, flame
lamp-post, 31–3, 171–3, 268
lapse, lapsing, lapsed out, lapse along, 12,
  115, 201, 235, 265
  see also falling, nut, seed
Lawrence, Arthur John, 44
Lawrence, D. H.: Works
  NOVELS
  The White Peacock, 1, 3, 23, 25, 26,
    29–30, 32, 39, 41–77, 79, 80, 81,
    103–4, 110, 111, 113, 114, 117,
    125, 128, 137, 142, 145, 147, 151,
    152, 155, 165, 168, 198, 207, 220,
    233, 235, 258, 260, 261, 266, 271
  The Trespasser, 25, 26, 27, 32, 39, 78–110,
    111, 114–15, 129, 130, 136, 147,
    151, 164, 173, 216, 260, 266
  Sons and Lovers, 1, 2, 3, 5, 7, 23, 25, 26,
    30, 31, 32, 33, 36, 39–40, 96, 111,
    112, 117, 120, 122, 125, 150–87,
    208, 210, 214, 233, 242, 258, 259,
    262, 263, 264, 266, 268, 270, 271
  The Rainbow, 7, 10, 44, 81, 137, 141,
    187, 191, 192, 233, 238, 258, 262,
    264
  Women in Love, 7, 13, 25, 36, 223, 259,
    262
  The Lost Girl, 127
  Kangaroo, 226
  The Plumed Serpent, 8, 15
  Lady Chatterley's Lover, 3, 24, 122, 127,
    151, 215, 257

  SHORT STORIES
  'A Prelude', 23–4, 111, 146
  'A Lesson on a Tortoise', 113–14, 129,
    137, 146
  'The Fly in the Ointment', 113–14, 137,
    146, 263
  'The Old Adam', 123, 146, 165, 214
  'A Modern Lover', 40, 111, 112, 114–
    22, 125, 130, 146, 147, 165, 168,
    206, 214, 244, 247, 251, 263, 264,
    271
  'Shades of Spring', 111, 112, 122–9,
    146, 147, 165, 168, 214, 263, 264

Lawrence, D. H.: Works – *continued*
SHORT STORIES – *continued*
'The Witch à la Mode', 111, 129–36,
  146, 147, 244, 261
'Love Among the Haystacks', 111, 112,
  123, 137–41, 142, 146, 214
'Second Best', 111, 112, 123, 141–6,
  147, 220, 254
'Daughters of the Vicar', 7, 23, 112,
  168, 185, 188–203, 209–10, 224,
  230, 259, 264, 268
'Odour of Chrysanthemums', 112, 125,
  129, 168, 188, 203–8, 210, 224,
  230, 259, 263, 264, 268
'The Prussian Officer', 34, 165, 211,
  212–23, 226, 239, 241, 263
'The Thorn in the Flesh', 112, 211,
  224–32, 241, 269
'A Fragment of Stained Glass', 264
The Prussian Officer (collection), 111,
  207, 211, 268
'The White Stocking', 112, 177, 233–41
'New Eve and Old Adam', 30, 34, 112,
  167, 169, 211, 233, 240–56, 257,
  259, 263, 264, 269
'Once', 263, 269
'St Mawr', 7, 258
'The Captain's Doll', 7
'The Escaped Cock', 193
'The Woman Who Rode Away', 127

OTHER WRITINGS
Twilight in Italy, 36, 241, 270
Phoenix II, 10, 257
Reflections on the Death of a Porcupine, 10
Love Poems and Others, 258
'Look! We have come through!', 203,
  259
'Women are so Cocksure', 210
Apocalypse, 193, 207
Lawrence, Frieda, 1, 34, 112, 155–6, 211,
  241, 242, 269, 270
  on DHL's art, 37–8
Lawrence, Lettice Ada, 43
Lawrence, Lydia, 122, 141
Lawrence-figures, 43, 82, 112–13, 114–22,
  122–9, 129–36, 142, 152, 240–56,
  265, 269
leading-shoot, 71
leaking, 95–6, 173; *see also* skin, dreams
Leavis, F. R., 3, 5–11, 12, 14–15, 18, 20,
  21, 27, 257
libation, 107–8, 121

life, 169, 249, 252, 254
  the mass of, 95, 96
  the House of, 95
  as candle-flame, 33–5, 36, 98
  the humming of, 99
  the sound of, 99
  bullet . . . into the heart of, 99
  most painful phase of, 118
  as fire, 116, 118
  life-warmth, 162
  l. wild at the source, 164
  one stroke of, 168
  fine jet of, 189
  l. with its smoky burning, 205
  children belonged to l., 206
  l. her immediate master, 207
  l. direct through his senses, 212
  man who fights with l., 213
  touched into l., 213
  firmer . . . with l., 218, 269
  out from everyday l., 221
  l. or not l., 221
  rouse into l. again, 222
  bring back the l., 245
  her l. for herself, 247–8
  elemental l., 249
  l. itself at storm, 250
  unity into his l., 253
  l.-current . . . in kissing, 259
  bursting with l., 269
  see also being, burning, fire, flame
light
  circle of, 31, 32, 33, 34, 135, 171–3, 262,
    266
  the mother as l., 32
  of the candle-flame, 33, 35, 178
  of the pressure-lamp, 35, 96–8, 162, 179
  of the moon, 35, 58, 180
  all the space of l., 170
  like a white l., 179
  big bright place of l., 221
Littlewood, J. C. F., 16, 18, 208, 257, 264
loins, 229, 261
London, 44, 73, 99
Lot's wife, 35, 103, 262

McLeod, Arthur, 152, 257
Madonna, 106, 110
  see also Virgin Mary, flowers (lilies)
manhood, 227
marriage, 44–5, 46, 76–7, 168–9, 187, 223,
  237, 253
Meredith, George, 133
metal, 91, 102, 262

Milton, John *Lycidas*, 116
mind, 33–4, 35, 105, 178, 195, 212, 224, 250, 251
  and body, 224–5
  see also consciousness, intellect
moon, moonlight, 12, 58–9, 66, 90, 106, 107, 108, 130, 131, 139, 149, 172, 179, 180, 181, 182, 184, 266, 267, 268
Morris, William, 128
motherhood, 46, 48, 76, 154, 207, 259, 260
mowers, mowing, 53, 56, 65, 71–2
mud, creatures of the, 73, 139, 259
Murry, John Middleton, 2, 4–5, 7, 11, 12, 40, 122, 152, 258, 266

neck, 238, 261
  as stem, 89, 135
  mouth on, 136
  sunburnt, 190
  nape of, 191
  the bend of, 213
  see also throat
Neville, George, 258, 266
Nietzsche, Friedrich, 4, 222
nut, 12, 202

oil on a dark stream, 247
Orion, 52, 116, 120, 149, 259
other, otherness, 125

Pan, 30, 42
Pater, Walter, 116, 262, 264
Persephone, 128, 263
perviousness (of the self), 32, 95–6, 133, 173
pit-dirt as mask, 23, 189, 199, 209
pivot, pole, 171, 174–5
plant, plants, 14, 65, 89–90, 105, 126, 248–9, 259
  see also bud, bulb, flower, nut, root, seed, stem, tendril
pleasure-pier, 250–1
priest, priestly, priest-like, 72, 76, 116
  priest of the sun, 94, 106
priestess, 28–30, 129, 130, 184, 186
'producing', 48
projection, 144, 146, 254

rats, 57, 62, 259
reaching across, 24, 141, 194, 200–1, 229
  see also gesture, hands, touch
rebirth, 192, 199, 202
  see also being

Resurrection, 192, 202, 226, 229, 230, 231
revelation, 191, 209, 227
rival, rivals, rivalry, 112, 117, 122, 123ff, 138, 143, 146, 149, 165, 214, 233, 243, 263, 265
rite, ritual
  of day and night, 107
  bathing, 86, 115
  washing, 94, 139–40, 190, 203
  gestures, 127, 134–5
  offering, 157, 159–60
  of passage, 232
  see also altar, annunciation, baptism, communion, hands, initiation, libation, priest, sacrifice
roots, 249, 252
  disengage her r., 248
  r. straining at their hold, 248
  blind source, 249
rot, rotting, 45, 61–2, 70, 74
ruddy
  of the moon, 107
  of children, 172
  of Walter Morel, 177
  with the sun, 196

sacrifice, 40, 48, 50, 56, 72, 82, 91, 109, 121, 130, 132, 145, 147, 156, 159–60, 163, 166, 181, 186, 265
  of Arabella, 158
  self-s., 36, 40, 159–60, 161
salt, pillar of, 35, 106, 262
sap, 90, 92, 93
second-best, 46, 50, 112–13, 142
sea, 90, 91, 106, 107, 115–17, 147, 250, 251
  and sunlight, 102, 109
seed, 12
  bitten by the sunshine, 89
  death of, 192
self, the, 10, 13–14, 244, 250, 252, 260
  being one's own s., 126, 232
  s.-assertion, 168
  old s. transcended, 191
  he was himself, 201
  she was beyond herself, 201
  death of herself, 201
  they were themselves, 232
  slipping away from herself, 235
  get outside himself, 255, 256
  see also being, I
self-consciousness, 212, 241, 250
self-responsibility, 48, 228, 237
servant, suffering, 213

service, 48, 50, 190, 194, 197, 204, 215, 226–8, 229, 232
shell, 218, 250
shoot, 12
side, sides, touching o's, 55, 64–5, 87, 139, 185, 261, 267
skin
  sunburnt, 24, 53, 64, 142, 213–14, 261
  white and unblemished, 64, 190
  smooth and clear, 185
  white as milk, 205
  permeable, 31–2, 133
slag, 102
source, 249
  life wild at the s., 164
  at her s. . . . connected, 248
space
  starting at the breast, 170, 173
  springing from him, 246
  between people, 248, 271
spontaneity, 37
stars, 31, 52, 107, 116, 120, 127, 147, 164, 175, 191, 259
  see also evening star, Orion
stem, stalk
  tense with life, 89
  strong white s., 135
sun, 12, 31, 72, 90, 106, 109, 110, 116, 117, 147, 149, 175
  associations, 35, 36, 98, 179, 184
  and fatherhood, 52, 65–6, 114, 184
  priest of the s., 94, 106
  'look, my pretty', 157
  s. had given him to her, 157
sunlight
  the death of, 72
  sweet flow of thick s., 74
  sea and s., 102
  thick heavy golden s., 113
sunset, 113, 114
sunshine, 92, 102
  bitten by the s., 89
  the s. in you, 95
symbols, symbolism, 131–3, 135
Symonds, J. A., 116, 122, 264

tarn, the, 10, 37
tendrils, 12
Tennyson, Charles 'The Lady of Shalott', 30, 261, 264
'there', 152, 163, 165, 209, 224, 229, 230, 232, 237, 241, 244, 253, 265, 269
  see also 'with'

thought, 40, 220, 247, 251
  t. like wild geese, 104
  like butterflies, 104
  like ants, 105
  like bees, 105
  t. not life, 118
  gripped . . . by t., 178
  nothing to do with t., 191
  not . . . t. that represented him, 247
  see also consciousness, intellect, mind
throat, 238, 261, 263
  fingers at, in, 67, 165
  as stem, 89, 135
  mouth on, 129, 135
  offered to attacker, 135, 219
  face on, 164
  of flowers, 181–2
  strong thin t., 219
  shirt unfastened at t., 228
  thumbs on, 262
  see also neck
thumb, thumbs
  tucked under the fingers, 83–5
  t. on your throat, 262
tide
  flushed t., 115
  t. of his soul, 192
  t. in the blood, 247
  see also wave
Tolstoy, Leo *Anna Karenina*, 47, 80
touch, 12, 49, 53, 70, 140, 143, 147, 176, 206, 207, 214, 248, 267
  touching death, 65
  t. of trees, 66
  as electricity, 12, 55, 87, 90
  touched into life, 213
  connection between two lives, 259
  continual soft touchings, 259
  touching things, 259
  t. of flowers, 259
  he had touched her, 267
  see also arms, hands, kissing
transfiguration, 190–1, 230, 266
trees, 26, 45
  kinship with, 66
  dying t., 67, 71, 89
  sycamore's leading shoot, 71
  rotting t., 74

unknown, the, 34

vampire, 96, 108, 133, 147
  see also kiss

vein, veins
  death in, 65–6
  sunlight in, 91–2
  body like a swollen v., 136
  stimulation in his v., 142, 148
  see also blood
vermin, 51, 57, 61–2, 64, 70, 117, 126–7, 143, 263
Virgin Mary, the, 109, 157, 194, 197, 230, 265–6
  see also Madonna, annunciation

Wagner, Richard, 80, 103, 261
washing, 94, 139, 147, 185, 189, 199, 202, 203–5, 208, 232, 263
  see also bathing, ritual
Waterfield, Lina, 266
Waterhouse, 'The Lady of Shalott', 63, 261
waves, 91–2, 116, 199, 246f., 250
  see also tide
wedding-ring, 233, 242, 270
white, 12
  w. light, 35, 179, 180, 181, 262

w. moonlight, 108, 180
w. lilies, 180, 181
w. roses, 183
w. virgin scent, 184
w. and slender, 222
will, 102, 189, 193–5, 197, 199, 215, 225, 242, 250, 252
w. to live, 91
woman's w., 106, 129
individuality as w., 161
the higher W., 189, 195
w. to love, 199
second w. in him, 229
wine
  of communion, 107–8, 121
  spilled w. = thwarted desire, 147
witch, 28–30, 129, 130, 134, 271
witchcraft, 96, 263
'with', 100–1, 163, 201–2
  see also 'there'
Woolf, Virginia, 75, 81
Wordsworth, William, 21, 268

Yeats, W. B., 231, 264